The Sociology of Rural Life

The Sociology of Rural Life

Sam Hillyard

Oxford • New York

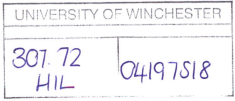
First published in 2007 by
Berg
Editorial offices:
1st Floor, Angel Court, 81 St Clements Street, Oxford, OX4 1AW, UK
175 Fifth Avenue, New York, NY 10010, USA

© Sam Hillyard 2007

Berg is the imprint of Oxford International Publishers Ltd.

Library of Congress Cataloging-in-Publication Data
Hillyard, Samantha.
 The sociology of rural life / Samantha Hillyard.
  p. cm.
 Includes bibliographical references and index.
 ISBN-13: 978-1-84520-138-8 (cloth)
 ISBN-10: 1-84520-138-8 (cloth)
 ISBN-13: 978-1-84520-139-5 (pbk.)
 ISBN-10: 1-84520-139-6 (pbk.)
  1. Sociology, Rural. 2. Sociology, Rural—Great Britain. I.
Title.

 HT421.H44 2007
 307.720941—dc22   2007015882

British Library Cataloguing-in-Publication Data
A catalogue record for this book is available from the British Library

ISBN 978 184520 138 8 (Cloth)
ISBN 978 184520 139 5 (Paper)

Typeset by Avocet Typeset, Chilton, Aylesbury, Bucks
Printed in the United Kingdom by Biddles Ltd, King's Lynn

www.bergpublishers.com

For John

Who reads Howard Newby today?

Contents

List of Tables

List of Abbreviations

ALF	–	Animal Liberation Front
ANT	–	Action network theory
BAP	–	Biodiversity Action Plan
BASC	–	British Association for Shooting and Conservation
BBSRC	–	Biotechnology and Biological Sciences Research Council
BFSS	–	British Field Sports Society
BRASS	–	ESRC Centre for Business Relationship, Accountability, Sustainability and Society, UK
BSA	–	British Sociological Association
BSE	–	Bovine spongiform encephalopathy
CA	–	Countryside Alliance
CAP	–	Common Agricultural Policy
CBBC	–	Children's British Broadcasting Corporation
CLA	–	Country, Land and Business Association (formerly the Country Landowners' Association)
CPHA	–	Campaigning to Protect Hunted Animals
CPRE	–	Council for the Protection of Rural England
CRC	–	Cobham Resource Consultants
CRE	–	Centre for Rural Economy, University of Newcastle upon Tyne, UK
DEFRA	–	Department for the Environment, Food and Rural Affairs
EC	–	European Commission
ESRC	–	Economic and Social Research Council
ESRS	–	European Society for Rural Sociology
EU	–	European Union
FMD	–	Foot-and-mouth disease
GCT	–	Game Conservancy Trust
IFAW	–	International Fund for Animal Welfare
HE	–	Higher education
HEFCE	–	Higher Education Funding Council for England
HSA	–	Hunt Saboteurs' Association
ICI	–	Imperial Chemical Industries
IGBiS	–	Institute for the Study of Genetics, Biorisks and Society, University of Nottingham, UK

IHR	–	Institute for Health Research, Lancaster University, UK
IOE	–	World Organisation for Animal Health, International Office of Epizootics
IRS	–	Institute of Rural Studies
ISG	–	Independent Scientific Group
LACS	–	League Against Cruel Sports
LM3	–	Local multiplier 3
MAFF	–	Ministry of Agriculture, Fisheries and Food
NERC	–	National Environment Research Council
NFU	–	National Farmers' Union
NGO	–	National Gamekeepers' Organisation
PACEC	–	Public and Corporate Economic Consultants
PRA	–	Participatory rural appraisal
RAC	–	Royal Agricultural College
RDA	–	Rural Development Agency
RELU	–	Rural Economy and Land Use research programme
RSPCA	–	Royal Society for the Prevention of Cruelty to Animals
RSS	–	Rural Sociological Society (US)
SFP	–	Single farm payment
SCCS	–	Standing Conference on Countryside Sports
SSRC	–	Social Science Research Council
UCL	–	University College London
VLA	–	Veterinary Laboratories Agency

Acknowledgements

Many colleagues directly or indirectly contributed to this project. They include undergraduate students in the University of Nottingham's School of Sociology and Social Policy, postgraduate students inside the Institute for the Study of Genetics, Biorisks and Society (IGBiS) and colleagues including Tracey Warren, Tim Strangleman, Ellen Townsend and Graham Cox. Alice Phillips and Gill Farmer in IGBiS provided administrative support and good humour and IGBiS's director, Robert Dingwall, supported my initial transgression into the rural and contributed to an earlier version of chapter six. New colleagues at Durham University have helped in the later stages. The text benefited enormously from the comments of an anonymous referee.

Chapter 3 draws on data from an Economic and Social Research Council funding project (grant no. L144 25 0050), chapters 4 and 5 upon a RELU grant (RES-224–25–00111) and chapter 7 upon research funded by the University of Nottingham's New Lecturer's Fund (grant no. NLF3062). The views expressed here are those of the author and not necessarily of these funding bodies. Chapter 6 was supported by the University of Nottingham's summer internship scheme in 2002, a research project conducted with Elizabeth Morris and the cooperation of the librarians and the head teacher of the Darlington infants' school. Chapter 4 is a modified version of a paper presented to the European Society for Rural Sociology in 2003. I would also like to thank the gamekeeper for permission to use the photographic data set discussed in chapter 6. Any errors or omissions in the book remain my own.

In the tradition of recognising that there are finer things in life than sociology, thanks are finally due to John Hensby – and of course J & F.

SHH, Lincoln, October 2006

Introduction

This text offers a critical introduction to the sociology of the rural. It draws upon classic and contemporary UK rural literature and the theoretical and methodological approaches dominant in each. As a means to ground the discussion, three case studies of three contemporary rural issues are explored. The approach applied across the book is one that is informed by interactionist theory and ethnography, building upon the rising status of qualitative methods in rural geography, and offers an alternative to the popular approaches of political economy and postmodernism.

The emergence of rural sociology lies with the origins of the discipline of sociology itself towards the end of the nineteenth century. The charge to explain the impact of profound structural changes upon social ties and networks meant that the first sociological accounts were not merely rural, but urban and rural – the two dimensions went hand in hand. Hence Tönnies's (1955) – the founding father of rural sociology – twin concepts of *Gemeinschaft und Gesellschaft* (community and association) were just that: defined by the very distinctions between them. Whilst Tönnies's contemporary, Geog Simmel, moved to address the emerging phenomenon of the industrial city (Simmel 1971), they faced similar theoretical challenges. Centrally, this was to explain the implications of tremendous technological advances and to translate the impact of profound economic restructuring upon human associations.

One hundred years on, rural sociology is now quite different and far less prominent within the parent discipline (Hamilton 1990). The text unravels the process by which this decline or marginalisation occurred, to see if there is a future for a rural sociology and in what directions useful rural sociological work may be pursued. Such a task has long been perceived to be highly problematic:

> There has been an ultimately futile search for a sociological definition of 'rural', a reluctance to recognize that the term 'rural' is an empirical category rather than a sociological one, that it is merely a 'geographical expression'. As such it can be used as a convenient short-hand label, but in itself it has no sociological meaning.
>
> (Newby 1980: 8)

Newby sought a sociology of the rural that was also engaged with the business of theorising as 'there can be no theory of rural society without a theory of society

1

tout court' (Newby 1980: 9). The text explores how 'the rural' has been conceptualised. The examples and literature used here are largely UK-based; however, the wider issues of theory and method may appeal to international audiences concerned with rural matters.

The first two chapters trace the history of rural sociology, commencing with very early sociological work (such as Tönnies), and introduce a basic knowledge of essential sociological terminology and the development of the discipline. The text positions each sociological and geographic analysis within its disciplinary context and paradigm, in order to view the dominant theoretical and methodological ideas and approaches of the time. It considers, from the perspective of each theorist, what they consider to be happening and why; how order is achieved; the implications of their conclusions; and what they have defined as the key variables or concepts. The second chapter unravels why 'the rural has frequently been regarded as residual' or less fashionable within sociology and draws upon more contemporary works from within the vibrant discipline of rural cultural and social geography (Newby 1980: 9). The final three chapters explore substantive issues in the countryside, informed by the theoretical and methodological conclusions of the opening chapters. The topics addressed are necessarily selective among the many sub-fields of rural studies (such as rural sustainability, rural development, social exclusion and poverty). They are the 2001 foot-and-mouth disease crisis, the hunting debate and game shooting. The first will be of interest to international readers interested in the social implications of disease outbreaks. The latter two address two country sports that, whilst unique to the UK in form, will strike interesting comparisons with research on hunting and shooting in countries such as the US, Sweden, Spain and France. The text locates itself primarily within the UK, which is, of course, located within the framework of EC directives, most notably the CAP. The context is therefore one in which the UK is influenced by European and global trends in agriculture and consumption. All three of the substantive issues addressed in the final chapters are instances of conflict in the countryside and therefore may appeal to those studying political sociology or modern forms of collective behaviour and social movements.

The text aims to equip students with the ability to critically examine social issues relating specifically to rural areas, and also to encourage students to explore the theory–method dialectic underpinning sociological studies of rural life. The final chapter draws together the conclusions reached in each chapter to ask how the legacy left by rural researchers can further our conceptualisation of the discipline of rural sociology. Fundamentally, the text challenges whether there is a future for a 'rural' sociology and, if so, in what form it could appear.

The current research framework is positive for rural studies more broadly. The £20 million joint funding initiative on rural economy and land use between the ESRC, BBSRC and NERC is a demonstration of the importance of understanding modern farming and also the social and economic lives of people in rural areas. This is fully warranted in a context of significant reform of the Common

Agricultural Policy (CAP), the full impacts of which for the UK are yet to emerge. Such a context of change highlights the need for rural research and this text seeks to contribute to these ongoing debates.

The Structure of the Book and How to Approach the Text

The text assumes no prior knowledge or familiarity with sociological concepts; each chapter progressively offers a series of key terms or vocabulary that will inform the text as a whole. Therefore, newcomers to social science more generally may benefit from an engagement with the opening chapters, in which key theoretical and methodological terms are explored and defined. The more experienced reader may move directly to the substantive chapter of choice, with the only warning that the analysis in each substantive section is informed by the preceding, emergent critical analytic approach. Those wary of theoretical commentaries may look towards the chapter summaries, where these developments across the book are most explicitly summarised.

The structure of the text follows a series of sociological analyses. The first chapter traces the beginning of urban/rural discussions, beginning with the classical commentaries of nineteenth-century theorists, such as Ferdinand Tönnies, Emile Durkheim and Max Weber, and the growing perception of significant differences between urban and rural societies. The chapter then concentrates upon the UK context and the challenge to the urban–rural bipolar model by scholars such as Ray Pahl. Pahl's work and a number of authors responsible for championing rural sociology, such as W.M. Williams and most notably Howard Newby, take the chapter into the late twentieth century. The chapter considers their work, the implications of the decline in agriculture as the key employer in rural areas, counter-urbanisation and the phenomenon of the suburbs. The absence of rural research in one of the first American departments of sociology is also briefly considered and the growth of rural sociology in the 1930s and its emphasis upon social policy and empirical research are described. The nature and meaning of the 'rural' in contemporary Britain are explored through an evaluation of early community studies (Williams 1963) and more explicitly rural studies (Newby 1977a, 1985). The chapter concludes by considering the most prolific sociological and comprehensive contributor to rural sociology – Howard Newby – most notably his *Deferential Worker* (Newby 1977a) thesis. Comparisons are made between rural studies and developments in sociological theory (the interaction order) and method (qualitative and ethnographic approaches to studying the social world) of this time. The chapter finally considers the critical legacy laid down by Newby in his later works (Newby 1978, Newby et al. 1978).

The second chapter brings us up to date by considering, in the light of the absence of an explicitly rural *sociology*, the emergence of alternative theoretical approaches in rural geography over the past thirty years. It considers the recent 'cultural turn' towards unravelling the theoretical, epistemological and personal histories underpinning rural research via a selection from the work of eminent figures such as Terry Marsden and Paul Cloke. Through Cloke (a geographer), the text reflects the impact of the 'cultural turn' upon rural geography that has drawn some inspiration from postmodernism and away from the overtly Marxist approach that informed Newby's later work and Marsden's early contributions. The rich legacy this work offers to sociology – despite sociology's movement beyond the impasse of postmodernism during the past decade – allows the relative theoretical and methodological strengths and weaknesses of various accounts in rural studies to be viewed. The new territories into which they have taken rural research are evaluated in the chapter's conclusion.

Chapter 3 then marks the point at which the book considers more substantive examples of contemporary rural debates and issues. This chapter offers a case study of the impact of the 2001 foot-and-mouth disease (FMD) epidemic to demonstrate the problems facing contemporary rural communities and the current state of the countryside. This chapter will therefore appeal to readers in countries also affected by the 2001 epidemic, such as The Netherlands, Ireland and France. Rather than attempting to offer a definitive overview of what has become a substantial body of literature, it draws upon a selection. The selection reflects a variety of conceptual and empirical approaches to the impact of the FMD epidemic. The chapter argues that collectively, these quite varied studies serve to offer many dimensions of understanding a profoundly complex issue. As rural areas have become more intricate in the twenty-first century, rural research has produced theoretical and empirical innovations in order to best capture the rural's complexity.

Chapter 4 continues the text's application of case studies to explore a substantive issue in the contemporary countryside. It focuses upon a contested issue, that of the hunting debate. Again, a sample is drawn from the literature, although the question of hunting has not attracted the same level of attention as the impact of FMD. The sample is purposefully diverse and includes government or research council funded projects by Milbourne and Cox, an analysis of hunting as a new expression of rural protest by Woods and new data looking at the expressions of rurality underpinning the position of pro- and anti-hunting lobbies by the author and also Burridge. Finally, a more traditional analysis of the economic contribution – or lack thereof – to the UK is evaluated. The conclusion of the chapter raises some questions as to how rural researchers have approached contested issues in the countryside.

Chapter 5 considers the topical question of game shooting in the UK. It evaluates how game shooting has been studied by a relatively scarce research literature. It considers both a sample from recent academic studies and also a report by a leading opponent of shooting. The debates surrounding game shooting share many characteristics with that of hunting and many fall outside the remit of the social sciences, for example ecological work. The chapter explicates pro, anti and academic analyses and also studies that on a surface level seem unconnected but raise highly relevant and related questions. The chapter's conclusion suggests that the social aspects of shooting have been neglected and it posits a few methodological approaches that could make such a contribution. It also questions whether the relative neglect of game shooting by the academic community is a result of excessive political correctness.

Chapter 6 continues the themes of chapter 5 in its advocacy of new methodological techniques for engaging in rural research. It outlines alternative methods from which to engage with the rural in contemporary society. It presents two different analyses of visual representations of the rural and critiques and evaluates whether the visual is a useful addition to the portfolio of research methods available to the rural researcher. The examples it uses are from children's literature and a photographic data set of gamekeeping work. Whilst not as holistic in the picture that they provide as some of the literature sampled in previous chapters, they nevertheless offer opportunities to challenge the taken-for-granted perception of rurality. Such an approach offers one way to ensure that a sociology of the rural avoids theoretical and methodological stagnation.

The text concludes by drawing the debates in the preceding chapters together and looks, in an overview, at the future of rural sociology. It considers, in the light of the preceding discussion and case studies, whether sociology has a contribution to make to rural studies and what principles could inform such a sociology. Has sociology changed in the 100 years since the first analyses of rural societies emerged to the degree that one should now speak of rural sociologies? What future direction could a future sociology of the rural pursue?

Learning Tools

The text offers a series of learning tools at the end of each chapter to enable students to self-assess their knowledge. These take the form of a number of questions, brief biographies of key thinkers and their ideas and a glossary of key terms as they emerged. The questions will invite students to compare and contrast the research styles and findings of rural research and thinking since the nineteenth century and, in doing so, invite them to progress their knowledge and understanding of the field as a whole.

–1–

'A Problem in Search of a Discipline' (Hamilton 1990: 232): the History of Rural Sociology

Tönnies and Nineteenth-century Commentaries on the Rural

Tönnies's (1955) [1887] seminal work, *Gemeinschaft und Gesellschaft*, is often appealed to as a starting point from which to begin to theorise the rural, indeed, to the extent that Newby (1977a) labels him the father of rural sociology – albeit whilst also perceiving him to be the father of the community studies approach. Tönnies's writing, in retrospect, can be seen as part of the new emerging discipline of sociology, which itself was influenced by the impact of the agricultural revolution. Tönnies's work therefore provides a useful starting point from which to view how rural societies have been characterised by sociologists in the past.

Ferdinand Tönnies (1855–1936)

The context of the second half of the nineteenth century and what came to be termed the industrial revolution[1] presented a challenge for the very earliest sociologists: namely, how was society understood before the transformation; and how could it be best conceptualised subsequently? Tönnies was writing in a context of the emergence of sociology as a discipline in its own right, alongside significant figures such as Hegel, Comte, Spencer and Marx. However, Tönnies is perhaps best situated among the second wave of writers to emerge in the new field of sociology. In France, his peers included Emile Durkheim and, in Germany, Simmel and Weber.[2]

Tönnies characterised the rise of urban industrialism – and its associated demographic shift from the country to the city – as involving a loss of community. His text, published in 1887, *Gemeinschaft und Gesellschaft* applied these two, twin terms to describe the contrast between pre-industrial and post-industrial societies. The rise of the urban city was instrumental in this process:

one could speak of a *Gemeinschaft* (community) comprising the whole of mankind ... But human *Gesellschaft* (society) is conceived as mere coexistence of people independent of each other.

(Tönnies 1955 [1887]: 38)

So, immediately, Tönnies's (1955) analysis contained a critique of the impact of industrialisation upon social relations. That is, the disruption of removing people from the familiar context of the rural to the anonymity of the city led, inevitably, to a loss of interactional associations between social factors. The cumulative effect of this was, for Tönnies, *Gesellschaft*. Tönnies's concept of *Gesellschaft* refers to the large-scale, impersonal, calculative and contractual relationships that, according to Tönnies, were increasing in the industrial world at the expense of 'community' or *Gemeinschaft*. The latter was more than familiarity and continuity, but also:

a totality which is not a mere aggregation of its parts but one which is made up of these parts in such a manner that they are dependent upon and conditioned by the totality ... and hence as a form possesses reality and substance.

(Tönnies 1955 [1887]: 40–41)

The two, twin concepts therefore invite points of contrast and comparison that can be, loosely, characterised as shown in Table 1.

Table 1 Tönnies's (1955) twin concepts of *Gemeinschaft* und *Gesellschaft*

Gemeinschaft	Gesellschaft
Community	Society/association/organisation
Real, organic life	Acts as a unit outwardly
Acts as a unit outwardly	Imaginary and mechanical structure
Intimate, private and exclusive living together	Public life – it is the world itself
	One goes into it as a strange country
Bound to it from birth	Mechanical
Organic	Exists in the realm of business, travel or sciences
Should be understood as a living organism	Commercial
	Transitory and superficial
Old	New as a name as well as a phenomenon
Pre-industrial	Post-industrial
	Responsible for the decline of 'community' in the modern world

Unravelling these concepts in a little more depth, however, allows some insight into whether Tönnies's (1955) analysis was indeed a critique of industrialisation, or rather a balanced account in which the respective advantages and implicit problems associated with each form of social relations are present. In relation to *Gemeinschaft*, social relationships were defined as intimate, enduring and based upon a clear understanding of each other's individual position in society. That is, a person's status was estimated according to whom that person was, rather than what that person had done. However, such relationships were relatively immobile, both geographically and socially (up and down the social scale). Therefore, in that respect, status was ascribed (that is, relatively fixed at birth) rather than achieved (based on merit or performance). The *Gemeinschaft* society, as characterised by Tönnies (1955), was therefore less a meritocracy than a relatively closed community. As Lee and Newby (1983) noted, such societies were relatively homogeneous, since well-recognised moral custodians, such as the church and the family, enforced their culture quite rigidly. Sentiments within this form of society placed a high premium on the sanctity of kinship and territoriality. At its core, *Gemeinschaft* was the sentimental attachment to the conventions and mores of a 'beloved place' enshrined in a tradition which was handed down over the generations from family to family and therefore both the church and the family were more important and much stronger in pre-industrial society. Derived from this form of social relations were enduring, close-knit relationships, which were in turn characterised by greater emotional cohesion, greater depth of sentiment and greater continuity – and hence were ultimately more meaningful.

In summary, *Gemeinschaft* implied close ties – both economic and emotional – to one geographic locale, but at the same time these were closely intertwined with a depth and richness in personal social relations.

In contrast, *Gesellschaft* was, broadly, everything that *Gemeinschaft* was not. The move towards industrialism and urbanism, for Tönnies, was associated with an increase in the scale, and therefore the impersonality, of society. This impersonality enabled social interaction to become more easily regulated by contract (as opposed to obligation and expectation), so that relationships become more calculative and more specific. However, they were also more rational, in the sense that they were restricted to a definitive end and constructed with definite means of obtaining such ends. That is, social relations were laid bare under a contract system and the implicit web of obligations and ties of *Gemeinschaft* negated by the explicit brokering of work and roles.

However, as a consequence the associational qualities of *Gemeinschaft* were also negated and most of the virtues and morality of 'community' were lost under industrialisation. Therefore Tönnies's (1955) is a critique against the utilitarian's society of rational individuals: that is, that individuals, once disconnected from the close form of association to be found prior to industrialisation, lost the stability or moral centre that characterised the *Gemeinschaft* way of life. Writ large, the replacement of *Gemeinschaft* by *Gesellschaft* relationships was ultimately a prerequisite of the rise of capitalism and hence of the rise of nineteenth-century industrial society. In this sense, Tönnies (1955) provided an early critique of the impact of capitalism upon human forms of association – the impact of macro structure change as analysed in terms of its impacts on the meso level. The importance of Tönnies's contribution to sociology, and rural sociology more explicitly, is therefore closely aligned to the historical timing of his work. Tönnies's own writings (across the years 1880–1920) were of a time when sociological writing was university-based, and little interaction or dialogue took place between countries (with the exception of America), unlike the present day. Nevertheless, there were also significant commentaries on the rural stemming implicitly from his contemporaries' work. Durkheim's concepts of mechanical and organic solidarity, Weber's lecture on capitalism and rural society and early American sociology's urban orientation and the developing emphasis upon social policy are briefly considered here.

Durkheim's Distinction between Mechanical and Organic Solidarity (Distinctions between Rural and Urban Societies)

Durkheim's concepts of organic and mechanical solidarity contain many parallels with Tönnies's concepts of *Gemeinschaft und Gesellschaft*. Tönnies developed his concepts many years before Durkheim's (1984) [1893] *The Division of Labour in Society* and, as such, arguably informed Durkheim's later concepts of mechanical and organic solidarity.

Durkheim is often seen as a one of sociology's more conservative thinkers, particularly when contrasted with Marx. However, Craib argues, 'he was nevertheless a reforming liberal or socialist in political terms' (Craib 1992: 14). Durkheim's methodological approach or position as to the correct approach to the study of sociology is beyond the remit of this book, although this clearly informed the concepts and distinctions that emerged from his work.[3] Two of the most notable of these are his distinctions between mechanical and organic solidarity. These concepts are discussed in his text on the increasing division of labour to be observed in capitalist society. Mechanical solidarity in primitive societies was based on the common beliefs and consensus found in the collective consciousness. The new form of order in advanced (capitalist) societies is based on organic solidarity. This was based on interdependence of economic ties arising out of differentiation and specialisation within the modern economy.

The context, like that of Tönnies's time, was the period of change following the industrial revolution in Britain and Europe and its impact upon social relations. Durkheim, like Tönnies, perceived this to have effected an 'evolutionary change in society from one form of social cohesion to another and in particular the role of individualism in modern societies' (Craib 1992: 15). However, unlike Tönnies, Durkheim did not perceive such a shift with the sense of pessimism implicit in Tönnies's interpretation. Rather than the shared beliefs which Durkheim perceived traditional (i.e. pre-industrial revolution) societies to characterise, the division of labour in people's working lives formed a new bond or contract between social actors. That is, the division of labour created economic dependence upon one another and this formed the new social bond and maintained the equilibrium.

There is a danger of confusing Durkheim's emphasis upon the division of labour as taking upon the same significance as Marx's emphasis upon the ownership of the means of production. Unlike Marx, Durkheim does not take the economy to be the driving force of his analysis of social relations. However, the core ontological assumption underpinning his analysis of society was that a shared moral basis was necessary to the social order (that is, to ensure the continued smooth running of society). Somewhat confusingly, Newby (1980) reflects on Durkheim's use of mechanistic and organic descriptors, and finds organic more evocative of a rural way of life:

> The use of the word 'organic' emphasizes the elision between the aesthetic and the eco-logical on the one hand and the social on the other. It obviously derives in part from its connotations with the land and fertility.
>
> (Newby 1977a: 16)

There are, perhaps, a few reasons underpinning Newby's (1980) interpretation, which inverts the romanticised view of traditional ways of life as synonymous with the rural. First, Durkheim was, to borrow Craib's (1992) term, 'drunk' on the concept of society. Society was, in this sense, the new, modern, industrial society that he sought to analyse and explain, rather than the traditional, pre-dating society. Therefore, the more positive, consensus-based modern society may trans-late more positive characteristics. The other, and perhaps more interesting in rela-tion to the concern here with rural sociology, is the more explicit continuum visible between rural and urban in Durkheim's analysis. Craib offers a useful summary:

> Strictly speaking 'mechanical solidarity' is not itself a form of social structure but it is the form of solidarity found in 'segmented societies' – societies originally clan (kinship) based but later on based on locality.
>
> (Craib 1992: 66)

Here the emphasis is upon geographic locality and a type or form of social rela-tions. This is far more explicit than is the case in Tönnies's analysis, as will later be discussed with reference to the work of Ray Pahl. In the work of Durkheim, therefore, we can detect an emphasis upon locale as a significant influence upon the social characteristics of the society residing there. However, Max Weber's analysis serves to take the notion of locale further, for in imprinting upon the cul-tural values or outlooks of an individual it ultimately becomes removed from any fixed geographical context.

Weber (1970) [1904] on Capitalism and Rural Society in Germany[4]

Weber's (1970) commentary of rural societies is based on a lecture he delivered in 1904. Whilst the essay goes on to specifically address Germany rural society (in particular the differences between the social formations of the east and west) he discusses the condition more broadly, including the English and American situations as well as that of mainland Europe. Weber argues that rural areas are distinctive and therefore that they warrant sociological attention:

> Of all communities, the social constitution of rural districts are the most individual and the most closely connected with particular historical developments.
>
> (Weber 1970: 363)

Weber's (1970) approach is therefore historical in his attempt to capture the complexities of the phenomena of rural societies. Like Tönnies, he finds that the rural is in decline:

> For a rural society, separate from the urban social community, does not exist at the present time in a great part of the modern civilised world. It no longer exists in England, except, perhaps, in the thoughts of dreamers. The constant proprietor of the soil, the landlord, is not an agriculturalist but a lessor; and the temporary owner of the estate, the tenant or lessee, is an entrepreneur capitalist like any other.
>
> (Weber 1970: 363)

The link between urban and rural (like Tönnies and indeed Marx) is the impact and phenomenon of capitalism and its relative impact upon farming. The spread of a capitalist ethic is Weber's (1970) particular concern and the manner in which land comes to represent not only agricultural opportunities but also social status. To buy or own significant tracts of land, he argued, also acts as 'an entrance fee into this [higher or elevated] social stratum' (Weber 1970: 366). However, Weber's (1970) interest lies in the shifts within agriculture within his own native country, Germany. Particularly, his analysis focuses upon the differentiations of farming intensities between east and west regions of Germany. He argues that the increasing value and social status of land is significant:

> by increasing the capital required for agricultural operations, capitalism causes an increase in the number of renters of land who are idle. In these ways, peculiar contrasting effects of capitalism are produced, and these contrasting effects by themselves make the open countryside of Europe appear to support a separate 'rural society'.
>
> (Weber 1970: 366–367)

He argues that this serves to differentiate between the old system of farming, which could be loosely described as the old, economically independent aristocracy, and the new urban capitalist emphasis upon the possession of money. The result is a form of conflict, as 'the two social tendencies resting upon entirely heterogeneous bases thus wrestle with each other' (Weber 1970: 367). In this there are many echoes of Durkheim's distinction between mechanical and organic societies. The 'rural community, aristocratically differentiated' is akin to the mechanical solidarity Durkheim associated with pre-industrial revolution societies (Weber 1970: 372). Even more particularly, 'the density of population, the high value of land, the stronger differentiation of occupations, and the peculiar conditions resulting therefrom' are evocative of the organic solidarity that Durkheim argues exists in modern industrial societies (Weber 1970: 372).

However, the pessimism in the shift that Tönnies, Durkheim and Weber trace is not necessarily framed in negative terms in the interpretation offered by Weber. For example, 'the former peasant is thus transformed into a labourer who owns his means of production, as we may observe in France and in southwestern Germany' rather than the preceding situation where they were owned or ascribed a status by the lord of the manor or Junker (Weber 1970: 367). In this sense, Weber's (1970) interpretation is less tinged with the nostalgia that has been perceived in Tönnies's work and, as the chapter will demonstrate, subsequent community studies.

The thrust of Weber's (1970) argument lies in the social history he conducts of Germany, rather than the inherent characteristics of the different regions themselves (although this is addressed to a certain degree). Weber argues:

> The establishment of extensive operations was facilitated, for the eastern landlords, by the fact that their landlordship as well as the patrimonialization of the public authorities had grown gradually on the soil of ancient liberty of the people. The east, on the other hand, was a territory of colonization.
>
> (Weber 1970: 376)

Weber (1970) therefore suggested that the traditions of these two regions were different and that, for example, these manifested themselves in the way the land and peasants were managed. For example, the 'eastern and western landlord differed when they each endeavoured to extort from their peasants more than the traditional taxes' (Weber 1970: 376). The older, 'mutual protection, the jurisdiction of the community' was a feature of the west. However, the result was that the east was more resistant to development than the west and more influenced by old, aristocratic traditions, the eastern farmer being more associated with a gentleman's lifestyle than that of working the land. Weber concludes, 'for Germany, all fateful questions of economic and social politics of national interests are closely connected with this contrast between the rural society of the east and that of the west with its further development' (Weber 1970: 384). There is, therefore, the suggestion that rural society is somewhat behind that of the new emerging forms of social relations. However, this is to some degree countered in the very importance that

Weber attaches to understanding these differences and the way the rural is significant to his analysis. The rural, for his sociology in this lecture, is a significant sociological concept for understanding social relations.

Having considered the European analyses of rural change offered by Tönnies, Durkheim and Weber, the chapter now turns to consider, very briefly, the American situation.

American Sociology

Newby (1980) addressed the issue of why rural sociology had become a vibrant research field in the US context and not that of the UK. Newby (1980) found that early American sociology was primarily urban in orientation and yet was then followed by an emphasis upon rural issues from a social policy dimension. Most significantly, Newby found it to be more reactive in its research than proactively seeking to theorise the changes in rural society (Newby 1980), a criticism that has also been levelled at more recent British rural research (Hamilton 1990). The discipline has developed on both sides of the Atlantic;[5] however, it became more community-based here and more oriented towards agriculture (at least initially) in America. For a summary of the most recent analyses offered by US sociologists in rural America, see Rural Sociological Society (RSS) (2005). RSS (2005) found that (1) the rural population is becoming more diverse in terms of its advancing age and increasing Hispanic population, (2) rural economies have been significantly transformed in the past decade (in terms of increasing dependency on the agriculture industry, declining manufacturing, increasing reliance upon service industries and a lack of high-skill and high-wage jobs), (3) rural communities, especially those within commuting distance of larger areas, are experiencing high physical growth, which must be balanced with protecting the natural environment, and (4) while new opportunities are being created in rural communities, poverty persists at alarming levels relative to urban and suburban areas (Consortium of Social Science Associations 2005).

The focus here is upon the UK context and the directions that UK rural sociology has most recently developed. The particular concern is the long-term impact of the decline in the significance of the rural for sociologists and its implications for the future of a theoretically and methodologically sophisticated analysis of contemporary rurality. Therefore, considering the importance attached to the rural by key, founding thinkers in the history of sociology, why the rural has not continued to attract such attention warrants examination. This relates to the interpretation, or legacy, of Tönnies's work by subsequent sociologists.

Tönnies's Legacy

The enduring impact of Tönnies's work has been the two models of society (pre-industrial and post-industrial). The twin concepts of *Gemeinschaft und Gesellschaft* served to represent the profound changes sweeping across nineteenth-century Europe and distinguish post-industrial revolution society from its more feudal precursor. However, Tönnies's analysis is generally perceived to be a pessimistic analysis of the consequences of these changes. That is, the breakdown of traditional social order is implicitly feared, as *Gemeinschaft* is defined as an important source of stability in society. Nevertheless, Tönnies's concepts of *Gemeinschaft und Gesellschaft* explored the transition from the 'communal' organisation of medieval society to the 'associational' organisation of modern, industrial society. In addition, he sought to give proper sociological attention to the creative and constructive role of individual action in producing its central cultural values – in contrast to the anonymity of Durkheim's model.

Re-evaluating Tönnies

The danger in interpreting Tönnies's contribution lies in the ready links made between his twin concepts and their relationship to urban and rural locales. The automatic mapping of these two concepts along a rural–urban continuum is misguided, as Tönnies was not referring to any particular social group (be it rural or urban) when he wrote *Gemeinschaft und Gesellschaft*, but to forms of human association (Lee and Newby 1983). Rather, Tönnies (1955) was careful to argue that both relationships could be found in rural and urban settings. The emphasis was upon understanding how our sense of place depends upon social organisation and it is this analysis that is significant as one of the earliest forms of sociology to engage and unravel such a connection (Lee and Newby 1983). It is important to understand that Tönnies's concept of *Gemeinschaft*, although it included locality, went beyond to encompass a type of relationship that could – at least potentially – characterise the whole of society.

There are therefore a series of ambiguities and difficulties arising out of Tönnies's (1955) seminal work. In terms of theorising the rural, we remain in something of a theoretical vacuum as fundamental questions remain as to the significance of the rural for sociology. Nevertheless, several useful concepts have emerged: locality, local social system and communion, although the exact nature of their interconnections remains unclear. These concepts and the attention of other important figures, such as Durkheim and Weber, in the development of sociology make the rural worthy – if ambiguously – of sociological attention.

Rural Sociology following Tönnies

Tönnies's concepts have been considered and the innovations in Tönnies's approach to the study of society, alongside other emergent conceptualisations of a distinct rural society from Durkheim and Weber. Whilst neither a formally phrased nor a fully theorised model of the rural has been promoted by such authors, what is it in this legacy that later causes Newby to argue that rural sociology remains a prisoner of its own history? At what point does this fault lie? Somewhat unfortunately, it lies in the way Tönnies's original concepts of *Gemeinschaft* and *Gesellschaft* have been subsequently employed, which was alluded to earlier in the chapter. Essentially, Tönnies's intention that they describe forms of association, rather than actual social systems, has been ignored and the twin concepts have been taken as clear-cut, distinct concepts. Tönnies's original emphasis holds that, in purely formal terms, *Gemeinschaft* included any set of relationships characterised by emotional cohesion, depth, continuity and fulfilment, whereas *Gesellschaft* referred to the impersonal, the contractual and the rational aspects of human association. However, by conceiving them as conceptually distinct, they have become reified, that is, they ceased to be tools of analysis but rather became viewed as actual social structures that could be observed and enumerated – and verified through fieldwork.

Secondly, and as a result of this first point, the two concepts became identified with particular settlement or geographic patterns: *Gemeinschaft* with the rural village and *Gesellschaft* with the city. Whilst Tönnies had been largely careful to regard the twin concepts as forms of association that, while differentially distributed across society, were present to varying degrees in all types of social structures and organisations. Nevertheless, the sustainers of the rural–urban bipolar continuum are easily viewed through the rash of essays or empirical works that mapped out the characteristics of 'urban' or 'rural' ways of life. Such studies included Simmel's (1971) [1903] 'The Metropolis and Mental Life', the Chicagoan Wirth's (1938) 'Urbanism as a Way of Life' and Redfield's (1947) 'The Folk Society'. More explicitly in the UK, the sociological community had developed its own set of sub-disciplines; the one most closely aligned with the rural also shared an empirical emphasis and the restrictions of its own theoretical inheritance. To update Newby's observation, it was as if the early forms of rural sociology were constricted in two senses: from Tönnies's misinterpreted legacy and from the inherent difficulties of the community studies approach. It is to the emergence and the epistemological underpinnings of the community studies approach that the chapter now turns.

Community Studies

Newby (1977a) finds Tönnies to be the founding father of rural sociology 'just as elsewhere I have described him as the founding father of community studies (Bell and Newby 1971) ... But then, it has always been believed that *real* communities were to be found in the countryside' (Newby 1977a: 1333, fn. 9, original emphasis). Newby's identification that Tönnies is an important reference for rural sociology and also for community studies research brings with it the ambiguities in Tönnies's work: that is the pessimism and sense of loss implicit in Tönnies – a negative tone that is shared by the community studies genre. As Newby notes, the community studies approach charted the decline of a 'spirit of community' and such a decline offers an excuse to explain a whole host of contemporary social problems. Therefore the sense of loss that made *Gemeinschaft* forms of association so desirable is shared by the desire for community and for security and certainty in our lives – that is, for identity and authenticity that have been lost in a modern industrial society. The implications of this use of Tönnies's work are twofold. First, the ambiguities of Tönnies's analysis are also continued within the community studies genre; essentially, what is actually meant by community (and indeed how has it been 'lost')? Secondly, sociology as it emerged in the UK was widely seen in Britain as a science for understanding and resolving social problems (Crow and Allan 1994). These were deemed largely to exist in the cities, and to be concerned primarily with issues connected to housing, health and education (Hamilton 1990: 229). The emphasis upon specifically rural research was therefore, almost by omission, seen as an unproblematic environment – a bucolic idyllic way of life, far removed from the pressures of capitalism. The chapter now draws upon some explicit examples – both modern and more contemporary – in order to draw out some of the critiques that emerged relating to the community studies genre.

The Emergence of Rural Community Studies

The most general of definitions identifies that the community studies approach consisted of a range of studies conducted between 1940 and 1960. The history of the approach has been addressed elsewhere (Frankenberg 1969, Bell and Newby 1971, Lee and Newby 1983, Crow and Allan 1994). However, Crow and Allan (1994), as the most recent, are able to mark the distinctions between the decline of community studies work and the plethora of studies conducted from the 1950s through to the early 1990s and both in urban and rural locales (Crow and Allan 1994: xxiv–xxv). The focus of rural community studies preceding its decline in the 1970s was, as Lacey and Ball (1979) observe in relation to the sociology of education, upon the changing social structure of Britain in the post-war period (Bell and Newby 1971, Lacey and Ball 1979). Centrally, this concerned social class and relied upon empirical research of, but not exclusively, rural areas. Lee and Newby (1983) summarise these studies as sharing a series of themes: gaining a clear picture of the place under enquiry; defining the social structure of the community; examining change and whether it was perceived to be positive or negative; the loss of the traditional social order (what could be considered to be *Gemeinschaft*). In relation to explicitly rural studies, attention was focused upon working-class life (the demise of traditional working-class community), through an investigation of the centrality of family farming, a consequence of which was a neglect of the locally powerful (Bell and Newby 1971). It is therefore possible to see that such an approach ran the risk of offering an analysis that was more retrospective than proactive in its attempt to theorise the rural. In effect, it has often been found to offer more descriptive than critical accounts of communties.

This section uses a number of rural studies that have been identified as defining examples of the genre and have shaped subsequent research in order to explore the contribution of the approach to rural studies more generally. The studies are Williams (1963), Pahl (1966) and Newby (1977a). Particular attention is paid to: the focus of the individual studies themselves; the methodological approach applied; the study's historical context; and, finally, the study's contribution to the genre and towards the development of the theory of rurality.

Williams (1963)

Williams, along with Frankenberg (1957) and Littlejohn (1963) attempted a distinctively British form of rural sociology, albeit within prevailing the paradigm of 'a rather functionalist "community studies" and its derivatives' (Hamilton 1990: 229). Williams's (1963) case study of 'Ashworthy' (a pseudonym) in the West Country followed on from his earlier study of a rural village, 'Gosforth' in Cumbria (Williams 1956), but the more mature work is the focus here. Williams was a geographer by training, having studied under a founding contributor to Welsh anthropology and the community studies genre, Alwyn Rees (Bell and Newby 1971). Rees had already conducted rural research himself (Rees 1950) and Williams's work can be seen to have been influenced by that genre. The focus of Williams's (1963) study rested upon traditional themes of: landownership/occupations; population change (the exodus from the land); family and kinship; kinship and social life; and religion/household type. Therefore the emphasis within the study was upon studying the impact of demographic change – the detailed effects of rural depopulation on family and kinship. The selection of the case study site – what could be said to be the 'typical' English village – was conceptualised as one with a population of between 500 and 700 and the concept of 'rural' defined as one in which the village was underpinned by a primarily agricultural economy.

Immediately, it is the threat of decline (depopulation) and locale (a village in an agricultural context) that are central to his approach.

The methodological approach of the study was necessarily concerned with the detail and nuances of village life – or rather family life. Williams (1963) therefore conducted fieldwork, in the summer of 1958, which included four individual family case studies and a 'map' of one couple's 'kinship universe', and he also attended a funeral. The studies emphasised the importance of the landholding system (for instance the problems of continuity of land ownership across same family generations) as well as that of social class distinctions within the parish itself. Bell and Newby (1971) evaluated that Williams gives 'a fine analysis of social class divisions in the community, but it is static rather than dynamic' (Bell and Newby 1971: 164).[6] In this, Bell and Newby (1971) reveal one of the main critiques of the community studies approach – that it suffers from an excess of description at the cost of analysis. The social impact of the changes Williams (1963) details is not addressed, for example how social relationships within the parish as a whole have changed as well as internal or family relationships (Bell and Newby 1971).[7] Bell and Newby (1971) then contrasted Williams's (1963) with Littlejohn's village case study (1963). Whereas Williams (1963) found elements of *Gemeinschaft* relationships and poorly developed class structure, Littlejohn (1963) found an extremely hierarchical class system, in which relationships were impersonal, contractual employer–employee relationships and therefore not characterised by *Gemeinschaft*. Whereas Williams (1963) found change to be taking place under the veneer of stability, Littlejohn (1963) perceived that social change was not a result of urbanism and that social class was more important for the community as a source of identification. Littlejohn (1963) therefore benefited from his more historical approach and framework, through which he was able to take the view that national changes were impacting upon the local, rather than any encroaching urbanism that underpinned Williams's (1963) analysis.

Bell and Newby (1971) through the contrast with Littlejohn highlight the drawbacks implicit in the mainstream community studies approach. Williams's (1963) Ashworthy study is an exemplar of the early form of community studies – its strengths and weaknesses. Williams's (1963) concerns were with a dynamic model of rural development, in which a wide range of factors, both micro and macro, were included and his approach was broad and multidisciplinary, rather than a narrow and specialist focus. Such an approach was admirable in its scope, but nevertheless in retrospect can be said to be something of a snapshot. For instance, the modern ethnographer's emphases upon immersion and long periods in the field are both absent (Pole and Morrison 2003).[8] However, there is a risk of evaluating Williams (1963) using contemporary criteria, when his style of research was – for its time – novel in its emphasis upon qualitative alongside quantitative material. Indeed, if we consider Hargreaves's (1967), Lacey's (1970) and Newby's (1977a) studies, considered to be exemplars of the early championing of qualitative methods, they contain a much larger proportion of quantitative data than would now characterise a contemporary ethnographic monograph (Hillyard 2003a). Therefore the criticisms of the community studies approach, which are sum-marised in table 2, potentially fail to engage with the objectives of the original studies themselves. Rather, they reflect their own contemporary concerns and as such ontological and methodological preoccupations. That is, they measure early community studies work by benchmarks developed long after the studies.

Table 2 Criticisms levelled at the community studies approach to social research

- Rarely multidisciplinary; geographer, economist and sociologist
- Unsystematic use of methods
- Largely descriptive
- Non-quantitative
- Impressionistic data
- Inductive generalisations
- Results specific to community studies
- Non-comparable
- Non-cumulative

Sources: Lee and Newby (1983), Crow et al. (1990) and Hamilton (1990).

The early community studies were informed by the then dominant paradigm of the structural functionalist tradition of social anthropology, not the 'new' or inclu-sive ethnography that now characterises small-scale ethnographic research (Harper 1998, Pole and Morrison 2003). If the studies are evaluated in this light – in their historical place within sociology – some of their methodological vacillations can be seen as more the refinement of the emergence of a case study approach for soci-ology and that qualitative techniques had yet to acquire the status and sophistica-tion they currently enjoy within sociology. Therefore, studies were concerned with the 'health' of individual communities and few 'have been used to examine the theoretical presuppositions themselves' (Newby 1977a: 96).

The Critique of Community Studies

Sociology as a separate academic discipline was itself forged in the nineteenth century reaction to industrialization and urbanization of which the Romantic movement was a part. It therefore accepted uncritically the prevailing view of rural society as a system of stable and harmonious communities ... much more attention was paid to urban industrialism and its attendant social problems and evils. Thus in Britain academic sociology developed out of the Booth and Rowntree tradition of urban poverty studies, while *rural* poverty was virtually ignored; thus today urban sociology is a flourishing area of the discipline, while rural sociology is almost non-existent.

H. Newby, *The Deferential Worker* (original emphasis)

Tönnies's concepts of *Gemeinschaft* and *Gesellschaft* originally referred to forms of association, not types of settlement however, Tönnies had noted that, in the rural village, *Gemeinschaft* 'is stronger there and more alive' (Tönnies quoted in Newby 1977a: 95).

Thus *Gemeinschaft* and *Gesellschaft* were abandoned as concepts and became reified into actual groups of people 'out there', which could be observed and investigated (Newby 1977a: 95)

> Unfortunately, however, they were used largely to classify communities almost like so many butterflies, and contributed to the low-level fact-gathering tendencies of rural sociology, particularly American rural sociology.
>
> (Newby 1977a: 95)

Pahl (1968)

In a series of key papers published in the late 1960s, Pahl offered a critique of the importance of geographical locale and its correspondence to particular forms of social relations. Pahl doubted the sociological relevance of the physical differences between 'rural' and 'urban' in advanced industrial societies. Fundamentally, Pahl posited that no sociological definition of any settlement type (or locality) could be formulated. Therefore, any notions of a rural–urban or any other locality-based continuum are destroyed. As such, he considered the concepts of 'rural' and 'urban' to be neither explanatory variables nor sociological categories. He used evidence from his own empirical research community studies to show that, far from an exclusive continuum from *Gemeinschaft* to *Gesellschaft*, relationships of both types could be found in the same localities. As a result, in a key paper Pahl (1968) [1966] came to doubt the very value of the notion of a continuum even as a classificatory system:

> For a time these polar typologies, some sanctified with the authority of the founding fathers, served as a justification for those who have been guilty of ... 'Vulgar Tönniesism' of the 'uncritical glorifying of old-fashioned rural life.'
>
> (Pahl 1968: 265)

Pahl's (1968) analysis was informed by a different set of concerns from that of Tönnies, that is, more contemporary sociological concepts. Sociology, as well as establishing itself in the universities in the 1960s, had recognised the importance of social class for influencing social actors' experiences and, indeed, their very life chances. Pahl (1968) applied this new concern to the study of rural life and found the emphasis upon locale, when analysed in relation to social class, lacked explanatory power:

It is difficult to see how the features of size and density could possibly exert a common influence on rich and poor alike.

(Pahl 1968: 267–268)

It was social class, rather, that was a key influence in determining the lifestyle options available to social actors, rather than any characteristics inherent within a rural area:

Class is the most sensitive index of people's ability to choose, and that stage in the life-cycle determines the area of choice which is most likely rather than of the ecological attributes of the settlement.

(Pahl 1968: 268, original emphasis)

Expressed more simply, 'only the middle class have the means and the leisure to be able to choose "places" in which to live' (Pahl 1968: 270). Pahl's interest in social class drew him into locating the issue of class with other key institutions that shape social actors:

It seems to me that the *sociologically* most significant feature of this settlement type is the interaction of status groups which have been determined nationally – by the educational system, the industrial situation and so on – in a *small-scale* situation, where part of the definition of the situation, by the localistic cosmopolitan, is some sort of social interaction.

(Pahl 1968: 276, original emphases)

However, any accusations that can be levelled at Pahl (1968) in relation to structural determinism are countered by his concern to place the individuals within the social structure:

Whether we call the process acting on the local community 'urbanisation', 'differentiation', 'modernisation', 'mass society' or whatever, it is clear that it is not so much *communities* that are acted upon as groups and individuals at particular places in the social structure.

(Pahl 1968: 293, original emphasis)

Pahl's (1968) analysis dismissed the analytic usefulness of the rural–urban continuum. In its place, the proper object of sociological investigation and theoretical concern, for Pahl, was that sociological analysis should concentrate on the confrontation between the local and the national and between the small-scale and the large-scale:

It is the basic situation of conflict or stress that can be observed from the most highly urbanised metropolitan region to the most remote and isolated peasant village.

(Pahl 1968: 286)

The direction of Pahl's argument is that rural sociology could no longer afford to consider the 'rural' sector in isolation from the rest of society. In doing so, and eighty years after the publication of *Gemeinschaft und Gesellschaft*, Tönnies's tools of analysis had been restored to their correct ontological status. That is, Pahl had divested them of their confusing association with locality (Newby 1977a). Immediately, this would seem to suggest that there cannot be a specifically rural sociology and that 'any attempt to tie patterns of social relationships to specific geographic milieux is a singularly fruitless exercise' (Pahl 1968: 293). However, this utilises a narrow definition of rural – as that of geographical or physical space. Another conceptual direction within Pahl's work (and pursued by Newby) suggests a new theoretical direction for a rural sociology to engage. Certainly, rural sociology that was defined by the study of those living in a rural locale that were associated with an agricultural economy (such as Williams 1963) is problematic since the disappearance of agriculture's economic dominance in rural areas. That is, the occupational basis of the rural population has become less homogeneous in all advanced industrial societies. As a result, the subject of study and a core focus for past rural sociological work have disappeared – what can be said to be rural is in doubt. However, the solution is present in Pahl's (1968) reference to 'a village in the mind', to which newcomers expect the villagers to attend. In the event that they do not, villagers are said to be to blame for the loss of the village community (Pahl 1965). This serves to open up some interesting directions for future work – if it is not based on locale, but 'the mind' or cultural imagination of 'the rural'. This opens up the notion of community – in the new Web-based age – to a global scale. It also, on an interactional level of analysis, allows a great detail of sociological research to be done: what definitions of the situation come to be operationalised in rural areas? Who occupy official positions and are able to impose their definitions upon less powerful groups in rural locales? And with what consequence? These are themes that inform the rest of the text. They are explored in chapter 3 through FMD, in chapters 4 and 5 through country sports. Prior to this, the degree to which Newby champions and then falters in taking this theoretical agenda forward is examined. This then led the way to a new wave of rural research within social and cultural geography in the 1990s and the twenty-first century – and a reinvigorated theoretical agenda, albeit with methodological limitations. This also marks an important shift between rural sociology and geography.[9]

Newby's (1977a) Critique of Pahl

In his examination of Pahl (1968), Newby agreed with the importance of social structures within the analysis, but argued that Pahl's work that looked at demographic and economic differences between rural and urban was a misleading 'substitute' for the detailed examination of social structures. That is, Pahl (1968) had himself fallen foul of overemphasising the importance of geographical milieux. Newby perceived that Pahl was more interested in local/national confrontations. However, Newby took the view in retrospect that 'rural sociology could no longer continue to consider the "rural" sector in isolation from the rest of society' (Newby 1977a: 99). However, Pahl in arguing (rather than achieving in empirical practice) that the physical locale of the rural was not sociologically significant holds important implications. Newby saw that 'a further consequence of Pahl's argument was to leave a theoretical vacuum in rural sociology which has never been filled' and an argument that remains valid for present-day sociology (Newby 1977a: 99).

In this vacuum, Newby (1977a) does find that a marginal relevance continues to be attached to the rural, in that geographic location may influence local social structure, in relation to the constraints that it applies to that structure. Indeed, as Newby (1977a) points out, Pahl's subsequent work (Pahl 1975) on the city developed this point. Yet, 'to paraphrase Pahl, there is no rural population as such; rather there are specific populations which for various, but identifiable, reasons find themselves in rural areas' (Newby 1977a: 100). Newby (1977a) perceives that Pahl may have overstated his case in this respect: that geographic milieu may define patterns of social relationships through the constraints which it applies to the local social structure – for example, the so-called 'tyranny of distance', that is, social actors' access to one another and to scarce material resources that are regarded as commonplace in more densely populated parts of the country. Whereas Pahl took the view that any connection between this local social system and its 'rurality' is purely spurious, as it stems from the inability of the inhabitants to transcend the spatial constraints imposed upon them, Newby suggested that if social institutions are locality-based and if they are interrelated then there might be a 'local social system' worthy of sociological attention – which may be called 'rural'. Again, there are a number of empirically identifiable properties if social relationships and institutions are constrained in such a way as to render them locality-based. That is, there *may* be a 'local social system' – or mostly self-contained community – where spatial factors have some effect upon social relationships. This would constitute a reasonable field worthy of sociological attention.

However, Newby's argument located the problem or incapacity to a wider societal system of inequality and/or technological development, rather than something specific to the locality per se. Therefore, in terms of creating an intellectually distinct field of sociological investigation, Newby pursued a more traditionalist research agenda – but his doctoral research drew upon a more cultural analysis, in which the definition of the situation and the rural is more conceptually significant.

Newby and the Deferential Thesis

Arguably Britain's last[10] rural sociologist, Howard Newby is significant in his innovative application of the theoretical and methodological agendas of the day to rural studies. Whilst he made no claim to have solved the problem of the definition of rural sociology, his research offers an important legacy. Newby's most productive period of research was during the early 1970s through to the late 1980s and there are three general stages that warrant consideration before his work's significance for contemporary rural sociology can be evaluated. This section, necessarily selective considering the scale of Newby's output, considers his doctoral research (later published as *The Deferential Worker*) and then later, more essayistic work, which moved to comment more broadly on the rural (Newby 1985). The following chapter moves to consider his last major empirical research project, conducted with colleagues at Essex (Newby et al. 1978b) and which marked a shift in his theoretical orientation.

Newby's theoretical model for his doctoral work was directly influenced by Goldthorpe et al.'s work on the affluent worker (Goldthorpe et al. 1968a, b). Goldthorpe's core conclusions were that the working classes were not, despite their relative affluence, becoming more like the classes above them. The significance of the affluent worker study is that it identified a non-conflictual working class (as opposed to the conflictual imagery of the traditional proletarians). The affluent workers participated less in the community, held an instrumentalist approach to their working lives alongside continuing to support trade unions and to vote Labour. Newby applied this analysis to a rural setting, specifically the farm worker, which was the focus of *The Deferential Worker* (Newby 1977a). It was therefore the experience of long-term farm workers, rather than immigrant ex-urbanites, which at the outset made *The Deferential Worker* more an occupational sociology than a generic piece of rural sociology. That is, Newby's conceptualisation of the rural was not the direct focus of the study and in those terms successfully avoided reifying the geographical locale of the rural as many previous rural studies had done. The study is better classified as an empirical study into the theoretical problem of workers' false class consciousness than what can be said to characterise the rural.

A distinction within his approach was his concern to examine social relations as they played out at interactional level. As such, he addressed some of the difficulties inherent in earlier community studies research but, more significantly, his analysis was also informed by Raymond Williams's (1973) work on the penetration of the rural idyll into the British cultural imagination. Williams's text, *The Country and the City* (1973), is a critical analysis of the representation of the rural in literature. The influence of Williams's work is therefore implicit but a powerful influence throughout Newby's critical approach to rural studies and it served to take his analysis beyond the accusations of descriptive narrative levelled at the community studies tradition. Borrowing heavily from Williams (1973), Newby critiqued the association of the English countryside with 'harmony, settlement, virtue, retreat, community, innocence, identity, retrospect', which are then contrasted with a parallel set of ideas associated with the city (Newby 1977a: 17–18). Newby (1977a) therefore shared Williams's (1973) concern to cut through the nostalgic sentimentality applied to the rural. For example, despite the tremendous change that can be said to have influenced rural England, such as mechanisation, the break-up of large landed estates since the First World War and significant rural depopulation, rural England continues to occupy a reified status in the cultural imagination:

> Ever since England became a predominantly urban country, rural England has been regarded as the principal repository of quintessential English values … Its reputation as the epitome of England's green and pleasant land has been aided by thousands of Constable paintings hung in department stores up and down the country.
>
> (Newby 1977a: 11, 12)

Newby then applied Williams's cultural analysis to the social situation of farm workers and argued that 'there has been a refusal to recognize the problem of rural poverty in the midst of this splendidly bucolic existence' (Newby 1977a: 12). His analysis drew upon a variety of cultural references, such as popular fiction's representation of the rural workers (Gibbons 1986 [1932]), in which farm workers are 'alternately ignored and caricatured in the public consciousness' (Newby 1977a: 11). Newby's approach is therefore an interesting combination of theoretical agendas and concerns. On the one hand, there was Williams's cultural analysis and on the other the influence of Goldthorpe's more traditional, sociological, class-driven agenda. When applied to the specific case of the farm worker, the combination served to penetrate the low-paid economic circumstances of the farm worker and their definition and interpretation of their own situation. Newby concluded that the myth of the rural idyll 'has affected the agricultural worker's interpretation of his own situation, for a general cultural approval of the rural way of life is something that an otherwise low-paid, low-status group of workers is grateful to adhere to with understandable enthusiasm' (Newby 1977a: 13). On a theoretical level, he argued that the persistence of the rural myth interlinks with 'important contradictions in unfettered capitalist development' (Newby 1977a: 19). Applied to the rural context, for landowners '[it was] because social control could be carried out on a personal, face-to-face basis that they were able to disassociate themselves from the consequences of their own actions' (Newby 1977a: 19). The combination allowed Newby's (1977a) analysis to reveal that 'the myth of rural retrospect thus became, consciously or unconsciously, an agent of social control' (Newby 1977a: 19). It was unravelling the exact manner in which these patterns continued to operate in agriculture in the 1970s that was the focus of Newby's (1977a) empirical research.

Newby (1977a): Locale and Methodology

His fieldwork was conducted in East Suffolk, a county with significant regional variations to the extent that 'no pretensions are made ... to portray the life of the "typical" agricultural worker – indeed this would be somewhat irrelevant since the object of study is not a group of workers but a set of theoretical problems' (Newby 1977a: 123). Whilst theoretical objectives can be seen to have informed the initial focus of the study, its methodological application is remarkably distinctive from the forms of social investigation dominant at that time. Newby's (1977a) methodology was 'deliberately eclectic' and he drew upon historical sources such as the agricultural and population census statistics, historical sources (both documentary and oral) and participant observation in addition to his own social survey (Newby 1977a: 123). In total, Newby interviewed seventy-one farmers and 233 farm workers in forty-four parishes in central East Suffolk between the first week of March and the third week of August 1972, during which he was resident in the field. The balance between the relative statuses accorded to these methods within the study warrants detailed examination:

> In effect the survey and the period of participant observation increasingly came to complement each other: insights gained from participant observation could be checked against survey data; on the other hand much of this data could often only become *meaningful* through the experiences gained from living with a farm worker and his family in a tied cottage for six months and gaining first-hand knowledge about the work and community situation. As the period of fieldwork continued, the participant observation became more and more important as many of the shortcomings of using interview material to obtain knowledge of relationships became apparent; nevertheless 'doing a survey' was a very good excuse for talking to farm workers and for prompting them to articulate their feelings about their own experiences which would otherwise have remained unstated.
>
> (Newby 1977a: 123–124, original emphasis)

It is clear that there was a significant interplay between these methods; the degree to which these methods informed Newby's analysis as a whole is more opaque.[11] That is, whilst the appendices contain copies of the social survey and Newby has written elsewhere about the fieldwork (Newby 1977b), his informal and discursive – and on occasion narrative – style tends to blend his argument and the results of his fieldwork in parallel. He concluded that farm workers and farmers participate in a system of social control, which he termed deference. What is significant about the deference thesis is that 'behind the everyday rituals of deferential behaviour there have frequently lain attitudes and motives which are quite the opposite' (Newby 1977a: 111). The exact meaning applied to deference by Newby (1977a) also warrants detailed explication:

'Deference' is generally reserved to explain at least this minimal commitment to 'deferential' forms of behaviour – otherwise 'quiescence' would suffice. However, differentiating deference from quiescence is far from easy, and not a problem to which sociologists have paid much attention, preferring to take it for granted that power relationships will, through some unexamined metamorphosis, automatically become moral ones over time.

These considerations have been highlighted by the work of Goffman to the extent that they cannot be ignored. Goffman has argued that what is necessary for the possibility of social interaction is merely an agreement on a definition of the situation which enables the participants to select correctly from their total repertoire of status positions and associated gestures and idioms. The process of maintaining this agreement is one of skewed communication: over-communicating those gestures, actions, etc. – what Goffman calls 'demeanour' – which confirm the relevant status positions and under-communicating those which are discrepant. Goffman called this process as 'impression management', which occurs while an individual is 'on stage'. However, when the role constraints are removed and the individual is 'off stage', only then can their identification with their 'on stage' behaviour be assessed.

(Newby 1977a: 111)[12]

The contradictions the deference thesis allows Newby (1977a) to unravel include the ironic observation that:

Many agricultural workers have seen their village overrun, as they regard it, by an alien, urban, overwhelmingly middle-class population, variously labelled as newcomers, immigrants, outsiders or, simply, 'furriners', who are viewed as having destroyed a distinctive rural way of life and a close-knit community in which 'everybody knew everybody else'.

(Newby 1977a: 20)

Therefore, 'it is the new urbanites, not the rural employers, who are blamed for the declining rural way of life' by the farm workers (Newby 1977a: 21). Indeed, even the landowners themselves 'share with their employees a quite sincere regret for a state of affairs that they themselves, in responding to market factors, have brought about' (Newby 1977a: 20). Newby's analysis permitted him to unravel the nostalgia expressed by respondents in relation to their work, alongside a critical appreciation that 'sociologically agricultural workers are "rural" only because the constraints of the labour and housing markets means that they must both live and work in the same locality' (Newby 1977a: 100). Newby's analysis therefore included the hierarchical authority structure of the farm and the highly unequal distribution of rewards between employer and employees and how deference serves to explain false class consciousness on the part of the farm workers constrained by their social situation. He identified a form of contractual bargaining or negotiation between these two groups. He termed this as paternalistic authority, which the landowners or farmers use to ensure the smooth running of the farm through their everyday interactions with the farm workers. The significance of Newby's approach can be seen to be theoretical and methodological: the latter in terms of the innovative use of qualitative methods and theoretical in terms of an analysis of small-scale micro-interaction alongside a macro, Marxist-influenced critique of capitalist relations. Newby reworked Goffman's concept of the total institution (Goffman 1961) into the notion of the 'total situation' in order to capture the constraint and systems of exploitation facing the farm worker.

The deferential worker thesis was derived from fieldwork, but Newby's later work employed a more reflective, historical approach to further develop the concept of deference and to locate the farm worker within the history of the English rural village. So, whereas in early Newby 'the analysis could be regarded as a piece of industrial sociology', his later work became a more overt form of rural historical sociology and commentary (Newby 1977a: 100). The following section considers one of Newby's last sole-authored texts and then draws it together with the deferential thesis to evaluate Newby's approach and its potential for subsequent rural studies.

Newby (1985): Change in the English Village

Newby here offers a different approach, which introduces no new empirical results but draws together his own research to offer a commentary on rural society. The text was more populist in tone and adopted a more historical approach. Newby argued that social changes were all rooted in change in agricultural industry – and its decline – as 'English rural society is no longer entirely, nor even predominantly, an agrarian society' (Newby 1985: 183), the result of which was that significant changes had occurred in the social and occupational composition of rural populations who were no longer dependent upon farming for their living. Newby distinguished those dependent upon agriculture for employment as the 'truly rural' and contrasted these with the ex-urbanite newcomers. The impact of this latter group also marked 'changes in the economic and social organization of agriculture. Social change in the village has therefore accompanied the upheavals in the nature of agricultural work itself' (Newby 1985: 183). Newby remained cautious in associating this transformation with a decline of communion or a particular quality of human relationship and meaningful social intimacy:

> The village inhabitants formed a community because they had to: they were imprisoned by constraints of various kinds, including poverty, so that reciprocal aid became a necessity.
>
> (Newby 1985: 154)

The focus of his analysis was upon the changing forms of association found in rural areas. This text differs from his doctoral studies in that he unravelled the historical legacy of the occupational community in order to contextualise its decline. His analysis began with the period between 1846 and 1873 and the 'rural-izing' process, in which the economic viability of much small-scale manufacture and domestic handicraft declined and the production of goods was transferred to the new system of factory production in the towns. The result for those workers remaining in rural areas was, inevitably, that 'farming was unquestionably the mainstay of the rural economy. The population of the majority of rural villages was therefore dependent upon agriculture for a living' (Newby 1985: 157). The bond that linked the village was not the rural location per se but employment. 'Because of its dependence upon a single industry the rural village formed what might be called an "occupational community" ' (Newby 1985: 157) (see table 3).

Table 3 Characteristics of the occupational community

- Isolated, self-contained community
- Fierce loyalty
- Own customs and traditions
- Sense of identity and morality
- Sense of certainty, clearer boundaries over what was and was not acceptable
- Sense of order and a sense of place
- A definition of community in both geographical and social terms
- The double-edge quality of the village in this sense was
  (i) Security for some, but
  (ii) A narrow and restrictive prison for others, 'shackling the individualist by the vicious pur-veyance of gossip and innuendo' (Newby 1985: 157)

Source: Newby (1985).

In his critique of social relations in the English village, Newby catalogues the class relations that underpinned the chronic poverty and cruel exploitation of workers in rural locations. The analysis draws in the importance of the physical organisation of land and its social consequences:

> the settlement pattern, with most villages consisting of the dwellings of agricultural workers and with the farmers scattered around the parish on their own farms but away from the centre of the village itself ... therefore, the employers, whether farmers or landlords ... were not part of the rural village community.
>
> (Newby 1985: 159)

The physical separation of worker and landowner created a distinct community among those resident inside the English rural village:

> there was another community, a locally based working-class subculture, which excluded 'them' in authority. This subculture represented the core of the occupational

community. It was basically a neighbourly association of kin and workmates, not dis-
similar to that which existed in many urban working-class neighbourhoods, but which
the outsider could find virtually impenetrable. It was sustained by the isolation of the
rural village, by the strong kinship links between the village inhabitants and by the
need for cooperation in times of family crisis ... it was forged out of the overlap
between workplace and village ... relationships established at work spilled into leisure
hours ... the accepted code of behaviour ... followed in the village also applied in the
work situation.

(Newby 1985: 159–160)

So the rural village was an extremely close-knit society, in which social
ostracism and gossip became extremely powerful ways of enforcing the values and
standards of village life. Status and prestige, unsurprisingly, are not entirely
derived from the world of work, so here the semi-public arena – the village pub –
becomes all-important as a site where work and the social life and news of the
village is discussed. The implications of this form of local social system and the
social relations within it hold implications for the farm worker. 'The integration of
the farm worker into this occupational community meant that it was his prestige
among his fellow workers and neighbours that mattered most to him' (Newby
1985: 161). This was based on a combination of work-based status and commu-
nity-derived prestige. For example, botching the task of ploughing a field would be
visible to all for the next six months so, as Newby (1985) points out, 'pride in the
job' was not based entirely on altruism.

The analysis Newby (1985) provides into this time period possesses two distinct
groups: working-class farm workers and the locally powerful, such as farmers and
landowners. Conflict between these two groups, whilst rarely rising to the surface,
was visible in 'covert expressions of resistance' and the rural underworld of arson,
poaching and 'subversive talk in the tap house' (Newby 1985: 162). Drawing upon
the deferential thesis, Newby highlighted the importance of the local landowner's
paternalism model of management, which served to smooth over divisions
between the two groups. That is, the ethic of the country gentleman or paternalism
of the local squire could be exchanged for the deference of local workers. For
example, charity and ostentatious acts of generosity accorded to the whole village
encouraged respect and gratitude. 'Gifts were the knots which secured the ties of
dependence ... community, as an ideology, was a gloss that was placed upon the
very rigid and authoritarian divisions within the village' (Newby 1985: 163).

Newby's (1985) analysis then moved to consider the early part of the twentieth
century, from 1912 onwards, and the invention of the internal combustion engine.
The context was one in which the drift from the land of agricultural labour continued and urbanisation also increased. However, this time period also marked a
point at which commuting from a village to an occupation outside the village
locale became a possibility. The attraction of the countryside for the new

phenomenon of the commuter included cheap housing (until the 1960s) and the continuing idealisation of rural life. Whereas in the epoch detailed by Newby in the earliest phases of the industrial revolution there had been a two-tier social class structure, this shift introduced a new group into the existing occupational community.

Newby (1985) detailed the manifold impact of this new group, newcomers who work in the towns, for rural villages. First, they brought with them an urban, middle-class, lifestyle, which was alien to the remaining agricultural population. As a result, newcomers did not make the village the focus of their social activities and they continued to make use of urban amenities whilst living in the village. Therefore both entertainments, socialising and even shopping tended to take place outside the village. In summation, 'the newcomer does not always feel it is necessary to adapt to the hitherto accepted *mores* of the village' (Newby 1985: 165), the result of which was that it soon became clear that everybody did not know everybody else. Ultimately, a new social division emerged within the village. Newby (1985) detailed this as consisting of members of the former occupational community retreating in among themselves, that is, becoming a form of community within a community. Newby (1985) terms this as an encapsulated community, which is resistant to any intimate contact with the commuters and second-home owners who increasingly comprise a substantial proportion of the rural village population.

The most important distinction Newby then went on to demarcate were two new points of contact and resentment: (1) housing and (2) the environment:

> Newcomers regard the countryside in primarily aesthetic and recreational terms … They tend to be unappreciative of the farm worker's skills, not out of malice, but because they simply lack the detailed knowledge of agriculture on which to base a judgement.
>
> (Newby 1985: 168, 169)

The result of this shift was that 'the criterion by which a farm worker could once obtain high status – skill at work – is therefore threatened with being overthrown' (Newby 1985: 169). In its place, Newby (1985) argued, was conspicuous consumption, that is, the urban basis for allocating status. The implication for those in the village remaining dependent upon farm wages was that they were simply unable to compete in the new differentials of size of house, car, consumer durables, furnishings and garden. The response of the farm worker, Newby argued, was to be the emergence of a new scale or hierarchy within the village:

> The agricultural worker, however, reacts to the possibility of being deprived of his former status in his own village by changing the rules of the competition … The basis of length of residence is one of the few ways in which local workers can retain any of their old status in the village.
>
> (Newby 1985: 169)

Writing over twenty years ago, the relevance of Newby's (1985) work for contemporary sociology needs to be evaluated and his analysis of the characteristics
of rural villages examined for relevance in the twenty-first century. Newby's work
can be assessed on three levels, that of theory, method and the legacy his work
holds for capturing the complexities of rurality. His early work was characterised
by a neo-Weberian theoretical approach (see *The Deferential Worker*), which was
then followed by a Marxist, structural analytic approach[13] (see *Property,
Paternalism and Power*), while in his work in the 1980s a more conversational, and
broader reflection was offered that encompassed rural society more broadly than
his earlier work (Newby 1980, 1985). Newby's turn towards a more explicitly
Marxist analysis (Newby et al. 1978a) is considered in more detail in the following
chapter – because this is not the most significant section of his contribution. His
theoretical shift away from the strong strand of interactionism in his earlier work
is an implicit critique of the lack of conceptual development within interactionist
approaches (Goffman 1983).[14] However, it is the synergy of method and theory in
his earliest work that offers the more fruitful legacy. The role and status accorded
his empirical research and the methodological innovations it contained are considered first.

The context in which Newby (1977a) conducted his empirical research was also
significant, albeit seen only with the benefit of hindsight. The timing of Newby's
fieldwork in the early 1970s coincided with and contributed to a historical shift
towards qualitative forms of research (Hammersley and Atkinson 1995, Pole and
Morrison 2003). Techniques, which had previously been the underdog to more sta-
tistically-orientated work, were moving to establish themselves as dominant
research paradigms in some sub-disciplines of sociology (Hammersley and
Atkinson 1995). Newby's (1977a) inclusion of qualitative methods alongside
quantitative techniques, but with equal if not more emphasis, can be compared to
methodologies emerging more broadly at that time in criminology (Young, J.
1971), within the Sociology of Education (Ball 1981, Burgess 1983) and in the
sociology of work (Oakley 1974) and an interest in symbolic interactionism (see
Rock 1979). It was upon the basis of the close, rich interactional data and
emphasis upon *verstehen* within his account that his analysis was derived. Newby
has also contributed to the wave of more reflexive pieces on qualitative research
(in the Bell and Roberts collection). This therefore places Newby as one of the first
in a new wave of ethnographic researchers emerging within sociology.

The role of theory within his account is more problematic to evaluate. In terms
of his citations, there is a clear interest and continuity with the traditional
approaches to industrial or occupational sociologies dominating sociology at that
time, such as Lockwood's *Blackcoated Worker* (1958) study. However, the
emphasis upon demeanour is clearly derived from Canadian sociologist Erving
Goffman's influence. Goffman's unravelling of a new arena warranting sociological attention – that of the interaction order – is clearly responded to in *The*

Deferential Worker. That Newby applied his fieldwork to explicate the nuances of face-to-face behaviour and interactional rituals as a means to critique the inequalities maintained through such relations is clearly (and emotively) expressed in Newby (1977b). Newby's approach is therefore very much a powerful critique of these relations as his more explicitly Marxist orientation in later studies. The approach he employed in his early work borrowed heavily from the very moral tone and critique often misinterpreted in Goffman's work (Hillyard 2004) and relied upon ethnographic research rather than narrative-style description. That symbolic interactionism continues to operate at the margins of mainstream sociology (Atkinson and Housley 2003) and that it defies easy definition or explanation (Rock 1979) undoubtedly contribute to why Newby is often more associated with Marxist approaches (Wright 2004a) than with Goffman's interactionism.

Nevertheless, there are a number of absences that are notable within his approach. These included the role and status of rural women, the elderly and young people and children. The latter two groups have now been engaged in research both as a deprived group within rural areas (Jones 1997, Leyshon 2002) and also as an empowered consumer group (Pole et al. 1999). Subsequent rural researchers (see Little 2003a, Leyshon 2004, Little and Morris 2004) have gone on to broaden the number of issues and themes examined in rural areas to include young people and women. There is now a wealth of literature on the role and status of rural women. Twenty years on from Newby, whilst he remains an instrumental figure within rural sociology, his influence has declined – or rather the relevance of the rural for sociology more generally. This can readily be seen in the way that the rural no longer features as an important element in introductory sociology textbooks (Fulcher and Scott 2003), whereas it had featured as prominently as the urban (Lee and Newby 1983). Most centrally, perhaps: is the dilemma that Newby did not resolve the difficulties inherent in attempting to define the rural – locale continued not to feature as the most significant feature underpinning his analysis as he shifted the focus on to rural Britain as a component of British life more broadly and the economic, technological, social and political milieu of which the rural is part. In that sense, the very relevance of 'rurality' remains open to question. Perhaps most important of all at that time, Newby extended the debate to include the concept of power and power relations inside rural areas – indeed, a development that may be somewhat neglected in contemporary studies of rurality.

A salient feature of Howard Newby's work as a rural sociologist was that he eschewed the somewhat nostalgic, romanticised approach to the countryside that had prevailed for so long. His work served to guard against the constant danger of excessive nostalgia and the tendency to take a highly selective and somewhat rose-tinted view of the 'good old days' for, in doing so, what actually has occurred and changed may be lost. Yet, whilst bearing in mind those reservations, the very persistence of this theme suggests we can't dismiss it as mere nostalgia – what seems to be underpinning it all is a critique of the present. It all seems to be an attempt to articulate, albeit vaguely, the private troubles people experience in everyday life in modern industrial society. This analysis up to the 1980s provided a context from which rural studies emerged and highlighted some of the key issues and gaps in these early approaches. Whilst there may be agreement that 'community' and rural life are a good thing, surprisingly, there is little agreement over what they actually are.[15]

Conclusion

The chapter has progressed the definition of the rural through the work of Tönnies, contributions from the community studies approach of the 1960s and significant critiques of that approach's study of the rural made by Pahl. The innovations of Newby's approach to the rural and omissions in his approach have been discussed. The conceptual shifts of how best the rural can be approached are now drawn together, as a precursor to the following chapter, which considers key figures in contemporary rural studies.

The three aspects of community have dominated studies of rural communities. The first of these was implicitly a critique of modern industrial society and the impact of modern society in terms of changing the structure and content of personal relationships. This is a pessimistic, negative analysis in which the impersonal and dehumanising aspects of modern life and a sense of social dislocation under the conditions of rapid social and economic change are emphasised. Community studies under this approach have a clear empirical charge to establish a factual basis for arguments about whether modern society does or does not suffer from a 'loss of community'. The concept of community is employed as a means to critique modern industrial society.

A second analysis associated community with localised social relations. That is, it also charts the decline of a form of relations, namely the importance of locality in forming the basis of modern social organisation. It explicates the erosion of small-scale and relatively self-contained lifestyles. The localised community had limited contact with the outside world and control over the core necessities of life – food, housing and employment – lay in local hands. Therefore, the lifestyles were fairly autonomous and there was a greater diversity of local traditions and customs.

The third echoes Newby's concept of the occupational community, where bonds had been established upon the basis of long-term residence, proximity and shared employment patterns. As a concept, this is equally applicable to rural and urban locations (see Wilmott and Young 1960, Bernard et al. 2001) and, for example, could relate to the redevelopment of many inner-city areas. This serves to highlight the importance of changing occupational structure as well as that of geographic proximity. As such, the importance of the rural location per se declines in importance compared with occupation patterns. The historical context of the decline of the traditional industries that characterised England as the 'workshop of the world' during and after the industrial revolution is significant in the pessimistic framing of such changes in terms of decline and loss. Returning explicitly to the concern here with rural settings, the shift is one in which an influx of ex-urban commuters into rural villages combines with the loss of former agricultural workers as the dominant form of employment within the locality. The result is that established patterns of village life – shaped around this employment pattern – are disrupted. Within this remains the problematic concept of community and its somewhat nostalgic definition. The desire for community seems to symbolise a desire for personal and social fulfilment: community as representing the good life, a utopian vision. In this sense, 'community' becomes a normative prescription. That is, it expresses the values of an individual concerning what life should be like (rather than what it actually is like). This demands that the loaded concepts of rurality and community be reworked and a more sophisticated definition offered.

Collectively, the chapter has suggested that community or rurality defined as a geographical expression, or a fixed and bounded locality that attracts a human settlement in a particular local territory, is not particularly sociological. Rather it needs to be viewed as a local social system, which represents a set of social relationships within a locality that can be studied. The social life of the area, the network of interrelationships established between those living in the same locality, should be explicated. However, nothing can be said about the content of those relationships, unlike *Gemeinschaft,* based on the unique qualities of that social system, but it does allow some empirical research to be carried out. Finally, and potentially most profitably, could be to approach rural and community studies as a type of relationship. This incorporates a consideration of a sense of identity between individuals, levels of mutual identification, an examination of 'community spirit' and – most importantly – the fact that this can be geographically widespread. We have seen that community as normative prescription has too often interfered with empirical description and that no systematic sociology of the community is yet available. That the community studies approach is labelled here as a tradition, despite recent studies (see Bell's 1994 *Childerley*), is largely due to its decline in fashionability. Such fashionability within sociology can be seen if the community studies approach – by definition, an empirical one – is placed into the historical paradigm through which the approach originated. The early 1960s community studies projects (see Stacey's 1960 study of Banbury) are informed by the structural functionalism characterising sociology at that time (Atkinson et al. 1993). Studies, such as Stacey (1960) and earlier, more explicitly rural studies such as Williams (1956), established rural sociology in a British context, based upon a premise that where you live defines how you live. Neither has a tidy classification to replace the rural–urban continuum been discovered – only a number of lines of enquiry on the relationship, if any, between locality, social relationships and a sense of identity (Donaldson et al. 2006, Pahl 2005).

However, associating such concepts with Pahl's notion of a 'village in the mind' and Newby's critique of the 'national village cult' (Newby 1977a: 17) allows media and communication and transport improvements to be incorporated into the examination of social ties and the consideration of important issues in modern society – of the nature and direction of social change. Therefore the relevance of community studies work has served to trace how the rural has progressively been approached theoretically and methodologically. Pahl's (1968) work not only corrected the over-exuberance of early readings, or misreadings, of Tönnies, but also was an instrumental part of a new wave of studies – both urban and rural – seeking to theorise forms of association. This period of research, which can loosely be seen from 1950 to the early 1970s, has been termed by others as 'the old tradition of community studies' (Crow et al. 1990: 248). However, the contribution of the key studies that will be considered here in relation to the rural was instrumental in the new research paradigm of qualitative research that emerged within sociology and blossomed from the late 1960s onwards, but also in that it paves the way for an eclectic approach to examining the rural that can be said to inform rural studies to this day: the ethnographic turn. Sociology in the 1950s and 1960s had, largely, been characterised by an interest in social class, leading Lacey to observe that social class, like chips, came with everything (Lacey and Ball 1979). However, the manner in which social class was empirically researched diversified in the late 1960s and 1970s within a number of sub-disciplines within sociology.[16] In the early 1970s, notably announced at the 1970 BSA conference, a paradigmatic shift in the sociology of education took place, with the emergence of a 'new' sociology of education, which moved into new territories of exploring aspects of education that before had not received critical attention (Young, M. 1971, Brown 1973). Features such as the curriculum, interaction in the classroom and pupil–teacher interactions became critical areas of investigation. Similarly, the UK was influenced by the distinction between secondary and primary deviance made in the US and by the theoretical ideas of symbolic interactionism (Rock 1979, Burgess 1984).

This chapter therefore serves to bridge the work of Tönnies with that of the second wave of – more sophisticated – commentaries on the rural.

Chapter Summary

The chapter summarised the very earliest rural sociology and work of Ferdinand Tönnies. It then considered Tönnies's legacy and found that the manner in which his ideas were understood and utilised in early community studies work was problematic. Such studies tended to overemphasise the sense of nostalgia for the loss of community and the rise of the industrial age. Pahl's work presented an important antidote to that tendency. He and Newby from the 1960s onwards began to examine the changes taking place in rural areas and to advance the concept of rural sociology beyond a reliance upon geographic location. New concepts to emerge at this time were locality, social relationships and a sense of identity.

These theoretical advances within the sociology of the rural were paralleled by an increasing emphasis upon empirical fieldwork. This coincided with developments in the wide discipline of sociology where qualitative studies were 'coming home' and symbolic interactionism was inspiring research in other sub-disciplines. This enabled our understanding of traditional concepts such as social class to be explored in new settings and through different social forms. Newby's *Deferential Worker* thesis is one such example. By the end of the 1970s, rural sociology represented an active and inventive research field – both theoretically and methodologically.

Learning Tools

Questions

1. To what extent did empirical research characterise the work of the rural commentators discussed in this chapter?
2. In what era of sociological development would you place (a) Tönnies's and (b) Newby's work? Which theoretical interests informed their writings?
3. Describe and critically evaluate Tönnies's twin concepts of *Gemeinschaft* and *Gesellschaft*.
4. How have social scientists re-conceptualised the idea of 'the rural' over time?
5. Pahl's analysis of a rural–urban continuum merely returned Tönnies's twin concepts of *Gemeinschaft* and *Gesellschaft* to their correct ontological status. Discuss.
6. How does the community studies approach to the study of rurality differ from Newby's? Discuss with particular reference to their respective analyses of social class.
7. To what extent does Newby's work remain relevant for contemporary sociologists?

Key Thinkers and their Ideas

Ferdinand Tönnies (1855–1936)   Son of a prosperous farmer. Dismissed from Kiel University (1913–1933) by the Nazis for his attacks on their ideas. Argued to be the founding father of community studies and rural sociology. His distinction between 'community' and 'association' is echoed (in different ways) by Durkheim, Simmel and Weber (see Craib 1992).

Howard Newby (1947–)   A rural sociologist. Born and brought up in Derby, his father was a skilled worker at the Rolls Royce factory nearby. Much of his academic work has been within the locality of East Anglia. Based at the Department of Sociology, University of Essex between 1967 and 1988 as undergraduate, postgraduate research student, lecturer, senior lecturer, reader and professor. Latterly, Director and Chief Executive of the Economic and Social Research Council (ESRC), Vice Chancellor of the University of Southampton and Chair of the Committee of Vice Chancellors and Principals (CVCP).

Glossary

Community studies: approach to social research popular in the 1950s and 1960s. Largely informed by structural functionalist theoretical assumptions.

Deferential worker: Newby's conception of the farm worker and how, through their work and social relations with their employers, they come to take on a pro-work attitude.

Definition of the situation: Thomas's concept that, if men [*sic*] define their situations as real, they are real in their consequences. This emphasises the importance of individual actors independently interpreting their social situations and acting on that basis.

Gemeinschaft: community.

Gesellschaft: association.

Monograph: the report of research findings in a book.

Reflexivity: the monitoring by an ethnographer of his or her impact upon the social situation under investigation at every stage of the research process (i.e. not just in the field). See Atkinson's (1990) quote under constructivism in the glossary at the end of the book.

Rural geography: perhaps more geographically sensitive than rural sociology and perhaps more oriented towards social policy, environmentalism and quantitative techniques.

Rural sociology: sociological investigation of all matters rural. These need not be purely defined geographically (i.e. within a given region or locale) but can also be a 'state of mind' or definition of a situation. Rural sociology positions social theory more prominently than rural geography.

Rural studies: social science research engaging with all matters rural.

Rural–urban continuum: a bipolar interpretation of society, in which the differences between urban and rural settlements is emphasised.

−2−

New Issues in Rural Sociology
and Rural Studies

This chapter takes forward the rural research agenda emerging from the first chapter and examines the work of more recent rural researchers. Chapter 1 summarised early sociologists' engagement with rural studies and how subsequent scholars then developed this body of knowledge. This chapter continues the analysis of Newby's work, but focuses on his later work. This distinction reflects a change in theoretical emphasis between his early and later work. Following Newby, an important move is made to consider rural studies more broadly than a specifically rural sociology.[1] In recent decades, the expansion of rural geography stands inversely proportional to sociology's engagement with rural matters. The text therefore moves to draw in research work by rural researchers, some with sociological backgrounds but primarily geographers.

The scale of the literature in rural geography speaks volumes on the vibrancy of the sub-discipline. There are many options and avenues to explore: for example, the role of community development from a developing world/colonial perspective; work on rurality that emerged in the mid-1990s by Keith Halfacree and Rachel Woodward; and more specific commentaries on gender in rural locations by Sally Shortall, Jo Little and Rachel Woodward. Alternatively there are themes of social exclusion explored by Mark Shucksmith and rural sustainability in the work of John Bryden that offer direct continuities with the themes of the declining role of agriculture in rural areas and questions as to what can feasibly take its place. The very breadth of these further areas of specialist rural research demonstrates the expansion of rural geography work and the expanded number of issues occupying contemporary rural researchers. It also renders a comprehensive review of all rural literature (sociological and geographic) beyond the scope of this text.

Fortunately, the text is not claiming to offer an overview of all rural studies – both sociological and geographically oriented (if such a task be possible). What is the concern is the theoretical and methodological concerns of geographers engaging with the rural. The two authors addressed in depth here (Terry Marsden and Paul Cloke) are only two among many alternative senior scholars working within the UK. However, both have clear links with early rural sociology and both moved on to define distinctive approaches to the rural. For example, the former demonstrates clear links with the Marxist orientation of Newby's early work and

Cloke has been closely associated with the cultural turn (although Murdoch would be another example) and has engaged with visual studies and written positioning/reflexive papers on the role and function of rural geography. There are many parallels between these interests and current preoccupations in sociology. Marsden and Cloke also both enjoy well-established and extensive research profiles. Indeed, there is a lesson here for future sociology, as the history and traditions of rural geography share many areas of overlap, although the disciplines do not necessarily progress in similar directions.[2] The work of a younger generation of scholars within rural geography (Milbourne, Woods, Ward) is described in subsequent chapters.

The primary – and most substantive – aim of the text is to reinvigorate rural sociology (to draw the rural to sociology's attention). It is well served by examining the continuities or disjunctions between earlier lines of development. This second chapter takes two scholars within rural geography in order to speak to the sociology community first and foremost and that of rural geography second. It necessarily draws upon rural geography work so heavily because rural geography research has flourished whilst rural sociology is largely absent from the curriculum in UK sociology departments, and this exposes how rural sociology is currently unfashionable in the UK.

Rural Sociology and the Legacy of the Post-war Period

Hamilton, albeit writing fifteen years ago, was moved to observe that there is a 'virtual absence in Britain' of rural sociology (Hamilton 1990: 225). His account relates to 'different organisational and institutional contexts' and 'historical experiences' after the Second World War (Hamilton 1990: 225):

> Post-war Britain *was* concerned about the agricultural sector. But it was a concern focused on the strategic role of agriculture, rather than the social changes accompanying industrial modernisation: the issue was food security ... in which the sociologist – if he or she did have a role to play – could only play second fiddle to those whose role was to increase agricultural productivity – the scientists and the agricultural economists.
>
> (Hamilton 1990: 228, original emphasis)

Hamilton argues that the 'post-war dream of increasing food output' served to shape different disciplines' treatment of the rural (Hamilton 1990: 228). Whilst relations between government (in the form of the Ministry of Agriculture, Fisheries and Food, MAFF) and farming unions (the National Farmers' Union, NFU) were drawn closer, this served to distract attention from the social implications of the drive towards an intensive agriculture:

The very success of the NFU in its corporatist links with the state maintained the fiction that academic attention on agriculture and rural society should be devoted to making the farm sector more 'efficient' and profitable, so that 'society's' interests in having a ready supply of cheap food could be served.

(Hamilton 1990: 230)

Neither were the agricultural economists oriented towards analysing the social impact of agricultural change, for 'they certainly had virtually nothing to do with rural society, or the impact of changes within agriculture on the society, culture, politics, economics or environment of the rural areas in which agriculture took place' (Hamilton 1990: 229). Sociology's failure to engage with rural issues was heightened by the comparatively new institutional status of sociology within the university system at the time. Hamilton argues that 'sociology really had no purchase on the British academic world until the early 1960s – and then only as a sort of American import, or somewhat esoteric intellectual dalliance practised largely by central European *émigrés* and their tiny coteries of graduate students' (Hamilton 1990: 229). On the charge that sociology lacked theoretical depth, Hamilton associates this with the form of sociology practised in its earliest form in Britain:

Sociology was also widely seen in Britain as a science for understanding and resolving social problems. These were deemed largely to exist in the cities, and to be concerned primarily with issues connected to housing, health and education.

(Hamilton 1990: 229)

Hence sociology was damned in two senses, marginalised by the lack of demand from the agricultural sector, from rural society and 'more significantly ... from the profession of sociology itself' (Hamilton 1990: 229).

The first attempts to analyse rural society have been considered in the opening chapter and they were, inevitably, shaped by the dominant theoretical preoccupations of that period, in Hamilton's eyes constituted 'a rather functionalist "community studies" and its derivatives' (Hamilton 1990: 229). Pahl (1968) and Bell and Newby (1971) reached similar conclusions:

For a time these polar typologies, some sanctified with the authority of the founding fathers, served as a justification for those who have been guilty of ... 'Vulgar Tönniesism' of the 'uncritical glorifying of old-fashioned rural life'.

(Pahl 1968: 265)

Hamilton (1990) further noted the conceptual dominance of social class within mainstream sociology following the early rural studies and how this also served to position the urban above that of the rural.[3] 'British sociology was pre-eminently concerned with class and occupational issues which were urban and industrial in their context' (Hamilton 1990: 229). Several examples illustrate this point; the 'preoccupation with male, industrial labour (management, professionals, the service occupations and women's work and social class position were also ignored), from which' in Hamilton's view as late as 1990 'British sociology has even now not fully recovered' (Hamilton 1990: 229).[4] The implication for rural sociology was that only a narrow set of issues was addressed within a 'conceptual agenda [that] had little or no room for work which did not treat questions such as social mobility, class consciousness' (Hamilton 1990: 229). As a result, 'rural sociology in the UK … has remained marginal and transitory' and secondary to the prominence of agricultural economics (Hamilton 1990: 228).

The new challenges Hamilton identifies lie with a new set of structural cleavages over environmentalism and amenity pressures: land-use conflicts and the 'newer' rural agencies and voluntary organisations[5] that have arisen following the 'relative demise of the dominant "productivist" paradigm in agriculture' (Hamilton 1990: 231). In terms of the state of change experienced within the countryside, it remains as compelling a site for sociological study as at the time of revolutionary change that attracted Tönnies's attention. The new danger, Hamilton argues, lies in the concentration upon single issues, and he refers to the work of Phillip Lowe and Graham Cox, which he perceived to be more in line with an 'environmental' tradition and as such 'limited by its grounding in policy issues' (Hamilton 1990: 231). However, the most penetrating criticism Hamilton levels is the prevalence of single-issue rural research that fails to 'provide the basis from which to construct a coherent and more general model of British rural society, and the changes which it is undergoing' (Hamilton 1990: 231). This focus on single issues, rather than theories or methodologies, shares one of the flaws of the old community studies tradition of the 1960s.[6]

The sting of such criticism is downplayed in Hamilton's overview of sociology more broadly and in his argument that sociology had itself become more diverse as it matured:

> Sociology itself has become less rather than more disciplinary as a social science and far less 'paradigm-orientated' than in the 1960s and 1970s. It is more and more implicated in cross-disciplinary work, and open to theoretical influences from many different intellectual fields.
>
> (Hamilton 1990: 231)

Hamilton's own argument seems somewhat contradictory – critiquing diversity when sociology itself had become more diverse – but, regardless of whether Hamilton attended to the logic of his own argument or not, he raises a serious question in his claim that 'in Britain, rural sociology continues to be a problem in search of a discipline' (Hamilton 1990: 232). Have rural studies become fragmented to the extent that no significant conceptual development has taken place following Newby? Or, alternatively, a reflection of the interdisciplinary nature of the issues facing rural studies?

Newby et al. (1978)

Hamilton (1990) positions Newby as a neo-Weberian but, whilst this may categorise his early work (see *The Deferential Worker*), his subsequent empirical research is progressively informed by a neo-Marxist, structural analysis (see *Property, Paternalism and Power*). This later, major empirical work (Newby et al. 1978b) is considered here as it marks a significant disjuncture with his previous work (Wright 2004a) and has influenced later rural researchers' analytic approaches.

The focus of *The Deferential Worker* upon the conditions, working life and social networks of the agricultural worker was shaped by Williams's (1973) recognition of the way the division between town and country has penetrated our everyday perceptions of the countryside to the degree that it shapes our expectations when we encounter rural relationships first-hand. It was Newby's assertion that this is even to the extent that it affects agricultural workers' interpretations of their own situation. The study was therefore a direct criticism of the functionalist overtones of mutual dependencies and the general analogy made between society and the human organism. Rather than a natural order, in which each aspect of society supports the functioning of the system as a whole, Newby moved towards a more conflict-based theory. By addressing the question of social stability and how the increasing profitability of farming has continued to remain in the hands of the few, Newby engaged with social and political controls. His study therefore contained both micro-theoretical concerns, the agricultural workers' understanding of their social situation, but also macro issues of inequalities and the playing out of economic divisions of wealth. Therefore, it is possible, at this stage, to conceptualise Newby's theoretical framework as neo-Weberian, as Hamilton (1990) does; yet it is also shot through with more Marxist concerns for how fundamentally the economy plays out in social relationships and ideological hegemonies.

Newby's later theoretical concerns continued to explore a more Marxist-oriented analysis (Newby et al. 1978). Newby's output, unlike Goffman, whose work he draws upon heavily in *The Deferential Worker*, included many jointly or team-authored papers with his colleagues in the sociology department at Essex.[7] The focus of a project with Bell, Rose and Saunders was again upon social inequalities:

> The concept of property refers not to the inherent quality of external objects *per se*, but to the socially and legally defined rights which attach to such subjects. It is in this sense that various conceptions of property ownership become highly relevant to the consideration of social inequality in contemporary rural society.
>
> (Newby et al. 1978b: 25)

Their analysis of traditional paternalism (the culture of the gentlemanly amateur) was contrasted with an emergent, alternative model of management (that of professional expertise and modern scientifically based agribusiness). Paternalism achieved authority over the workforce via the use of traditional forms of authority outside the work situation to obtain identification with their employees. This is ideological, employers managing their workforce in an organizational sense (such as the day-to-day practical running of the farm), but ideologically through providing definitions of the situation and transmitting a series of values and beliefs that are conducive to social harmony on the farm. This included a constant interpretation of the work situation in a way that would reinforce harmony and identification achieved through the premium placed on personal and pervasive interaction/face-to-face interaction. Newby et al. (1978b) capture the values and beliefs that the farmers promoted through a number of metaphors, such as team, family, community and partnership. This is in order to generate identification with the aims and methods of the farming enterprise and, at the personal level, a sense of stable harmony, cooperation, shared pleasure in the work and *Gemeinschaft*:

> Once the correct team spirit is inculcated ... then the whole system will run reasonably smoothly. Farmers will be pleased to consult their workers for they will usually be given the advice they want to hear.
>
> (Newby et al. 1978b: 175)

This analysis of complete ideological hegemony shares the conclusions of Newby (1977a). The innovation lies in their updating the thesis and the encroachment of such alien influences as the mass media, the 1944 Education Act and expansion of compulsory secondary education and the welfare state's weakening of the work ethic in the post-war period. Newby et al. (1978b) conducted new research to complement the data on farm workers in the deferential thesis funded by the then SSRC. The research team conducted interviews with farmers and landowners and traced the manner in which larger farms and the increased scale of business resulted in the loss of opportunities for sustained personal contact between employer and workforce. Their analysis suggested that employers take steps to try to mitigate the consequences, and this would seem to account for the increasing degree of involvement in the lives of workers outside the course of work, whereas on smaller farms contact in the work situation is often so continuous that there is no need, or even desire, to continue it outside:

> Ultimately the structure of the [farmer's] relationship with his workers, however matey its content, is an extremely hierarchical one ... He must convey the correct mixture of social intimacy and social distance which will enable the exercise of his authority to proceed smoothly. Much of this involves the ostensibly petty nuances of behaviour – demeanour rather than articulated speech.
>
> (Newby et al. 1978b: 179)

Newby et al. (1978b) are careful to clarify their findings with the caveat that whilst all farmers produce for the market, by no means all farmers behave in what they termed a 'market-orientated' manner. Their analysis linked the type of farmer with the size of their property or holding. The larger the holding, the more explicit, or contrived, social relations between employer and workforce became:

> Most farmers are quite prepared to construct an intricate web of paternalistic labour relations in order to obtain the identification of their workers; on the smaller farms this will occur spontaneously out of the much closer involvement of employers and employees in the work situation, whereas on the larger farms it is often a matter of con- scious or unconscious policy.
>
> (Newby et al. 1978b: 189)

The context is one in which Weberian rationalisation has signalled a shift 'away from justifying authority in terms of tradition towards legitimation in terms of knowledge and expertise' (Newby et al. 1978b: 30). The concerns of Newby and his colleagues are to unravel the different types of farmer and the forms of mana- gerial relationship they operate with their staff. They categorise this in the terms indicated in table 4.

Table 4 Typology of East Anglian farmers

		Market orientation	
		Low	High
Degree of direct involvement	Low	1. Gentleman farmer	2. Agribusinessman
in husbandry	High	3. Family farmer	4. Active managerial
farmer			

Cell 1: Traditional landowners; 'gentleman farmers'; local; second most educated
Cell 2: Agribusiness men; largest farming companies; most educated; linked to expansion
Cell 3: Family farmer; standard of living as much as the drive to profit; local
Cell 4: Active managerials; highly instrumental; closely involved
Source: Newby et al. (1978b: 182).

Newby and his colleagues are offering the simple correlation between type of farmer and the size of their farm holding and the 'legitimating ideologies but- tressing the stability of social life' that ensure the smooth running of the farm business (Newby et al. 1978b: 25). Echoing the deferential thesis, Newby et al.'s (1978b) account is interesting for the manner in which it utilises concepts drawn from the tradition of symbolic interactionist and Thomas's oft-cited emphasis upon the social actor's definition of the situation. In their analysis of the relationship between landowners and their employees, the emphasis was upon the landowner inculcating his workforce:

Embedded in the very concept of paternalism is the notion of dependence upon the moral judgement of others and how they define the prevailing social situation.

(Newby et al. 1978b: 28)

To cite Thomas in the original, the origins of Newby's thinking are clear:

Not only concrete acts are dependent on the definition of the situation, but also gradually a whole life-policy and the personality of the individual himself follow from a series of such definitions.

(Thomas 1928: 42 [1928])

However, the manner in which this is mapped on to wide social relations orientes the study into an analysis of social stratification,[8] rather than providing a study in rural or occupational sociology. The focus is upon the influence of farmers and landowners, as this far exceeds their physical number or presence. So the focus is quite clearly upon capitalist farmers and their privileged location within the wider class structure. Like Newby (1977a), the position of farmers (like farm workers) is located in the class structure of British society as a whole. In this sense, Newby and his team's emphasis is far more upon the issue of social class, which dominated sociology at that time, than the playing out of such forces upon an occupational group or upon the fine nuances of face-to-face behaviour that informed Newby's doctoral fieldwork. This is evident in the relative status accorded different methods within the study. Therefore, the qualitative techniques (interviewing farmers using questionnaires) employed within Newby et al.'s study (1978b) seek to cast light on much wider social processes than other contemporary studies using interviews as a key means of data collection. Participant observation is absent and indeed the number of interviews is reduced from Newby's (1977a) original work from 233 to 198 in the later work (Newby et al. 1978b). The emphasis is upon the different rhetorics of ownership ('outlooks on life') expounded by farmers (both tenant farmers and owner farmers), and their orientation towards the market and the social class of their friendship networks are among the other factors Newby outlines. These are also positioned historically in terms of the number and size of agricultural holdings in England and Wales at that time.[9]

The steps towards a more Marxist analysis is apparent in the attention paid to the working through of landownership and how this translates into 'ideologies of property ownership [that] contribute to a system of "natural" inequality in the countryside which can remain an extraordinarily prevalent feature of the taken-for-granted perception of rural society' (Newby et al. 1978b: 25). Here, again, is the question of how the inequalities of the current system are maintained and recreated – what sociologists term the problem of order. Employing Gramsci's notion of hegemony, attention is again paid to the 'sedative effects of paternalism' through which farmers attempt to obtain the identification of their employees via a web of paternalistic relationships outside the work situation itself (Newby et al. 1978b: 28). So the farmer is ultimately exercising 'ideological control as well as fulfilling material needs' (Newby et al. 1978b: 28).

Property, Paternalism and Power (Newby et al. 1978b), whilst not pursuing the potential of the qualitative techniques of *The Deferential Worker*, takes forward the theoretical ideas of the latter and the:

> inherently hegemonic nature of traditional authority which defines the prevailing 'rate of exchange' as legitimate. It is precisely by defining the relationship as a free and fair exchange that it is stabilized.
>
> (Newby et al. 1978b: 29)

However, the ontological emphasis has clearly changed to become more explicitly informed by Marxist thinking and an emphasis upon:

> The different forms of property, upon the social conditions of existence, rises an entire superstructure of distinct and peculiarly formed sentiments, illusions, modes of thought, and views of life.
>
> (Marx, cited in Newby et al. 1978: 24)

Following Newby, sociological interest in rural studies declined markedly. Therefore, the chapter broadens to consider other social science work that has examined the rural – namely social and cultural geography – and how the rural has been researched towards the end of the twentieth century and into the twenty-first.

Marsden

In a series of papers and books analysing the rural, Marsden's work represents a significant contribution to rural studies (Marsden 1993, 1995, 1999, 2000a, b). The centrality of his status within what could be loosely defined as rural geography stems from not only the expanse of his writings, but also his collaborations in many of those enterprises with other rural researchers – those within the School of City and Regional Planning, in which he is currently based, and beyond. This central position within the rural research network therefore makes it important to consider his work in terms of how rural studies has been taken forward in the past ten to fifteen years. Substantive areas of investigation have included sustainable rural development, food policy and consumption. This chapter draws upon the positioning pieces written in that time, rather than articles or chapters explicating specific research projects.[10] Necessarily selective, Marsden (1998b) and the farming piece (Marsden and Murdoch 1998) of a special journal issue are drawn upon here.

The territory in which Marsden (1998b) was commenting was far more advanced in terms of the expansion of agriculture and the concern towards food security that characterised the post-war period. Marsden (1998) argued that the context was now one of a differentiated countryside and significant rural spatial change. Underpinning these shifts were several forces of development: Marsden placed an emphasis upon what could be labelled traditional, mass food markets, the newcomer of quality food markets, agriculturally related changes[11] and also rural restructuring. Whilst such concepts appear, at first glance, to offer a holistic picture of agriculture at the end of the century, Marsden's theoretical interest precludes any ready generic theory of the rural. Indeed, he actively levels theoretical questions concerning the governance of rural space at a regional level, as the vision of a differentiated countryside suggests that integration and holism may be problematic. Marsden (1998b) therefore makes a call for government regulation to vary according to the significance of local or even non-local networks.

Marsden's (1998b) article is concerned to offer a theoretical commentary on how best the rural can be conceptualised. Beyond a purely theoretical concern, however, he also calls for a rural development policy and further a regional policy that can account for the internal and external conditions of differentiated rural spaces. Such differentiation demands 'new conceptual parameters' that can account for the redefined roles that emerge and the developmental trajectories of different rural areas (Marsden 1998b: 107). At the centre of these changes is the decline in 'agricultural hegemony' (Marsden 1998b: 108). In its place, is 'the "post-productionist countryside" ... 'where the certainties of agricultural production as the traditional 'rural hub' are giving way to a much more polyvalent rural scene and regulatory structure' (Marsden 1998b: 107). Whilst this is a general change, Marsden is concerned to analyse 'the degree to which *different* rural areas are developing contrasting strategies of adjustment and compromise with both the state and the wider economy' (Marsden 1998b: 107, original emphasis). The most important institutions in this context of change are therefore state, economy and regulation and the site at which they play out relates to land use. Attention must therefore be paid to:

> The interaction between types and levels of regulation and the degree to which social formations react to, as well as influence these, is most clearly expressed in land development issues and processes.
>
> (Marsden 1998b: 108)

However significant these new changes' long-term impact was to be, Marsden considered agriculture and land-based relations remained influential, as 'agricultural and broader land-based social and economic relations still have a significant hold on the shaping of regulation, and on *the processes by which rural areas are differentiating*' (Marsden 1998b: 108, original emphasis). The structure of Marsden's (1998b) analysis followed 'four distinct types of rural social and political formation' (Marsden 1998b: 108). This 'four-fold ideal typical classification' had been developed through a series of papers between 1993 and 1997 and is therefore a useful illustration of the developing line of Marsden's conceptual thinking. Landownership, echoing Newby et al.'s (1978b) interests, was again important. Marsden took the view that 'rural property rights, their exploitation, development and commoditization have been shown to be an important locus around which social and economic change occurs' (Marsden 1998b: 108). However, change occurs at 'different speeds and in different directions according to local and external combinations of relationships operating in rural localities ... the rearrangements of agricultural and non-agricultural property rights [centre] around new consumption and production dynamics' (Marsden 1998b: 108–109).

Marsden's (1998b) theoretical stance therefore addresses macro and micro concerns – or rather their manifestation at a meso level. The terminology shares much with a neo-Marxist approach, in which economics, regulation and state are primary concerns. The terminology, however, has shifted from such explicit concerns of ideology and social class to a new emphasis upon the 'multi-dimensionality of these processes of change either in terms of external dynamics or local response mechanisms' (Marsden 1998b: 109). So his call for a clearer understanding 'of the processes which are *making things different* in the post-productivist countryside' provides scope for more localised networks to also play a part (Marsden 1998b: 109, original emphasis). Marsden's (1998b) interest in 'how different local and non-local combinations configure in different rural spaces' therefore moves away from accusations of structural determinism that accompany more traditional Marxist-influenced models.

The theme of conflict and its manifestation in the rural, however, is clearly present, as no assumption is made 'that these processes [of change] will necessarily interact harmoniously to produce an integrated and functionally coherent rural space' (Marsden 1998b: 109). The key players are 'dominant social formations' and 'regulatory authorities' (Marsden 1998b: 109). In this sense, Marsden summarises the form of analysis he is offering as incorporating lateral differentiations (between rural spaces) and also vertical connections (between wider markets, housing, tourism, leisure and food chain relationships). Whilst this serves to progress his debate, as he points out, beyond the dualistic assumptions of rural land development with an agricultural or non-agricultural focus, it remains very much a structural analysis. The challenge, utilising this perspective, is to use an analysis of vertical chains to interpret 'the variable regulation and particularly economic governance of rural space' (Marsden 1998b: 109).

Marsden uses 'four dynamic spheres of development' (Marsden 1998b: 113), or constituents, of the debate in order to comment on how rural governance can be best analysed. Moreover, rather than simply offering an analysis, he is also concerned to actively question which are 'the most effective ways to regulate the differentiated countryside in the post-productionist context' (Marsden 1998b: 109). The four key dimensions (or spheres of influence in the differentiated countryside) he identifies are (1) mass food markets (both national and global), which relate to intensive production. (2) The use of rural space for the 'quality' food markets and products. As such products are defined locally to be targeted at the 'careful consumer' directly, inevitably this is more beneficial to some areas than others and they are therefore incorporated in different ways into quality food markets. (3) The third aspect considers development outside or only related to agriculture. This acknowledges more recent phenomena of diversification, the creation of new networks at local, regional and national levels. Marsden further associates these with the vagaries of the urban wealthy and what he terms 'rounds of rural fetishism' leading ultimately to 'the continued urbanized construction and commoditization of the rural', which will also vary in their diffusion into rural areas, for example with a range of variously costed activities, where deprived and employment-hit areas are most pressured to accept planning (Marsden 1998b: 112). (4) The fourth sphere of influence is explicitly non-agricultural developments where there has been rural restructuring. Marsden labels this 'the exploitation of the redefined rural resource', considering this to constitute unpleasant developments, which are more easily achieved (and therefore concentrated) in deprived areas of the countryside where employment opportunities are scarce (Marsden 1998b: 113).

As a theoretical approach, Marsden (1998) offers an intriguing framework. The terminology and the emphasis lend themselves to a Marxist orientation. However, the combination of lateral and vertical influences betrays an overtly structural analysis. Whilst not addressing the minutiae of interactional worlds and relations, the four spheres of influence that Marsden engages with are 'specific strands of commodity and network relationships' (Marsden 1998b: 113). It is together that they are significant and become 'agents for the further generation and momentum of social and economic changes in these spaces' (Marsden 1998b: 114). Therefore, Marsden's is a macro approach, but one within which such agents can be seen to be 'jostling for dominance at the more micro-spatial levels' (Marsden 1998b: 114). In addition, the definition of the rural moves away from one purely associated with agriculture and also away from strictly geographical, or physical, definitions of rural localities:

> Rural spaces which are caught up in different *webs* of local, regional, national and international supply chains, networks and regulatory dynamics.
>
> (Marsden 1998b: 114, emphasis added)

This in turn creates the empirical challenge to understand these new patterns and social actors and institutions within the new framework:

> Different local/non-local social configurations of networks and actors are developed, and these are aligned to the separate development spheres identified here. These configurations allow relative power to be distributed in different ways, such that the power

geometry of each rural space creates different governance and regulatory issues and processes.

(Marsden 1998b: 114)

Therefore, both structural and local concerns are present within his analysis, which moves towards 'integrating local *and* external processes and assessing how they are expressed in different regional ruralities' (Marsden 1998b: 115, original emphasis). However, the synergies between structure and action within Marsden's (1998b) account are negated somewhat by his further layering of two major dimensions: supply chain regulation and institutions. The degree of regulation within the four spheres is therefore primarily dominated by economic and political concerns. The example he provides of this is that land-use planning has become a major regulatory arena. Whilst he moves to argue that 'bottom-up or top-down approaches are not sufficient on their own' (Marsden 1998b: 116), we can also see that on a theoretical level, whilst he claims that 'the "at a distance" influence of external actors and their effects upon creating demands for rural resources' are significant, the approach is a political-economic one, in which actors are marginally positioned both in the spheres of analysis and ontologically (Marsden 1998b: 115). Whilst this could be perceived as a critique of the growing rhetoric about enhanced local participation the government has employed, he nevertheless argues that 'rural development policy needs to accommodate the realities of external and internal regulatory connections ... [in order to] create a "third-way" for rural development policy' (Marsden 1998b: 116). There is no assumption that all rural spaces are integrated or homogenous, indeed they may potentially be in intense competition, the ideal type or model towards which Marsden moves is one in which 'rural resources – social and natural – are to be successfully integrated and sustained' (Marsden 1998b: 116). The shift with an approach to rural research Marsden's analysis offers is one that resists perceiving 'the rural at a national level [as a] policy sector in itself, given the complexity of the supply chain and development processes outlined here' (Marsden 1998b: 116). Nevertheless, it remains useful at a broad, structural, albeit meso, level of regional analysis and Marsden advocates such a 'strategic spatial planning approach on a regional basis' (Marsden 1998b: 116).

The general approach Marsden employed, as considered briefly here, contrasts with Newby and the old traditional community studies approach quite markedly. Their theoretical suppositions differ quite radically and as such there is not a great deal of continuity. The structural functionalism of the early community studies writers is absent, itself mirroring a move away from such approaches within sociology itself, as are the interactional sociology nuances within Newby (1977a). However, there is evidence of progression from earlier treatments of the rural. That is, the critical approach underpinning Newby's more Marxist-oriented later work can be viewed in some of the terminology and conceptual emphases in Marsden's earlier work (Marsden 1986) and again in the work considered here (Marsden

1998b). However, most notable within the transition is the manner in which Marsden has reconfigured his approach to incorporate local relations within a more general structuralist framework. The shift is therefore one towards a more meso emphasis, a differentiated conceptualisation of rurality and a layering of different key spheres of influence. What Marsden has achieved is to look at the rural in its totality – whilst acknowledging local differentiation – and has therefore pushed forward the theoretical challenge to represent the rural. He has also avoided any naive or excessive dependence upon viewing the rural purely in agricultural or geographic terms or as a bipolar continuum. In the considerable portfolio of books, chapters and articles which his work comprises, there has also been an active empirical research agenda. Specific focuses have included food, diversification and corporate retailing and food provision. Therefore, his work reflects a commitment to empirically informed theory. However, within such an emphasis, more structural, policy-level interests dominate over that of micro, interactional nuances. It is the latter that the chapter now addresses and the work of Paul Cloke and rural geography's engagement with postmodernism – the 'cultural turn'.

Cloke

The work of Paul Cloke, latterly of the School of Geographical Sciences at Bristol University, offers a contrast to Marsden's approach and has engaged substantively with geography's 'cultural turn' and therefore his work provides a useful way to bring the debate up to date. Cloke, like Marsden, has made a substantial contribution to the body of knowledge available to rural social scientists. These include edited texts (Cloke 2003) and joint-authored texts (Cloke and Little 1997, Cloke and Perkins 2002, Cloke et al. 2005,) in addition to numerous articles, both individual and collaborative (Cloke and Perkins 1998, 2000, Cloke et al. 1998a, b, Cloke et al. 2002, Cloke 2005). In facing such a substantive body of literature, the selection considered here draws from positional pieces (see Cloke and Thrift 1987) and a reflective article (Cloke et al. 1994).

Cloke and Thrift (1987)

The focus of this article was to challenge the taken-for-granted perceptions of existing rural studies and as such is a useful insight into the preconceptions and assumptions of the approach to rural geography that Cloke has pursued. They criticise, what they term as 'self-reinforcing traditional wisdoms' (Cloke and Thrift 1987: 322). They argue that these 'traditional concerns' lie with the analysis of class conflict (as Lacey and Ball 1979 also observe) as manifested through inter-class conflict of 'locals versus newcomers'. Evaluating Newby's work, they position him inside this older tradition:

Newby's own work has explained the apparatus used by farmers to ensure their hege-mony over agrarian labour (Newby, 1977a) and has related property relations within capitalist agriculture to the maintenance of political power (Newby et al., 1978 [here 1978b]) and to environmentalism and countryside planning (Newby, 1980).

(Cloke and Thrift 1987: 322)

The innovation within their approach was an emphasis upon intra-class conflict, that is, class conflict within classes, not simply just between them. Three shifts or developments within the rural informs their analysis:

three other social relations have developed which have invested the members of certain class fractions, already part-formed by the capital–labour relation, with new causal powers with which they can differentiate themselves from other class fractions.

(Cloke and Thrift 1987: 323)

So their analysis is one that retains some causal similarities with the neo-Marxist flavour of Newby (and indeed Marsden) and a concern for capital–labour relations. However, it is how these forces are played out at the more micro level of social relations that is also important. The three shifts or new directions that should concern rural researchers include, first, the increased complexity of the division of labour and its organisation. For instance, Cloke and Thrift cite the rise of large corporate and state bureaucracies as such examples. Secondly, and stem-ming from this first point, is that the skills necessary to run such organisations (particularly those involved with running bureaucracies or organisations) have been captured by 'fractions' of labour power and made subject to educational cre-dentials. That is, not all social groups have equally benefited from the rise of such service industry sectors and the middle and upper classes have manoeuvred to maintain their advantage within the social system: the result of which, for Cloke and Thrift (1987), is the rise of mass consumption. Combined with the previous two points this holds the implication that 'certain fractions of labour power are better able to appropriate the means of consumption' (Cloke and Thrift 1987: 323). That is, those in positions of power and privilege continue to occupy those positions.

The result of this shift is that a new, or at least modified, approach to the study of rural societies becomes necessary and this links directly with the concern of this chapter: that is, the place of the rural within contemporary society and how to best theorise about these changes, in the same way that Tönnies had theorised about the changes the industrial revolution had brought about in human forms of associa-tion. Cloke and Thrift (1987) engage directly with this matter by examining the very notion of social class and its relevance for the study of contemporary society.

Cloke and Thrift highlight a series of problems with class analysis in the then late twentieth century. They highlight the 'contingent nature of class formation', viewing it as contingent on the way it is both structurally (macro) and experientially (micro) defined and recreated. Within this interaction between macro and micro concerns are the complex combinations of both conflict and compromise between groups; there is no straightforward mapping of one dominant social class upon the social structure. Most notable is the sea change in the basic class structure, centrally the growth of the middle class and the new boundaries as to where social class distinctions can be made. They draw these first two points together and conclude that there has been a general growth in the population and as such this has increased the diversity within classes. It is this new intra-class diversity to which they attach importance:

> *intra-class conflicts* have become important, both in their own right and because these conflicts can shape classes by undermining or strengthening their organisation'.
>
> (Cloke and Thrift 1987: 324, original emphasis)

Therefore, as a result, Cloke and Thrift argue that:

> Intra-class conflict is a significant motive force in the economic, social and cultural constitution of rural areas, one which has too long been ignored.
>
> (Cloke and Thrift 1987: 324)

The framework they employ is one that appeals to both macro and micro sociological concerns: the latter even more so when they go on to describe the various forms of cultural capital, or resources, that classes may possess. They term these the 'assets' that classes appeal to or employ and it is in this wider interpretation that each asset comes to embody (or reveal) an exploitative social relationship. First, they describe 'capital assets', which are quite simply the ownership of the means of production. The second are organisational assets and build these from the way in which production is organised, especially in bureaucracies. Finally, they describe skill or credential assets and the possession or lack thereof, which is significant. It is the manipulation, or use, of each of these three assets that, according to Cloke and Thrift renders each group within the social class structure with a different ability to take up a share of the 'social surplus' (Cloke and Thrift 1987: 322): that is, to wield power in contemporary social relations and society.

Cloke and Thrift (1987) are therefore employing a conflict theory and they apply this to a particular case study or context to explore these processes on the ground. Their paper goes on to concentrate upon a study of the middle class in rural southern England, or what they term the service class (which then consists of three subgroups: the expert manager/expert supervisor/expert non-manager). 'The service class can come into conflict or alliance with all of these [other] classes or class fractions' (Cloke and Thrift 1987: 326). The features of the growing British service class that make the group an important site for investigation, relate to the causal powers they accumulate from three separate, but related, sources. These are enumerated in table 5.

Table 5 Service class sources of influence

1. Favourable position in the economy, based on: highly skilled and well-paid jobs in the service industries; membership of primary labour markets in bureaucracies; a degree of freedom of decision at work; considerable spatial mobility; ability to use educational credentials to access service class privileges and exclude other fractions.
2. High income generates a high propensity to consume and, in turn, goods producers, allowing the service class to impose its consumption preferences upon these producers, target them.
3. Possesses political power and increasing presence in the machinery of the state, i.e. disproportional representation in local political positions, hence attaining an ability to present sectional issues like conservation and heritage as community issues.

Source: Cloke and Thrift (1987: 327).

We can see the influence of Bourdieu's work on habitus here (Bourdieu 1973) in that cultural capital is concentrated in some classes, the result of which in this case is that 'the service class is increasingly able to impose its interpretation of Britain on Britain' (Cloke and Thrift 1987: 327). The impact of this, for Cloke and Thrift, is that this class's definition of rurality suffers from a 'halo of historicism' or nostalgia, which seeks to recreate a past image of the countryside or at least that it be conserved (Cloke and Thrift 1987). In this we can also see echoes of Williams's (1973) analysis of the reified status accorded the rural in contemporary culture. Interestingly, and potentially in a contradictory manner, Cloke and Thrift 1987) position this alongside the need for the countryside simultaneously to be adapted to present-day needs – namely the need to consume and, for instance, the demand for the provision of all modern amenities (a modern-day example of which could be broadband Internet access).

Cloke and Thrift (1987) put forward this interpretation, or reworking, of the concerns of rural researchers, and they further provide a conclusion as to the impact of the steady stream of service class members making their way into the countryside and changing it upon their arrival. Like Newby (1985), they take the view that the service class has served to crowd out other classes through rising house prices and, secondly, that once enthroned in their rural dwelling they also lobby against further building in rural locations (appealing to conservation and heritage values). We can see here that, following the logic of this perspective, con-trols over the green belt are therefore examples of class conflict.

In summary, Cloke and Thrift (1987) offer an interesting positional piece. They critique the predominant concept of social class that had dominated previous engagements with the rural by social scientists. However, in their reworking of the notion of social class, they have not thrown the baby out with the bath water in the sense that their analysis does not seem so far removed from the work of Howard

Newby and his deconstruction of the maintenance of social class inequalities (by means of deferential paternalism). It could be argued that this is part of a tendency among social scientists to encounter new techniques of social research and seek to integrate or rework them into their own analyses. The result is not as new as the rhetoric surrounding the analysis may suggest. However, a more significant onto-logical shift is one that has occurred more recently in relation to the advent of post-modern systems of thought. Cloke is one example of a geographer who has engaged with postmodernism and the chapter now looks at his interpretation of the 'postmodern turn', for want of a better term. The question remains, however, to what extent such a 'turn' has provided an insight into the phenomenon of the rural and if, indeed, it contributes to its further theoretical refinement.

Cloke (Cloke et al. 1994)

Cloke (Cloke et al. 1994) is a biographical piece that has been written in 'a self-reflective mode' (Cloke et al. 1994: 149). The chapter by Cloke, in an edited col-lection that offers similar reflections by other geographers, offers an opportunity to position Cloke in the wider frame of changes in the discipline, in terms of the fashions and trends in the wider social sciences. This relates exactly to the concern to unravel the ontological and methodological suppositions underpinning his analysis of the rural. Cloke (Cloke et al. 1994) discusses his long-standing interest in what he summarises as rurality, rural change and rural governance over the past nineteen years. His express objective is to give an account of his preoccupations and attitudes towards rural change, for instance, to ask (and answer) what fires his 'geographical imagination' (Cloke et al. 1994: 149). He discusses the influences, experiences, theories, social relationships and spatialities informing his 'interpre-tation of people and places' (Cloke et al. 1994: 149).

As discussed earlier in the chapter, the rise in the popularity of qualitative research methods was very much contemporaneous to Newby's (1977a) doctoral fieldwork and also the rise in methodological collections, such as Bell and Newby (1977). This engagement with qualitative approaches has also been shared by geographers, and the research context Cloke (Cloke et al. 1994) describes is one in which the usefulness and legitimacy of ethnography[12] as a research technique are growing within human geography. Ethnography, for Cloke, 'is both a research practice and an interpretative practice' (Cloke et al. 1994: 150). That is, he under-stands that ethnographic methods also entail ethnographic outcomes and that these are informed by particular theoretical predispositions. Ethnography is not purely a research method, but also contains an epistemological emphasis upon the creation of certain forms of knowledge. Cloke expresses this aspect of ethnography as:

> a description of the daily practices of people both in their social situations and in the
> wider context of history and culture. Such descriptions have had to cope with the idea

that different individuals will have different, and even competing, experiences and will represent themselves differently.

(Cloke et al. 1994: 150)

Cloke is implying that 'the ethnographic project is about a *production* of the real rather than about how to discover it, and that ethnography thereby concerns the practice of *writing* culture rather than revealing it' (Cloke et al. 1994: 150). He recognises in this process that there is a need to 'acknowledge the self as integral to the process of constructing and interpreting texts' (Cloke et al. 1994: 150). The task Cloke (Cloke et al. 1994) sets for himself is to problematise the operation of the ethnographer's self – and ultimately the kind of knowledge that ethnography produces. He poses three central challenges or questions of ethnography: where one can speak from; to whom one speaks and why one speaks at all. Cloke (Cloke et al. 1994) labels this activity, or challenge, as 'autoethnography' (which serves to, somewhat unproductively, recreate terminology already existing in sociology) and we can see in the sociological literature that this is a form of reflexivity (see glossary at the end of the book). Reflexivity begins to look at how a story is read and how it is written. Cloke argues (1) that both of these are mobile and (2) that they have political implications: for instance, the manner in which a particular story (that of the writer) is elevated in story writing (to borrow his terminology) above others' stories.

Cloke (Cloke et al. 1994), like commentators within sociology (see Coffey 1999), argues that there is a need to be clear about (1) the positioning of the self, although Cloke frames this as where the self is positioned, and (2) whether the self is a textual or physical entity. This warrants further explication. Within ethnography, Cloke is arguing, there is a tension of experience between the ontological (what he labels as experience as a separate realm of existence, gendered/race/class) and the epistemological (what he views as the conditions of possibility: the discursive and what is used to politicise the ontological). The language and style of Cloke's (Cloke et al. 1994) writing in unravelling these concepts is unhelpful in explicating what are extremely important debates for social scientists. In translation, what Cloke is attempting to get at is the need to challenge the taken-for-granted ('make the familiar strange' to use the more oft-cited phrase within the sociological methods literature) – or to find alternative points of view from those of the politically dominant. He phrases this as a defamiliarisation of the taken-for-granted because 'any assurance of ontological importance should be regularly challenged' (Cloke et al. 1994: 153). It is Cloke's (Cloke et al. 1994) argument that both the experiential self and the politicisation of experience need to be challenged if alternative points of view (or definitions of the situation) are to be unravelled. To summarise, Cloke's (Cloke et al. 1994) notion of self-reflection is both direct (based upon individual experience) and indirect in the placement of one's experiences into pre-existing categories (pre-existing theories or ideas about the social world). The argument is that, in order to have both, there is a need to theorise where we speak from, whilst also deconstructing these theoretical spaces to keep them from becoming fixed, in order to keep the self's role useful for interpretative reflection. So, for Cloke, self-reflection involves (1) an ontology of self, what he terms 'personal positionality' and (2) theoretical reflection about 'broader categories of discourse' (Cloke et al. 1994: 152).

Together, these two aspects combine to provide an account of what Cloke terms the 'essential spaces' (Cloke et al. 1994: 152) underpinning the accounts ethnographers offer about our social world. The challenge in ethnographic research is to keep challenging our interpretations, rather than enforcing them. Cloke is here placing the researcher right into the very construction of an academic account or analysis. The phrase he uses to describe the researcher is 'an agent of culture in process'. The argument he is employing is very similar to the arguments taking place earlier in the ethnographic research literature (Atkinson 1990), although the terminology is perhaps less clear and certainly not shared. This line of development, for Cloke, however, takes him to a very different line of discussion from that of sociologists' and ethnographers' reflections. That is, Cloke (Cloke et al. 1994) develops an extended essay or exploration into his theoretical and personal preoccupations with the rural. The extent to which this furthers the conceptual development or refinement of the rural and studies of the rural is addressed at the end of the chapter.

Cloke's Biography

In this section of the discussion, Cloke (Cloke et al. 1994) unravels his Christian, white, middle-class upbringing in a North London suburb, his training at Wye College (prior to its amalgamation into the University of Central London) and highlights the dominance of 'positivistic and planning traditions of human geography' at that time (Cloke et al. 1994: 157). Cloke's account argues that, at this stage, his approach to rurality was submerged in the somewhat orthodox training, or educational experience, that he received at Wye. This was then followed by a lectureship in geography at St David's University College, Lampeter, in West Wales. The features of his time in Wales that Cloke selects as pertinent in his reflective 'journey' (again, to use his terminology) were both subjective and intellectual: subjective in the sense of not really belonging, as an Englishman, in rural Wales and through seeing 'poverty, alternative lifestyles, the search by in-migrants for different forms of rural idyll, and the social and geographical isolation of remote living for the first time' (Cloke et al. 1994: 158). He summarises this as the emergence of his 'socialist Christian viewpoint' and says that it was further informed by his personal involvement with college politics (Cloke et al. 1994: 158). From these influences, he began to develop an insight into representation, lines of decision-making and democracy.

For Cloke (Cloke et al. 1994), this collectively instilled an interest in the implementation of policies and led to an increasing engagement with power and political economy and change. He held the view that, at that time, there was little work on rural areas applying such a broad, political-economic perspective (or the study of capital restructuring) in the mid-1980s. Here Cloke reveals that his theoretical preoccupations in the 1980s emphasised social class:

> Class relations are not only the end-product of foregoing rounds of capital accumulation and restructuring, but also serve to mould the characteristics of ensuring iterations of these processes.
>
> (Cloke et al. 1994 [1989]: 160)

Cloke is employing a definition of the rural that runs along a continuum, or 'spectrum', rather than separate entities of urban or rural, so here he is avoiding the naive bipolar representation of rural and urban critiqued by Pahl (1968). In its place is an emphasis upon the unevenness of change in the countryside. This leads him to conclude that such change should be represented in terms of rural geographies, rather than a single rural geography. Cloke's research style marks something of a shift from that of Marsden, which was considered previously, in that his emphasis upon ethnography distances him from accusations of a neo-Marxist and reductionist view of social actors. Cloke further outlines what he considers to be a current tension in his work and, perhaps, one that is also visible in Newby's analysis, that is, a tension between 'interpretative stories' and accounts of human agency and 'meta narrative' or more political and economic structures (Cloke et al. 1994: 162). This is exactly the interface between macro and micro structural concerns, echoing the bridging of these two interests in Newby's earlier work. Like Newby, Cloke's research preoccupations are with the interconnections between the exercising of power, issues of conflict and the incompatibility of different cultural rural idylls. More simply, it is the positioning of sociocultural concerns alongside those of the political economy:

> Contemporary society is messy and complex in nature, yet we felt that rural places could be categorised (indeed are so categorised by some of their residents and visitors) according to the specificity of people and place without divorcing that place and those people from wider sets of changing relations.
>
> (Cloke et al. 1994: 167)

So, in marked contrast to Marsden, Cloke is concerned to see how these forces play out at a much more interactional level. He seeks to understand 'the ways in which the meanings of rurality are constructed, negotiated and experienced' (Cloke et al. 1994: 165). Whilst they both emphasise a lack of uniformity within rural spaces, Cloke positions these more equally within his analysis, that is, a multiplicity of versions of rurality, those of policy, lay and academic discourses. The challenge Cloke therefore faces is to blend such micro and macro concerns and he has addressed this most recently through the concept of commodified rural spaces.

Commodified Rural Spaces

The key notions or ontological assumptions underpinning this approach contain many echoes of postmodernism,[13] but Cloke is very careful to retain links with his Marxist-derived interest in political economy: that is, 'how rurality is being constructed by a relevant group of interests' (Cloke et al. 1994: 169). Commodified rural spaces refer to the consumption of rural spaces: for example, through tourism and through the representation (potentially, the enshrinement) of rural spaces in tourist literature. The concept's roots lie with Marx. In its original sense, it means the point at which an object assumes an exchange value that is over and above its use value. Hence, it becomes associated with 'judgements of worth which are socially and culturally constructed' (Cloke et al. 1994: 169). Marx's metaphor that the opium of the people was religion is critically reworked. Cloke's theoretical representation of the contemporary social world is not the postmodern plurality, but somewhat similar:

> Society is geared towards the production of spectacle and that the social and cultural constructs of commodity (including in this context commodities of the rural or the countryside) should be seen in that light ... the production of illusive and artificial counterfeits of real objects and relations.
>
> (Cloke et al. 1994: 169)

For Cloke, the definition of the rural is in flux and subject to conflict in terms of power and in the cultural realm. The new theoretical emphasis of Cloke's conceptualisation of a commodified rurality is power over both material and imagined conceptualisations of the rural. In consuming the commodity, it is translated into the abstract and the contact with relationships or original objects can be lost or obscured: that is, 'the countryside is being commodified in such a way as to go well beyond the real objects and relations of the places, sites and buildings concerned' (Cloke et al. 1994: 171). This is a form of fetishism of commodities, through which 'rural attractions are using representations and iconographies which are related neither to the particular place, site or building nor to its landscape or history' (Cloke et al. 1994: 171). However, in this cultural analysis, Cloke also maintains his commitment to the analysis of social inequalities. The focus also draws attention to 'notions of power both over the imagined and over material and cultural conditions' in understanding rural life (Cloke et al. 1994: 172). For example, 'dominant social constructions of rurality may include cultural notions of idyll which render rural poverty, rural deprivation and rural disadvantage basically as contradictions in terms' (Cloke et al. 1994: 175). Therefore, Cloke is emphasising that 'the rural idyll can be bought and sold, such that power and wealth underlie the ideology of the idyll' (Cloke et al. 1994: 177).

In this sense, Cloke offers a more sophisticated treatment of the role of ideology, even hegemony, and seeks to update Gramsci's work and improve Newby's model of the paternalistic management of the workforce. Cloke's work also sits well with more contemporary treatments of community by sociologists such as Delanty (2003). Although largely urban in focus, many analogies can be made with more rural communities. For example, whereas Newby (1985) was more concerned to detail the end of the occupational community upon rural communities and the impact of urban incomers, Delanty (2003) combines these changes with ones taking place on a global scale. Hence, he offers the analysis of community as a sense of place and belonging that originated in Tönnies's work and progresses this through to understanding communities not in a purely geographic sense but also a virtual one. The tone of his analysis also avoids some of the inherent nostalgia that was present in early community studies approaches in the US in the 1930s and also in early community studies work in the UK such as Williams (1956). Theoretically, therefore, the very idea of community is far broader and is derived from geographic location, shared occupation, shared identities (both majority and minority or liminal) and those transcending national boundaries. The impact of technology is, of course, heralded as a major driver in this process.

Delanty's (2003) ideas, like Cloke's, are useful in that they allow a more fluid understanding of community and rural spaces to be employed. This will be a theme returned to in subsequent chapters that examine social relationships that are in conflict, experiencing crises or utilising new forms of technology. As Newby (1985) noted the impact of the invention of the internal combustion engine upon commuting distances (enabling urbanites to live in the countryside but continue to work in the cities and towns), new technologies such as email and the telephone will be seen to be a significant carrier of social processes. Both Cloke and Delanty emphasise a transformational community – and not a static one:

> The notion of community as a 'symbolic construction' suggests a too affirmative sense of community, neglecting its capacity for cultural transformation. It is in this stronger constructivist sense that I argue community is communicative – communicative of new cultural codes of belonging.
>
> (Delanty 2003: 191)

In Cloke, key rural sociological themes, somewhat ignored by Newby, are incorporated, such as the 'structuring of opportunities and the experiencing of lifestyles' (Cloke et al. 1994: 181). The new question in the light of this theoretical shift gives rise to the question as to whether the analysis is so far removed from the critique of capitalism underpinning Newby's work and the early Cloke that the ontological baby has been thrown out with the bath water. In this instance, the continued emphasis upon power would suggest not. However, in methodological terms (even epistemological ones), Cloke has served to 'go beyond "giving voice" to the exploration of the powerful and the influencing of policy-makers' – which answers Cloke's original question of what, to whom and for what purpose he speaks (Cloke et al. 1994: 181). As Goffman expressed it, the concern is to research

> hierarchies of credibility [and to conduct] unsponsored analyses of the social arrangements enjoyed by those with institutional authority ... who are in a position to give official imprint to versions of reality.
>
> (Goffman 1983: 17)

Conclusion

This chapter has considered new issues currently facing rural sociology following Newby. In doing so, the extent to which the rural remains an important area worthy of social science research has been analysed. The relevance of the rural for contemporary society is undoubtedly secure in the light of the new wave of researchers commenting upon rural matters. Whilst two established figures have been considered here, the work of alternative scholars such as Michael Winter and Philip Lowe appears in subsequent chapters. The following chapters address substantive rural issues and the literature in these fields draw in new authors making innovative developments in rural geography. For example, in the work of Jo Little, we can see important attention being paid to the neglect of the role of women in the rural economy (Little 2003a) and, in Michael Woods's recent publications, important political questions have been raised about new social movements in the countryside and the mobilisation of traditionally disparate interest groups (Woods, M. 2002, 2003). Methodologically, Martin Phillips and, in the US, Douglas Harper have contributed to the establishment of the visual sociology analytical technique in the rural arena (Harper 2001, Phillips et al. 2001). Jo Little has also highlighted the value of qualitative techniques for gaining a detailed insight into previously marginalised and powerless rural groups and others (Little 2003b). The innovations to rural studies made by these younger authors are clearly important. Some form of selection is necessary to ground the discussion in sufficient detail. The degree of choice reflects the vibrancy of rural geography.[14, 15]

The two introductory chapters have progressed the idea of the rural as engaged with by sociologists and geographers over the past 100 years and earlier. The decline of Marxist analyses and of the urban–rural bipolar model has been unravelled and the reconfiguration of traditional social divisions, such as social class, race and gender, considered. Finally, a new theoretical approach to defining the rural as a commodified space was briefly outlined. The core developments within rural sociology are summarised in table 6.

Table 6 Key thinkers and their ideas

Author/ discipline	Historical context	Theory/ ontological stance	Key terminology/ themes	Methodology	Treatment of the rural
Tönnies (early founder of emerging field of sociology)	Late nineteenth century; early industrial	Macro impact upon the micro, everyday social order; forms of human association	Impact of the industrial revolution; obligations to one another	Armchair theorising	Nostalgic? Continuum
Community studies (borders of sociology, social policy and anthropology)	1960s	Structural functionalism	Consensus	Large case study, village/ community. Multi-method. Longitudinal	Nostalgia
Pahl (sociology/ urban studies)	Mid-1960s+ Highly complex industrial society	Local/national is important; social class is related to capacity for choice/ freedom	Intra-class conflict; urbanisation	Case study	Rejection of the sociolog- ical worth of the rural
Newby (sociology)	1970s–1980s	Deferential thesis	Class conflict, paternalism, property and power	QT and QL Longitudinal	Sceptical
Marsden (sociology/ geography)	Mid-1980s+	Neo-Marxist, political- economy emphasis	Class relations, regionalism	QT (although not exclusively)	Important contribution to rural policy
Cloke (human geography)	Mid-1980s+; Global society; postmodern society?	Neo-Marxist, with postmodern overtones. Synthesis of the micro and macro	Sociocultural, power, intra- class 'fractions,' gender, race, disability, age	'Ethnography'	The rural continues to be salient. Also advocates regional analysis.

The contribution the two geographers discussed here demonstrate how theoretical and methodological innovations have been made in understanding rural areas in the later decades of the twentieth century. The pattern that has been traced opened with the decline of Marxist analyses, the rejection of a simple, urban-rural dualism and the impact of postmodern thought. As a result, contemporary rural studies and rural geography now engage with reconfigured traditional social divisions such as social class, race and gender alongside newer themes of age, ability, time and spatiality. The more recent engagement with the ontological anarchy of postmodernism[16] has also served to reduce some of the pretensions of over-claiming.

The brush with postmodernism has been at the risk of returning rural research to the same haphazard vacillation between concepts, tools and methods that characterised the early community studies genre. First, the danger in the cultural turn, narrative turn and postmodernist influence is to assume that 'anything goes' in terms of theory and methodology. Second, to equate ethnographic research with objective, dispassionate research is to overemphasise the insight that qualitative research approaches can provide into the social world. Whilst the synergy between the theoretical preoccupations of Newby's work with an image of rurality that is more cognisant of contemporary debates in social theory is to be advocated, there remains an important obligation to provide an analysis that is informed by contemporary theoretical and methodological debates, which provides an opportunity to cumulatively develop knowledge and also to offer a critical account that is underpinned by a moral analysis or concern with differentiations of power. An analogy is useful here.

Novelist David Lodge (1984) has one of the characters give an account that reading a text is analogous to a striptease. That is, the account is persuasive, it's leading you on, taking you down a certain route with the promise of ultimate revelation. And that's where the fundamental flaw resides. The character in the novel argues that perhaps we shouldn't be trying so hard to look for the 'truth', the categorical statement or meaning 'and instead of striving to possess it we should take pleasure in its teasing' (Lodge 1984: 27). The point here is that the engagement with postmodern thought, if taken to its logical conclusion, suggests that all knowledge is relative and no one account more privileged than another. However, contemporary ethnographers within sociology have responded to this challenge: first, by remaining mindful that all research techniques should be used with an awareness of the research traditions that underpinned their historical development; and secondly, and whilst acknowledging the nuances of differences in argument between the arguments employed by different ethnographers, the drive towards theoretical cumulation, however small, can underpin even small-scale research (Hammersley and Atkinson 1995). To refer to the work of Goffman again, we should continue our unfettered exploration of the social world and attempt to render visible the inequalities (both structural and interactional) through the reflexive use of eclectic methods, albeit modestly:

Only in modern times have university students been systematically trained to examine all levels of social life meticulously. I'm not one to think that so far our claims can be based on magnificent accomplishment. Indeed I've heard it said that we should be glad to trade what we've so far produced for a few really good conceptual distinctions and a cold beer.

(Goffman 1997: 261)

The second half of the book offers a series of case study analyses of recent prominent rural issues, with the intention of demonstrating the potency of a multi-methodological approach to a rural sociology that is underpinned by a critical framework and informed by the above obligations. The challenge of the next chapter, therefore, is to construct a particularly sociological analysis of the impact of the 2001 FMD epidemic and consider how this complements the existing body of knowledge surrounding the epidemic in 2001.

Chapter Summary

The opening two chapters have described and contrasted the theoretical supposi-tions of the key thinkers summarised in table and 6 considered how their work has served to progress our understanding of the rural. The literature on rural issues, with the decline of rural sociology in Britain following Newby, has indeed moved to become dominated by social and human geographers, such as Marsden and Cloke. This has moved the debate to address new issues facing rural sociology fol-lowing Newby's work and evaluate whether the concept of the rural continues to be a relevant analytic concept.

The conceptual apparatus available to the rural analyst has been enriched by the work of Marsden and Cloke. This included new terminology such as reconstituting rural spaces and commodified rural spaces. The chapter concluded with a caveat regarding the contribution of new terms to the debate: do they serve to take the debate forward or merely muddy the waters? Whilst the rising status of qualitative methods in rural geography offers an alternative to the popular approaches of polit-ical economy and postmodernism, what an interactionally informed analysis can offer for rural sociology in the twenty-first century is a question as yet unanswered.

Learning tools

Questions

1. To what extent have rural studies become the study of issues, rather than a holistic treatment of the rural?
2. Outline and assess the key characteristics of rurality as conceptualised by any one of the following:

    (a) Howard Newby

    (b) Terry Marsden

    (c) Paul Cloke

3. What benefits has an engagement with postmodern systems of thought accrued for rural sociology?

4. To what extent is the 'cultural turn' an appropriate metaphor for rural studies in the late 1990s and onwards?

Glossary of key terms

'Commodified rural spaces': where locales become subject to values, either economic or societal, without necessarily accruing any positive benefits.

Paradigm: A distinctive perspective that proposes a conceptualisation or explanation of phenomena that has been adopted into mainstream modes of thinking (i.e. become a popular way of thinking). See the end glossary for a full explication.

Postmodernism: the rejection of the possibility of grand theory – or indeed of reaching an explanation of the social world. A rejection, therefore, of the Enlightenment ideal of progress.

The 'cultural turn': the impact of postmodern thought in rural geography. This has included an emphasis upon 'otherness' and those groups neglected in past research. It has also prioritised more qualitative ethnographic research and reflexive thinking.

–3–

The 2001 Foot-and-mouth Disease
Epidemic in the UK

There are many issues or alternative debates in rural sociological circles (for instance social capital, governance, social exclusion, evidence-based policy, Water Framework Directive) at the forefront of rural debates. The case studies that are featured within the text reflect areas in which the author has conducted research and as such is better placed to comment. These case studies are a means to engage with a number of contemporary issues/concerns in the rural, which are grounded by the opening chapters' broad overview of the background of rural sociology: not to declare the current state of play in rural sociology.

Introduction

The foot-and-mouth disease (FMD) epidemic in the UK in 2001 is used in this chapter to demonstrate how an interest in the social aspects of rural issues has been somewhat neglected and also what insight exploring the social and cultural aspects of FMD can yield. The FMD crisis in 2001 is a useful case study as it exposed some of the problems facing British agriculture in the twenty-first century and this chapter seeks to show how sociology can complement the variety of methodological and theoretical analyses of the crisis and its aftermath. The FMD crisis has received a great deal of attention from the academic community and a wide array of resources and literature is available. The rich archive of data includes bioscience reflections on the transmission and virulence; political-economic-inspired analyses; intense media scrutiny; epidemiological modelling and predicting of the disease spread; linguistic analyses of the representation and cultural understandings of the disease itself; geographic analyses of the spread (and the highly mobile nature of livestock movements); the impact upon farming and farming-related businesses and the wide economy (such as tourism); photographic and visual archives of those face to face with the disease; the long-term health implications of the stress and trauma experienced by those encountering the disease; instances of political protest by interest and affected groups; the importance of the Web as a resource for those seeking to disseminate and also seek out information about the disease and its spread (such as the NFU and www.warmwell.com sites).

Furthermore, there are the officially sanctioned accounts of the disease offered by DEFRA analyses and agents, government reports and also local government reports.

This chapter is therefore necessarily selective. The discussion reflects the author's involvement in an ESRC-funded, two-year project that explored the social and cultural impact of the epidemic (grant no. L144 25 0050). Other literature is drawn upon for its innovative or penetrating application of methods and/or theory to unravel the complexities of the FMD crisis. The chapter concludes by raising a series of questions regarding the future of British agriculture and rural ways of life in the wake of the FMD crisis. These include comments on rural protests, ways of life and the long-term future of farming in the UK.

What is FMD? An Overview of FMD in 2001

FMD is an acute, infectious viral disease that is manifested in a fever and lesions in and/or on the mouth and hoofs. It affects cloven-hoofed farm animals (such as cattle, pigs, sheep, goats) but not horses.[1] In 2001, a confirmed case of FMD was announced on 19 February 2001, the first outbreak on the UK mainland since 1968. The last outbreak had run between 1967–68. In 2001, the last case was announced on 30 September. Unlike the 1967 outbreak, the 2001 crisis reached all parts of the UK including England, Scotland and Wales and also Ireland. In reaction and due to the highly contagious nature of the disease, British exports were immediately banned by disease-free importing nations. At home, the then Ministry of Agriculture, Fisheries and Food (MAFF) began to try to trace its spread and eliminate it by applying the traditional methods of slaughter and livestock movement restrictions. By the end of March, the disease was out of control as infected animals remained alive for days and served to contribute to further spread. In the UK media coverage was dominated by highly emotive images of rotting carcasses awaiting burial or burning atop pyres.

Academic analyses have produced a variety of assessments of the impact of the 2001 FMD crisis. Some figures reveal that 2,000 premises were infected, over 6 million animals were slaughtered and the cost to the public sector was £3 billion (National Audit Office 2002). Whilst such figures speak baldly about the scale of FMD in 2001, why has the FMD epidemic (and the term captures the scale of FMD more aptly than outbreak) received so much attention from the research community? Why did this epidemic attract so much attention in 2001 and why does it continue to be discussed in academic, scientific and policy circles? The case of FMD is complex, due to the legacy of historical treatments of the disease, the policy context and the very virulence of the disease itself. However, it also coincides with shifts inside rural societies and the place of the rural within society's cultural imagination. That is, the farming industry has changed in the time that has elapsed since the last outbreak of FMD on the UK mainland, policy has also begun to shift and, finally, the perceptions of agriculture and rural living have also been reconfigured. FMD served to bring some of these issues to the fore and this 'crisis' allows them to be examined and analysed. The chapter considers some of these changes and attempts to draw some conclusions about the way social scientists approached the problem of FMD and asks, finally, what rural sociology can learn from the applied case study of FMD in 2001.

FMD in 2001: the Scope of its Impact

The wider framework of European Union policy informed the situation in 2001. The EU insisted upon FMD-free status amongst its members. Further complicating the situation was that no 'all-purpose' vaccine for the disease was yet available and the vaccines on the market did not offer permanent protection. The diagnosis of the physical manifestations of the disease was also complex. It could first be identified only by visual inspection and symptoms appeared after nine days, whilst the animal itself would have been infectious after four days. This situation was complicated further in that there was no internationally recognised test available to distinguish between infected and vaccinated animals.

All of these scientific details concerning the virulence of the disease created problems in terms of its spread and diagnosis. However, the social and cultural contexts were also significant. The previous outbreak of FMD in 1967 had reached cattle and pig populations only, whereas in 2001 cattle, pigs and sheep were infected. The latter two were also subject to more movement around the country to reach their markets. Furthermore, sheep were managed on farms in radically different ways, for instance, the hefted flocks of Herdwick sheep in Cumbria are far removed from the management requirements of dairy cattle. Such nuances would prove extremely relevant to how the disease could be managed on the ground and the extent to which government officials and policy were cognisant of these changes. In addition, the standing of agriculture and farming within the cultural imagination of the country had been damaged by the BSE crisis and farmers had begun to be associated less with a profession that was feeding the nation and more one that was reliant upon state subsidies (Hillyard 2006). The changing nature of agriculture, away from mass production and towards more quality food markets (Marsden 1998a) made the market itself more diversified and made it difficult to predict how FMD would impact it, and there was the cost to associated industries (such as tourism) located in rural areas. The rural village itself was no longer an occupational community, numbers of workers in agricultural had declined and this served to widen the gap between urban and rural knowledges. Finally, the policies informing the government's handling of the disease derived from historic British interests now enshrined in EU policy. The FMD epidemic 2001 is an instance where macro, meso and micro concerns interplay alongside social, economic, science and policy questions. It is the latter macro issue of policy and the vaccination question that offer a starting point from which to progress to more social and cultural questions.

The Vaccination Question and FMD as an 'Economic Disease'

The vaccination question relates to the debate within government and farming circles as to whether vaccinating animals against FMD can effectively manage FMD. Relevant to the debate was the prohibitive cost of vaccinating all susceptible animals and that the vaccination would not eradicate the disease itself, as there was the risk of vaccinated animals continuing to carry the virus without showing the clinical signs, making long-term control difficult. Influencing the vaccination question was the effect of the disease upon livestock. Unlike BSE, for example, 95 per cent of FMD-infected animals recover within two weeks with little or no treatment and there was virtually no risk to human health. Yet FMD did have significant economic ramifications as it caused permanent reduction in meat and milk productivity in animals that had had the disease. The worldwide approach to or policy on FMD held that the disease must be eliminated and no exports were (knowingly) permitted for FMD-infected countries.

Collectively, all of these issues set a context predisposed towards the adoption of a slaughter policy (for infected cattle initially) as the only effective countermeasure, and the vaccination question was subjugated by economic concerns. Winter (2003) argues that the wider policy framework influenced how the implications of the disease were evaluated and which response strategy was favoured. The construction of FMD as an 'economic' disease (a disease that is controlled for economic and financial reasons, rather than purely animal health or welfare concerns) recognised animals' commodity status. The EU policy framework defined Britain's political obligations and protected its own markets. Table 7 reveals how the European standard of disease-free status was also significant for wider, global markets.

Table 7 Countries with outbreaks of FMD pre-2001

UK	1968 (430,000 animals slaughtered)
Canada	1952
USA	1929
Australia	1872
New Zealand	Never
Worldwide	30+ countries FMD active

Britain's concern to protect animal import and export markets required her to meet the World Organisation for Animal Health's (IOE) specific criteria, which favoured non-vaccinated animals. Countries could be classified as FMD-free after they had been disease-free for twelve months, used no vaccination for at least twelve months and had not imported vaccinated animals since the cessation of vaccination. In contrast, the requirements made of countries that had used vaccination were that they needed to have had no outbreak for two years, used an approved vaccine (complying with IOE standards) and employed a system of intensive surveillance for detection of any viral activity. In contrast, IOE conditions for regaining FMD-free status following an outbreak was only three months after the last case where stamping out and serological surveillance are applied (i.e. slaughter), or three months after slaughter of the last vaccinated animal where stamping out, serological surveillance and emergency vaccination are applied.

The UK was therefore under pressure to regain trading status sooner rather than later and IOE status was regained on 22 January 2002. However, the implications of the decision to avoid vaccination and to conform to a slaughter policy held important consequences for the impact and spread of the disease. Abigail Woods's (2002) work, based at the Wellcome Unit for the History of Medicine, Manchester University, unravels the policy history surrounding the slaughter policy. It was the slaughter policy – and the very right to slaughter – that proved to be one of the most contentious issues relating to FMD (Campbell and Lee 2003). Therefore, Woods's (2002) analysis takes us closer to understanding the social and cultural impact of FMD.

Abigail Woods (2002)

Abigail Woods (2002) argues that there has been a century-old preference for a policy of compulsory slaughter and that, throughout the twentieth century, officials had argued this to be the cheapest and most effective means of eliminating FMD from Britain. Their argument held that, whilst FMD had a low mortality rate, it inflicted permanent problems such as lameness, infertility and mastitis and caused reduced meat and milk production. The extremely contagious nature of FMD would reproduce this effect upon an enormous scale and result in huge financial losses. That Britain retains her disease-free status was seen as imperative. Vaccination, in comparison, could not eliminate disease as rapidly or as cheaply as the traditional policy and the speed at which occasional epidemics were stamped out was cited in support of the slaughter policy.

Woods (2002) emphasises that the pursuit of a slaughter policy can only be understood with reference to the political, economic and social context in which it arose. Professional, economic and political interests shaped the definition and uptake of disease concepts. That is, there was a relationship between the perception of disease and the measures thought necessary to control it and therefore the role of the laboratory in defining disease entities. She unravelled how in the nineteenth century FMD became a 'plague' and demonstrated how this contrasted with initial opinions regarding its avoidance and impact. For example, Woods (2002) traced the appearance of the disease back to 1839 and noted that the popular belief of that period was that FMD spontaneously generated under unhygienic conditions and as such led to the general opinion that nothing could be done to prevent it. Whilst it was known to be contagious and so could be prevented by isolation of infected animals, few farmers took such measures, acting rather on the belief that it was metaphorically best to 'get it over with'. In summary, in this period FMD appeared frequently and was not believed to be harmful and was also impossible to prevent (to the degree that is now perceived) – essentially an occupational hazard.

This perception changed following the cattle plague of 1865–7, an extremely contagious and fatal disease that medical researchers had failed to cure. The ongoing decimation of herds led to the controversial introduction of a slaughter policy and included movement restrictions and import bans from infected countries. The success of this policy regarding cattle plague also reduced incidences of FMD, challenging perceptions and suggesting that FMD was preventable, although this did not translate into policy at this stage.

The legacy of the nineteenth century shaped the treatment of FMD in the twenty-first century. Changes inside agriculture, conflicts of interests within the farming industry and agriculture's changing relations with policy and government had also taken place. For example, nineteenth-century pedigree breeders insisted that FMD was a disastrous disease, giving rise to permanent loss of condition and decreased fertility and that state control of FMD was in the interests of both farmers and consumers. The economics of FMD control underpinned political opposition. The pedigree breeders, often Tory MPs, sought import restrictions to bolster their own herds' value, whilst Liberal politicians, who were keen to ensure a reliable flow of cheap meat to the urban masses, opposed calls for the restriction of livestock imports.

The scientific understanding of FMD (or lack thereof) was reflected in disagreement upon the epidemiological aspects of the disease; whilst legislation continued to be piecemeal and ineffective, the regulation of FMD grew harsher (restrictions upon selling and movement) and the economic effects of control measures on farmers increased. Woods (2002) concludes that this produced a strong desire to avoid FMD altogether, not because of its clinical (or health and welfare) effects but due to the financial harm inflicted by legislative controls. In 1884, leading farmers defeated the Liberal government to force the passage of an act that prevented livestock imports from FMD-infected nations and, shortly after, the disease vanished from Britain.[2]

Woods's (2002) argument was that this led to a deep-rooted faith in the slaughter policy, whose origins dated back nearly 100 years.[3] Slaughter as a means of FMD control therefore came to achieve a virtually constitutional status, adopted unquestioningly each time the disease appeared, and formed the basis upon which the contiguous cull (discussed later) could be imposed in 2001. Immediately, Woods's (2002) questioned why was such controls (a legacy of the late nineteenth century) were virtually unchanged and automatically applied in 2001. The context of the rural in 2001, as has been unravelled in the preceding chapters, is markedly different from that of a century ago, and Woods (2002) noted changes in the role and status of the veterinary profession, in the nature of the international meat and livestock trade and scientific advances and innovations. In terms of the impact of FMD in 2001, this leads to a series of questions as to why MAFF adhered so firmly to the notion that slaughter is the best means of controlling FMD and how MAFF countered public opposition to slaughter and justified its continuation of this policy to the pro-vaccination lobby. Woods's (2002) historical analysis serves to raise social and cultural questions and begins to unravel why the 2001 FMD epidemic continues to attract the attention of academic commentators.

In the context of 2001 when FMD appeared again, the control policy in place had dismissed vaccination under the influence of groups such as the NFU and leading farmers. The power of the NFU in terms of influencing government policy has been documented elsewhere (Hamilton 1990, Woods, A. 2002) and left the Prime Minister, Tony Blair, unwilling to act without NFU consent. Somewhat unusually, and for reasons that will be explored later in the chapter, Blair instead chose a team of university epidemiologists' computer models. These models advocated a 'contiguous cull' of all livestock within the 3 km zone (regardless of whether they were infected or not) surrounding an infected farm and argued that this policy would control the disease.

The Government-sponsored Analyses

Three government-sponsored inquiries were announced on 9 August 2001 (Anderson 2002, Curry 2002, Follett Report 2002). The remit of the government-sponsored inquiry chaired by Follett (Follett Report 2002) was the scientific basis of the government's handling of FMD and introduced three further subgroups to address: surveillance and diagnosis; prediction, prevention and epidemiology; and vaccination. These reflected the way the government had allocated different remits to the three commissioned inquiries following the epidemic, in preference to one public inquiry. The Follett Report (2002) concluded that the paucity of high-quality information posed problems for modellers and those preparing risk analyses and made a more general comment that in future the public and politicians could not contemplate mass slaughter and culling on the same scale. In this sense, the Follett Report (2002) was more favourably disposed towards alternative strategies and this involved greater use of vaccination and as such future EU legislation would need to be amended. Similarly, the Anderson inquiry found that the vaccination option should form part of a future government strategy to deal with the disease and (until a vaccine is produced that can be used for routine purposes) emergency vaccine should be a first resort (Anderson 2002).

The third inquiry, chaired by Curry, held a broader remit to explore the future of farming and food (Curry 2002). The report was perhaps more of a manifesto for change than a reflection of changes already well under way in British agriculture. Curry (2002) called for a change in farming subsidies in favour of ecological and environmental grants rather than production subsidies (some of which can be viewed to have taken place with the decoupling of farm payments). Curry's (2002) emphasis largely advocated change in agriculture, rather than being explicitly FMD-focused, and can be seem as contributing towards a growing identification of the future of farming lying with diversification and sustainability. Collectively, the three government-sponsored inquiries positioned vaccination far more favourably for the management of future outbreaks. In the light of A. Woods's (2002) analysis, this was a sea change in policy.

Reactions to the Contiguous Cull

A number of disparities can be identified between the officially sanctioned accounts and the reactions of those commentators and farming communities 'on the ground'. The commentaries reflect the diversity of groups associated with or implicated in farming in the twenty-first century. They include political or support groups, such as those appearing on the Web (http://www.footandmouthdoc.com/; www.cullmaff.com; http://www.warmwell.com; www.fmdaction.com; http://www.action-footandmouth.co.uk); media reports in *Private Eye* (2001) and in a *Guardian* newspaper special (*Guardian* 2001). The contiguous cull proved to be the most controversial aspects of the government's handling of the crisis, and several farming and associated groups specifically addressed the issue. The 'Cull MAFF' website (http://cullmaff.com/demands.htm) is one such example and it posted a series of ten 'simple demands' that 'We, the British public, demand of MAFF and the Government' ('Cull MAFF' undated). The demands protested against the 'enforced culling of uninfected animals' including a differentiation between farmers, keepers of rare breeds or pet owners' stock. They also resisted the perception of animals in purely economic terms, arguing that animals 'are sentient beings and not just another commodity, to be destroyed at will to achieve a political or financial advantage' ('Cull MAFF' undated). In addition, they made a much wider point that government 'recognise that food production is about more than simply making a profit and is also an intrinsically valuable way of life with strong ethical and social merits' (ibid.).

The points of criticism on websites such as 'Cull MAFF' relate to specific issues of disease management systems (the compulsory contiguous cull) and much wider issues that allude to a government that failed to appreciate the value of the farming profession and to understand their way of life. This theme will be returned to at the end of this chapter, in the following chapter on the hunting debate and in chapter 6 on researching rural worlds.

A concern with the impact of FMD upon farming and the farming community was less explicit in a more politically targeted report on FMD by *Private Eye* (2001). The author, 'Muckspreader', focused on the political machinations and context underpinning the policy decisions made within government. For example, they emphasised the 'old boy network' of contacts existing between Krebs and the head of the modelling team at University College London, Professor Roy Anderson, and that this facilitated the modellers' introduction into the policy-making process and ultimately their promotion of a contiguous cull policy. The report took the view that the impetus for Blair's keen urgency to eradicate FMD was less a concern for farmers than the proximity of the timing of the general election (which was ultimately delayed), and this also fuelled Blair's interest in vaccination (*Private Eye* 2001). The report casts its net wider. As well as criticising the current Labour government, they also cited the MAFF incompetence (and lack of staff) as a result of the legacy of Thatcher's Conservative government and their cutbacks (for example, the number of MAFF vets had declined).

Oates (2002)

Oates (2002) used the World Wide Web as a means to analyse the reaction of farming communities to the epidemic. She focused upon the hard-hit counties of Cumbria, Durham, Northumberland and North Yorkshire and specifically the web pages of their respective county councils. Through this analysis, she was able to comment upon what information was disseminated or omitted, what audiences were targeted and how well their needs were met. The changing nature of the epidemic's spread necessitated a 'snapshot' of each county website and 11 August 2001 was selected – well into the epidemic – and each county contained both open and restricted footpaths.

Her analysis revealed that collectively the websites targeted walkers (unsurprisingly in Cumbria's case), visitors to the county, businesses and other community members as well as farmers. However, not all were present for every county. The Northumberland site, for example, had no pages for local business owners or other members of the community (Oates 2002). Oates (2002) summarises her findings in a table (see table 8).

Oates concluded that 'no site provided plenty of information for all of the audiences' (Oates 2002: 1205). She noted that 'almost all of the information was of a factual, often financial, nature ... there was very little content about *psychological*

Table 8 Amount of information for each type of audience

	Cumbria	Durham	Northumberland	N. Yorks
Farmers	Limited	Limited	None	Plenty
Walkers	Plenty	Limited	Limited	Limited
Other visitors	None	Limited	Plenty	None
Local business owners	Plenty	Limited	None	Limited
Other members of the community	Plenty	Limited	None	Limited
FMD discussion forums	Yes	No	No	No

Source: Oates (2002: 1204).

support to cope with the loss of animals and businesses and the distressing scenes' (Oates 2002: 1206, original emphasis). In terms of the quality of the information provided, Oates argued, 'nor did the four councils use their websites as a means to *increase democratic debate* in their community. The information provided followed the official Government line without offering alternative views' (ibid.). This was significant as:

> It must be remembered that there were many other websites with information or discussion forums about FMD. However, some information, particularly up-to-date information on footpath closure or re-openings, was *only* available from the county councils.
>
> (Oates 2002: 1207)

Oates's (2002) contribution to the FMD literature is her conclusions that websites such as local government pages are increasingly important in contemporary society and that the provision during the FMD epidemic was inadequate. Moreover, she suggests that the mere provision of information is insufficient and that support and opportunities to engage in the debate are also important. She cites Brigadier Birtwhistle's (an army officer commanding the FMD strategy in Cumbria) distinction that 'we need to connect with people, not just communicate, *connect*' (Birtwhistle 2001, in Oates 2002: 1207). Her own analysis shows the links between community and farming and also the psychological impact of the FMD epidemic. Echoing Delanty's (2003) reconfiguration of the meaning of community to extend beyond geographical proximity in the digital age, virtual communities demonstrate the importance of the World Wide Web during the FMD epidemic. For example, many farms were subject to movement restrictions and the farming community's capacity to create their own support networks. Whilst the number of farmers connected to the Web should not be overestimated, the very virulence of the disease and the speed at which it reached across the country made gathering the latest and most accurate information problematic. As Oates's (2002) work showed, this was not always available on local government pages, and the web pages (such as www.warmwell.com) were and continue to be sources of information, discussion forums and primarily farming-oriented.

Scott et al. (2004)

Scott et al. (2004) offer another analysis of the impact of FMD that expands upon the theme of community addressed by Oates (2002). Their broader focus considered the position of agriculture in the rural economy and society and themes of governance and partnership. They introduce case study data from Wales (119 telephone surveys, interviews with key informants and two comparative community case studies). The latter data set is drawn upon here in order to examine the social consequences of the FMD epidemic.

The case studies were of two small market towns in mid-Wales, Tregaron and Llanfair Caereinion, and they used participatory rural appraisal (PRA) methods. PRA involves four stages: in summary, interviews (with residents and business owners) and a feedback to a public meeting and then finally written consultations with key individuals. They identified that the trauma of FMD had 'left a residue on the rural social psyche' of both communities (Scott et al. 2004: 11): for example, 'widespread hostility and mistrust towards officials and their overall handling of the epidemic' (Scott et al. 2004: 10). More specifically relevant to the concern here to progress towards examining the social impact of the FMD epidemic and its implications for rural studies is their conclusion that 'the key issue highlighted by the FMD outbreak is the inextricable link between agriculture and rural tourism' (Scott et al. 2004: 12): for example, 'the intensity and form of land-use, and relations between the various hierarchical levels of governance which seek to influence rural economy and society' (Scott et al. 2004: 13). They advocate 'the need for more energetic study, perhaps in a broader interdisciplinary context, of the public good links between agriculture and tourism' (Scott et al. 2004: 11). It is this focus, albeit from an economic and then a more political-economic perspective, as offered by research teams from the University of Nottingham and the Centre for Rural Economy, University of Newcastle upon Tyne, that ius considered next.

Blake et al. (2002)

A research team based at the Business School Tourism and Travel Research Institute, at the University of Nottingham, used a computable general equilibrium model (a quantitative technique) to analyse the effect of the 2001 FMD epidemic on the UK economy. They were therefore considering the impact of the epidemic upon agriculture, but also upon tourism sectors, with specific reference to UK foreign, domestic (i.e. from within the UK) and regional tourism. Their analysis demonstrates that how the government and its agencies (MAFF and its re-emergence as DEFRA) handled the epidemic 'has much larger adverse effects on tourism than on agriculture' (Blake et al. 2002: 1). Some of the indirect impacts, what they refer to as 'inter-sectoral linkages' (Blake et al. 2002: 1), included (1) the imposition of 'restricted areas' (upon historic sites and tourist attractions), (2) the closure of the country-side (i.e. footpaths and waterways), (3) cancelled and/or postponed sports and public events (for instance hunting) and (4) the imagery of the mass slaughtering, burning and burying of animals, which had adverse effects on tourism. For instance, the hotels, catering and pubs sector saw an 8 per cent drop in revenue and they concluded that policy-makers needed to think beyond agriculture in their han-dling of future FMD epidemics and agricultural policies more generally. Their analysis led them to propose a series of recommendations, including the re-exam-ination of vaccination; the advocacy of an early warning system; a call for the improvement of animal identification and movement monitoring; and a self-financing insurance mechanism for the farming industry to cover future outbreak costs (such as compensation). They finally suggested that the likelihood of tourist activities contributing to the spreading of the disease should be established (a point that had been contested during the outbreak).

CRE

The CRE has conducted a number of research projects on the impact of FMD, funded by a variety of bodies. Rather than focusing on the more scientifically ori-ented of their papers (Donaldson and Woods 2004), economic and business analyses (Bennett and Phillipson 2004, Phillipson et al. 2004) or policy (Ward et al. 2004), we turn to Donaldson et al. (2006), who offer a summative account lit-erally five years on from the first confirmed case of the FMD virus. Donaldson et al. (2006) address three themes: disease control and management; changes to insti-tutions and policies; and compensation and rural economies. However, continuing Scott et al.'s (2004) note that FMD exposed the interdependencies between agri-culture and rural tourism Donaldson et al.'s report also addresses what FMD served to reveal:

> The FMD crisis seemed to challenge dominant representations of the countryside and its functions by illuminating underlying rural realities that normally remain hidden or implicit ... in doing so it laid bare a host of connections (local interdependencies and long-distance linkages between localities).
>
> (Donaldson et al. 2006: 4)

Their exploration of some of 'the unintended consequences of the crisis' pro-duced findings more focused on upland ecology (the proliferation of flowering plants following the removal of sheep from the fells), atmospheric emissions during cattle restocking and the transmission of bovine tuberculosis than upon rural studies per se. They conclude with a damning comment on DEFRA's policies and argue that the cart has been put before the horse:

> Defra is a large and sprawling ministry in which rural affairs have, perversely, been eclipsed. There remains a preoccupation with the well-being of farmers. National resourcing for rural development has been passed over to RDAs4 within England, but they have become preoccupied with 'city regions' and urban-based growth ... the future well-being of farming families depends on the success of wider rural development, and not the other way round ... The unanticipated outcome of the 2001 post-Election reshuffle was the creation of Defra with all its environmental protection and climate change responsibilities ... the treatment of rural affairs within central government has been marginalised as a result.
>
> (Donaldson et al. 2006: 17)

The CRE's contribution to understanding the impact of the FMD epidemic is considerable. Established in 1992, they have been able to generate a sustained level of awareness and commentaries on rural issues that permits such a long-term analysis of FMD's impact upon policy and the rural economy. The importance of generating a critical mass of rural researchers and continuity across various funded projects is a theme that will be returned to in the book's conclusion.

Mort et al. (2004) and Convery et al. (2005)

Mort and her colleagues' work continues with CRE's emphasis upon the symbiosis between families and rural development and progresses the chapter on to a micro-level focus of analysis. Based in the Institute for Health Research (IHR), Lancaster University and the University of Central Lancashire, Mort and her research team promote the importance of understanding lay knowledge and local responses to an understanding of foot-and-mouth disease, inside a community profoundly affected by the disease (Mort et al. 2004, Convery et al. 2005). Specifically they addressed the long-term health consequences of foot-and-mouth disease.

Mort et al.'s findings label foot-and-mouth disease in 2001 as a 'disaster', a definition they qualify by arguing that the disease was a 'substantial and enduring [source of] distress and disruption' (Mort et al. 2004: 7). Their fieldwork examined the health and well-being of rural people over a period of eighteen months via a variety of qualitative research techniques, including weekly diaries, in-depth interviews and group discussions. Their contribution to the debate surrounding foot-and-mouth disease was to highlight the impact of foot-and-mouth disease on the hard-hit area of North Cumbria and the explication of the 'chronic health' problems experienced by farmers and exacerbated by foot-and-mouth disease (Mort et al. 2004: 7). Mort et al. moreover argue that such problems remained 'invisible' to formal records:

The enduring and complex nature of events taking place in often scattered communities may have prevented statutory agencies from 'seeing' the foot-and-mouth disease epidemic as a human disaster.

(Mort et al. 2004: 8)

In their research Mort and her colleagues sought to problematise the perception of farmers and the complexities of their relationships with their livestock (Convery et al. 2005). They argue that images of farmers weeping over their slaughter of their stock were not hypocritical, rather 'that the distress displayed reflects severe and often poorly understood disruption to a complex *lifescape*' (Convery et al. 2005: 99, original emphasis). The concept of lifescape is a socially constructed one:

In the process of production people create their environments; in the sense that the environment is the embodiment of past activity and it is continually evolving, it is a 'work in progress'. The environment enters actively into the constitutions of persons; there is a mutually constitutive interrelationship between persons and environment, production is a becoming of the environment. The relationship between people, place and production system is thus complex and multiscalar.

(Convery et al. 2005: 101)

Their methodology – action research – sought to 'research *with* people and communities, rather than on them' (ibid., original emphasis). This emphasised the local knowledges and practices of those experiencing the FMD epidemic. Their findings argued that during the outbreak of FMD 'death was in the wrong place' (Convery et al. 2005: 104):

There was a clear breach of *normal* relations – whilst lambs are normally slaughtered, this is not when they are newborns, and so the rhythm and cycle of livestock farming relations was out of synchronization. The epidemic created fissures in taken-for-granted *lifescapes* which transcended the loss of the *material* (i.e. livestock) to become also the loss of the *self* (respondents' perceptions of identity and meaning associated with this *lifescape* were called into question).

(Convery et al. 2005: 104, original emphases)

Convery et al. introduce the interactional relationship between human and animals – what they term 'livestock farmer relationships' (Convery et al. 2005: 107). Their argument is that the FMD epidemic served to breach or disrupt that relationship and that this is vital towards understanding the economic and cultural impact of the disease. Through the use of the concept of 'lifescapes', they attempted to articulate a more rounded notion of farming life – as a 'whole way of life' (Convery et al. 2005: 107). They conclude:

The scale of killing during the 2001 FMD epidemic did transgress the emotional geographies of the farm as the place of livestock management and the abattoir as the place of livestock death, because death was in the wrong place, at the wrong time and on the wrong scale.

(Convery et al. 2005: 107)

Methodologically, action research is a goal rather than an outcome that can easily be achieved (indeed, perhaps it is better viewed as an ideal type). For example, can respondents be involved as partners in every aspect of their research process – even to the extent of selecting which quotations are included in an article and which are not? The researchers, nevertheless, compiled a rich data set of interviews with a wide range of rural respondents. These included farmers, farm workers, teachers, slaughtermen and local business owners. As such, they offered a community account, grounded in the context of the hard-hit area of Cumbria, and this complements the virtual analysis of Oates (2002) and the political-economic analyses of the CRE. Continuing the narrowing of the chapter's focus on to more micro-oriented concerns from that of the macro-analyses discussed earlier in the chapter, the focus now turns to examine the social and cultural impact of the FMD epidemic.

Nerlich et al.

Nerlich and her team based at the University of Nottingham employed a variety of methodological and theoretical ideas in order to reflect upon the scale of the epidemic's impact. These included a linguistic analysis of the representation of the disease in the UK media (Nerlich et al. 2002, Nerlich 2004, Nerlich and Döring 2005), the impact FMD had upon rural children (Nerlich et al. 2005) and the status and role of science within the policy to cull (Wright and Nerlich 2006). For example, Nerlich et al. (2002) accused the government of relying on 'frames' of belief on what to do in certain crises and that the case of FMD highlighted this problem. They found that metaphors of war and plague framed the issue of FMD because FMD had been mythologised as a 'plague' of some sort, and that eradicating FMD was in turn metamorphically expressed as fighting, and winning, a war. The culmination of these frames was that the slaughter policy adopted was couched in terms of these metaphors and that served to trap the government inside a single policy solution instead of searching for other possible solutions.

Nerlich's linguistic approach unravelled how policy problems and dilemmas concerning farming and the countryside were interpreted via particular frameworks that then served to inform how that given issue was treated. This was further applied to the analysis of focus group data with members of the public in an infected and non-infected region of the UK (Wright and Nerlich 2006). Their interest in everyday language and the wide questions of science surrounding an epidemic such as FMD led to their examination of the relationship between science and society. In this case, their findings did not support a deficit model of the public understanding of science, but rather that the public understanding of the public understanding of science warrants investigation. For example, their respondents discussed the disinfection of vehicles along rural roads – and the fact that the very effectiveness of this form of biosecurity was unclear.

Nerlich and Döring (2005) were similarly concerned to position the reflections of those experiencing the FMD epidemic first-hand centrally inside their analysis. They drew together the poetry that emerged in 2001 and in the wake of FMD. Their deconstruction of these poems enabled them to be seen as cultural artefacts that reflect opinions and active interpretations of the damage FMD inflicted and upon whom, but also in a more psychologically therapeutic sense of allowing such reactions to be expressed through the medium of poetry. Nerlich and her interdisciplinary team collectively applied a variety of methods and theoretical approaches to explore the many facets of the FMD epidemic's impact upon rural communities in the UK.

The range of research arising out of the epidemic, a necessarily selective number of which have been briefly overviewed here, has begun to reveal how an interest in rural sociology can be useful. That is, it enables rural events to be viewed in a broad manner and far-reaching consequences to be considered, for instance, that events in rural can also have a significant impact on other areas. The FMD epidemic demonstrates that a much broader appreciation of rural matters is needed in order to capture the plural, even reconstituted, nature of the rural and its intrinsic links with wider, more urban concerns.

This chapter has attempted to demonstrate that FMD was considered by most to have been mismanaged to an extraordinary extent, with the slaughtering of millions of farm animals that were in no danger and were of no harm. However, what is generally not realised is the historical framework that the epidemic has to be put within, and this serves to explain the actions of government, MAFF officials and leading farming groups such as the NFU. In relation to FMD, economic factors, along with a nostalgic, normative view of how the rural should be, are the reasons why policy problems arose concerning farming and the countryside. The problem with the economic factors is that the policies implemented did not look at the whole picture: the slaughter policy was intended to ensure that agriculture did not lose so much money, and yet the policy proved tobring about more significant costs in terms of loss of revenue to the country as a whole and the emotional damage sustained by farming and farming-related communities (Nerlich et al. 2005, Hillyard 2006). The government department in place at that time, MAFF, was separated from significant sectors that were clearly affected by its actions. This exacerbates the somewhat nostalgic view held of 'the rural' more generally. The rural remains an 'escape' – which is somehow magically detached and isolated from the strain and stresses of everyday urban life. Yet, as Newby (1985), Cloke (Cloke et al. 1994) and Marsden (1998b) remind us, the rural is not idyllic but also features poverty, exploitation and considerable differentiations of power. FMD served to demonstrate that the rural and urban are not separate entities, but inextricably linked.

A sample of the now considerable literature surrounding FMD has been engaged with here. The key sites of research work are summarised in table 9.

Table 9 A selection of academic analyses of the impact of the 2001 FMD epidemic

Research team	Approach	Data sets
IGBiS: Nerlich, Döring, Wright, Wallis, Dingwall, Hillyard	Linguistic, discourse analysis, science and society, sociology of measurement	CBBC (Children's BBC) online discussion forum/interviews/ focus group/web analysis
CRE: Lowe, Ward, Donaldson, Bennett	Political-economic, actor network theory	Business impact/policy context and background
BRASS: Campbell and Lee	Legality of the contiguous cull	Regulatory theory and policy
Wellcome Unit for the History of Medicine, University of Manchester: A. Woods	Historical, policy, veterinary profession	Historical and policy analysis
IHR, Lancaster: Mort	Qualitative	Interviews/diary-based study/action research

Conclusion

The range of material analysed here has not sought to capture all research work on FMD, but to cast insight into the future of British agriculture and rural ways of life in the wake of the FMD crisis. The very diffuse impact of FMD could not have been captured by any one research team, as explicated above, but all of the studies conducted by these units serve to begin to piece together comments on rural protests, ways of life and the long-term future of farming in the UK. Whilst individually they may seem disparate, for example in their terminology – 'lifescapes' (Convery et al. 2005), ANT (Donaldson et al. 2002), the 'sociology of measurement (Dingwall 2004, Wright 2004b) – they emphasised that the interconnections between the rural economy and the government and its agencies had become somewhat detached, both culturally and practically, from the contemporary countryside. The studies and their findings considered here clearly show that there were a number of existing policy problems and dilemmas that were emphasised by the FMD crisis in 2001. However, as Winter (2003) notes, the shifts inside government to reform MAFF were already under way before FMD. Therefore, FMD served to accelerate the emergence of DEFRA from the old Ministry. The post-war context in which Hamilton (1990) saw little scope for social issues to be engaged with and where the then MAFF and NFU were so closely intertwined has now changed to one quite remarkably different.

In terms of the lesson learned for the advancement of a sociological appreciation of the rural, FMD has in several senses reinvigorated the methodological challenge to capture the complexities of the rural. The status and contribution of social science research are now positioned more favourably alongside those of traditional methods employed by official agencies, such as DEFRA.[5] For instance, also relevant here is Wright and Dingwall's interest in the emerging field of the sociology of measurement (Dingwall 2004, Wright 2004b). So, to recap the conclusions of previous chapters, and to refer back to Tönnies's original descriptions of *Gemeinschaft und Gesellschaft* and the encroachment of urban values and lifestyles on previously remote and static rural areas, these ideas seem very distant in their relevance for contemporary rural society. Therefore, capturing a concept of 'the rural' for the twenty-first century remains problematic. The analysis of the 2001 FMD epidemic allows the interconnectedness of a number of themes to be seen: the political (policy), economic (as a key driver) and social impact (upon ways of life and notions of community and belonging). Any rural sociology, it seems reasonable to conclude, must attend to how people fit into any political-economic modelling of rural societies: that is, how people understand and respond to their circumstances; whether they resist or welcome change, or, indeed, both simultaneously.

The very business of theorising rural sociology – and the very concept of the rural – is therefore far from complete. What is important, and this is where I think Pahl makes a vital contribution, is to return to Tönnies's original argument that there is no simple bipolar opposition between notions of community and association (*Gemeinschaft und Gesellschaft*), but rather a continuum. What may be needed is a theory of rurality that is able to encompass such contradictions. Finally, Winter (2003) indirectly raises a particularly interesting question: that is, how such policy changes that followed the outbreak can remedy the perceived gap between policy-makers in Whitehall and those people living and working in rural areas. If we cast our minds back to 22 September 2002 and the 'Liberty and Livelihood' march, Winter (2003) points out to us that the march was actually able to mobilise a series of arguments (or, in another light, criticisms) about New Labour and its handling of the countryside in far more general terms than the apparent focus of hunting. It is to the hunting debate and rural protest that the following chapter turns.

Chapter Summary

The chapter examined the impact of the 2001 FMD epidemic in the UK. It drew upon a wide variety of analysis, from the macro (Woods, A. 2002, Blake et al. 2002, CRE) to the meso (Mort et al. 2004, Scott et al. 2004) and the micro (Nerlich and Döring 2005, Wright and Nerlich 2006). Collectively, these analyses showed how interconnected rural areas are in contemporary society. That is, FMD penetrated rural lives in a wide variety of ways, both during and after the crisis. The variety of methodological approaches applied to the study of the 2001 epidemic produced rich insights, but also runs the risk of becoming too single-issue-focused and failing to explicitly contribute to wider changes taking place. Donaldson et al. (2006) is an important exception in this case.

Learning tools

Questions

1. Critically assess the argument that the foot-and-mouth disease epidemic in 2001 was an economic problem.
2. To what extent did the mismanagement of the 2001 foot-and-mouth epidemic highlight existing policy problems and dilemmas concerning farming and the countryside?
3. To what extent did the 2001 foot-and-mouth epidemic act as a catalyst for change in the countryside?
4. How can the impact of the FMD epidemic be researched? Discuss with reference to empirical studies.

Glossary of Emerging Key Terms

Contiguous cull: the cull of cattle within a three-kilometre area of cattle diagnosed as infected.
Epidemiology: the study of the spread of a disease, often via the use of computer modelling, to predict the future direction of disease spread.
FMD: foot-and-mouth disease.

–4–

The Hunting Debate: Rural Political Protest and the Mobilisation and Defence of Country Sports

Introduction

Chapter 4 takes as its focus another substantive example drawn from rural studies. The opening chapters of the book demonstrated how sociological approaches have placed less importance on geographic location in understanding rural areas and progressively become concerned with identity, gentrification, commodification and the countryside as contested space (to mention only a few). This chapter focuses upon hunting in the British countryside, and hunting can be viewed as an example of where the countryside has become a contested space: for those supporting and opposing hunting. The literature that addresses hunting is vast and, rather than attempting to offer a definitive summary of all of the literature, the aim of this chapter is to emphasise what a sociological perspective can bring to such issues.

The introduction of the book expressed a concern with theory and method. This chapter will use a variety of literature to examine how hunting has been approached and seek to demonstrate what theoretical and methodological ideas have been applied. Hamilton argued 'there was no "demand" for this [rural] sociology – either from the agricultural sector or rural society, but more significantly, none from the profession of sociology itself' (Hamilton 1990: 229), yet the previous chapter on FMD showed that a variety of social science research was produced in reaction to the epidemic. In contrast, hunting offers an issue that has been approached by researchers without the catalyst of an epidemic, but within a context of rural protest and a government pledge to examine hunting. Furthermore, Hamilton (1990) raised a note of caution over the way single-issue topics tended to dominate the new wave of social researchers following Newby. This chapter considers hunting in terms of its activities; whether it constitutes a new social movement; the arguments underpinning the pro- and anti-hunting lobbies and whether they have been carried in the printed media; and finally the economic significance of hunting to the UK economy. The conclusions reached here will inform chapter 6, which seeks to expand the portfolio of research techniques available to engage with the rural.

Research and the Hunting Issue

Hunting with hounds in the UK was banned in 2004, when the Hunting Act came into force. Hunting is a field or country sport. Country sports encompass hunting, shooting and fishing. Shooting includes game, clay, stalking, wildfowling and pigeon decoying. Fishing includes trout and salmon as opposed to the different practices of course fishing. Hunting can be as diverse as fox, stag, deer, drag, bloodhound and mink hunting and ferreting.[1] The obvious point here is that 'country sports' is a broad church, and the chapter focuses upon recent social science empirical research on hunting. There is, of course, an important natural science literature in relation to foxes (see Harris 1993, Baker et al. 2002) and game shooting (see GCT 2005), in addition to reflections by participants themselves (Sassoon 1999, Shilling 2004). However, the chapter seeks to challenge whether Hamilton (1990) has a case that the academic community has evaluated the country sport of hunting via its own, dominant methodological paradigm and according to the agenda of the government, rather than seeking to explore the phenomena of hunting a priori.

The political interest in hunting with hounds has provoked some attention among rural sociologists and geographers (Cox et al. 1994, Cox and Winter 1997, Ward 1999, Milbourne 2003a, b) and also substantial media coverage. The chapter considers the findings of several – substantive empirical projects exploring hunting; the analysis of the 2002 'Liberty and Livelihood' march by academic commentators and also within the national press; an economic evaluation of hunting's contribution to the UK economy – and ends with an evaluation of the methodological and theoretical preoccupations of these studies. This chapter therefore also serves to introduce a number of new researchers not addressed in chapter 2 but who have increasingly emerged within rural studies since Hamilton's (1990) summary. They include Paul Milbourne (Cardiff University), Michael Woods (University of Aberystwyth) and Neil Ward (Centre for Rural Economy, University of Newcastle).

Milbourne (2003a, b)

Academic research into hunting has enjoyed something of a renaissance following the Labour government's hunting ban and as a consequence of the portfolio of research commissioned under Lord Burns's inquiry into hunting with hounds. Within the social science community, inquiry contracts were awarded to researchers at Cardiff University (headed by Paul Milbourne) and also at Bath University and to the Royal Agricultural College (RAC) consortium. Milbourne and his colleagues at the Department of City and Regional Planning, Cardiff University, along with Market and Opinion Research International (MORI), explored 'the effects of hunting with dogs on the social and cultural life of the countryside in England and Wales' (Home Office 2000). Broad in its remit, to explore their objective was therefore:

> firstly, ... what involvement or contact individuals in different hunt localities have with hunting and its associated social activities; secondly, to explore what impact hunting and these activities have on their lives; and thirdly, to examine attitudes towards hunting and related activities.
>
> (Milbourne 2003a: 161)

Milbourne's (2003a, b) emergent methodology included material supplied by the local hunts in his four study areas (Cumbria, Leicestershire, Powys and Exmoor), interviews with key local citizens (parish/community councils), structured interviews with 617 households across the four areas and final semi-structured interviews with a sample of participants from the structured interviews. His technique, in which he 'approached the issue of hunting from the perspectives of the broader rural community' is reflected in his findings, namely, the importance of understanding communities inside communities (Milbourne 2003a: 161). Milbourne's (2003a, b) conclusions addressed the means by which dominant discourses about hunting in hunt countries overcame local non-hunting residents' opposition to the activities of the local hunt. Milbourne's research remained firmly embedded in traditional forms of social research and made no claim to be ethnographic; nevertheless, his analysis serves to 'layer' the different cultures coexisting within rural communities. These different understandings of hunts and hunting practices within hunt countries were not always derived from first-hand participation or following the hunt:

> knowledge was not derived not from any personal participation in the practice, but from residence within the local areas that have long histories of hunting. Consequently, hunting had become an embedded part of the local rural social fabric.
>
> (Milbourne 2003a: 164)

Milbourne's insight into hunting lies with his conclusion that the cultural understandings of traditional rural activities, in this case hunting, are as diverse as the groups within that population. He reveals that 'dominant discourses of nature exhibit strong references to rurality and located within these natural discourses of rurality are powerful images of hunting' (Milbourne 2003a: 169). So here we come to see how attitudes towards hunting are derived less from first-hand experience than from dominant ideas of nature and 'passive knowledge of hunting' and rather complex socio-natural constructions of rurality (Milbourne 2003a: 170). This echoes Newby's (1977a) observation that, with the disappearance of the agricultural occupational community, the understandings and appreciation of traditional skills of rural employment also decline. For example, the all-too-visible furrows of a newly ploughed field are not the source of status within rural communities they once were (Newby 1985).

The central drawback to Milbourne's (2003a) study resides with his methodology. The means by which he sought to complement his survey data with interviews and the selection of indicators of social involvement are questionable. His sample for semi-structured interviews was drawn from those who had already participated in the household structured interview phase of the research and had indicated a willingness to take part:

> Potential interviewees were drawn from those residents who had responded to the household survey (617) and who had agreed to take part in the second phase of the research (231).
>
> (Milbourne 2003a: 162)

A sample of over 200 interviews is indeed substantial, yet Milbourne (2003a) remained reliant upon a largely self-selected sample on a highly contentious issue. Admittedly, one of his objectives was to counter the focus of previous studies of hunting that focused solely upon the participants – and elite hunts – to the neglect of those residing in hunt countries. Nevertheless, the manner in which he accessed the rural community and the indicators (which were selected in order to demonstrate the social significance of the hunt alongside other community activities) were far from reflexive (see glossary at the end of the book). For example, he concluded that the local public house and local church were more socially significant, on the basis that they had been frequented more regularly among his sample than hunt social activities or events. This was evaluated on the basis of participants who had visited them over the twelve months preceding the survey, admittedly with the caveat that the 'question asked related to social events specifically organised by the pub, and not those organised by other bodies and taking place there (Milbourne 2003a: 167). However, such events could constitute events as significant as an annual beer festival or a curry night at the pub or the flower festival or a funeral at the local church – none of which indicate that the church or pub occupies a regular or significant part of local residents' lives. Finally, he uncritically cites (much like Ward 1999) MORI polls funded by anti-hunting campaigning organisations (International Fund for Animal Welfare and the CPHA).[2] The bases of such surveys have come under attack from both pro- and anti-hunting organisations alike (Countryside Alliance 2004, LACS 2004a, b, c).

Milbourne's conclusions successfully placed hunting in its community context and drew upon case studies other than from elite hunts. Little more is revealed than that 'new middle-class groups are conforming to existing dominant cultures of hunting within these areas' (Milbourne 2003a: 169). On what basis this conformity is achieved remains unclear.

Cox et al. (1994)

An alternative approach to the study of hunting is presented in the work of Graham Cox. Cox, with Will Manley, Julia Hallett and Graham Smith at the RAC, examined 'drag and bloodhound hunting' on behalf of the Burns Inquiry and he has also considered the experience of hunt followers (Cox and Winter 1997). However, here I want to focus upon an earlier article based on empirical research in order to strike a contrast with Milbourne's approach. Funded by the National Trust, Cox et al. (1994) analysed red deer (*Cervus elaphus*) hunting and they demonstrate a more penetrating research style than that of Milbourne's (2003a, b) approach and their analysis includes an emphasis upon hunting terminology, rituals of dress and the nuances of membership.

Cox et al.'s (1994) opening argument is that knowledge of and participation in hunting need to be placed into their social contexts. Based upon a case study of two stag hunts in the south-west, Cox et al. (1994) sought to appreciate 'the irretrievably social nature of our being in the world and the knowledge we have of it' (Cox et al. 1994: 191). By applying Goffman's (1961) metaphor of the social institution, they highlighted the compelling nature of participating in hunting and argued that hunts also act as 'extraordinarily effective agencies of socialization' (Cox et al. 1994: 190). However, they were anxious to avoid the quite profoundly negative connotations of Goffman's (1961) original use[3] of the term:

> the total institution image is not an entirely appropriate one. For, although it is important to understand the part played by apparently rigid boundaries, it is no less vital to appreciate the extent to which the hunts are integrated with, and draw upon, wider sets of social relations.
>
> (Cox et al. 1994: 190)

So Cox and his team, like Milbourne (2003a), placed hunting within the structure of the wider rural community. However, for Cox et al. (1994), the concept of community was so intrinsic to his analysis that the analogy with the total institution was justified. For instance, 'hunting, for those that take part in it, has a paradigmatic quality that makes the delineation of community particularly compelling' (Cox et al. 1994: 191). The means by which such boundaries were established and maintained guided their approach. They argued that 'a satisfactory explanatory strategy demands that the analysis of social barriers occupy a central position' (Cox et al. 1994: 191). Therefore, geographic proximity to the hunt and personal familiarity with the hunt become less important than appreciating that, for participants, hunt country is non-spatial and 'a "country" of the mind' (Cox et al. 1994: 191).

Cox et al. (1994) therefore detail the rituals and practices of hunting. They make the case that it is vital to appreciate such nuances as 'many features of the social organization of hunting make it an exceptional case: not least the ritualistic aspects that are integral rather than incidental to the activity' (Cox et al. 1994: 191). They explicate such rituals through detailed example, the clarification of a litany of terms and the ordering of the hunting day and the hunt organisational hierarchy. We are provided with a rich account of terminology (tufters and harbourers) and dress (the distinction between rat-catcher and black coats) and so are able to unravel Cox's description of hunting as a total institution:

> Hunting is a world of elaborate ritual, reflected in the customs and practices associated with the activity of hunting itself, strict conventions concerning dress and the habitual use of an esoteric linguistic code. Like all ritual, this serves to confer a clear sense of exclusion for those not familiar with the mores of hunting. The uninitiated are, for example, typically immediately identifiable because of their inappropriate use of language.
>
> (Cox et al. 1994: 193)

Cox et al. further reveal that the organisational structure of the hunt is complex, as the 'distinction between members and subscribers is an important one; [for] membership can neither be applied for nor openly sought' (Cox et al. 1994: 194). The two case studies of two hunts further reveal details of the constitution of hunt subscribers (farmers make up 53 per cent of the economically active in the total sample) alongside geographical proximity of hunt participants. Cox et al., like Milbourne, found that not all local residents of hunt countries participate:

> the majority of Hunt followers live within the Hunt Country itself and that this country is rural in character and relatively thinly populated, it is nonetheless important to note that only a small proportion of the area's population are directly involved in hunting.
>
> (Cox et al. 1994: 199)

However, the means by which Cox et al. progressively build up a picture of a unique social hunt community is quite distinctive from that employed by Milbourne and his team:

> The social organization of hunting entails a succession of commemorative ceremonies that are almost entirely performative in character. The very particular kind of belonging that constitutes a lived sense of community is thus re-affirmed and given practical expression.
>
> (Cox et al. 1994: 204)

The emphasis here is not only upon the hunting community's actions, language and demeanour, but the manner in which they relate to the rural majority – who do not hunt:

Those who take part in field sports and reflect with any degree of seriousness on their activity cannot but be aware that many find it ethically unacceptable. Convinced, as they inevitably are, of their own moral rectitude, they are bound to consider themselves misunderstood by the very substantial majority of the population that neither lives in rural areas nor has any familiarity with what they consider quintessential rural ways.

(Cox et al. 1994: 200)

Within even this minority, stag hunting is itself relatively rare, as 'stag hunting is something of an esoteric activity and those who pursue it are very much a minority of a minority' (Cox et al. 1994: 200). Like Milbourne, Cox's methodology rested upon interviews with hunting households, but sought an understanding of the depth of participation in hunt social activities. For example, Cox outlines that 'hunts are socially least important to those who lived outside the hunting countries' by asking hunt subscribers how significant the hunt was for their social activities (Cox et al. 1994: 202). This is achieved by a list of thirty-three functions organised by one of the case study hunts. These range from the high-profiled (the winter and summer hunt balls) to bingo (Cox et al. 1994: 201). Further than this, subscribers, or any member of their household, were asked if they 'had been 'involved in the organizing or running' any of the events listed 'including clearing up afterwards'. The answers to this question show that no fewer than half of all respondents (48 per cent) had been directly involved in helping in some way at these functions. The figure is an impressively high one which indicates a distinctive cohesiveness amongst the hunting community'. From this Cox et al. conclude that:

Our evidence suggests high levels of involvement and cohesiveness encompassing the whole age range and providing numerous occasions on which people from isolated rural areas get together. There is, in that sense, a community that is based on shared activities as well as shared values.

(Cox et al. 1994: 203)

It is through this that we understand hunting as a total institution, which fosters a most particular distinctive form of belonging, 'despite the fact that those who hunt are often strongly connected to worlds beyond hunting and many do not reside within the geographical community' (Cox et al. 1994: 204). Therefore 'the hunting community, in short, proved to be characterized by 'totalizing' social and ideological relation' (Cox et al. 1994: 191).

Cox et al.'s (1994) methodology allows a more detailed understanding of the 'totalising' impact of membership of a hunting community and its terminology and practices. However, whilst style of dress, rituals and hunting practices are described and placed within a social network, little is revealed as to what hunting means to individual participants. The principal aim of Cox and his colleagues' project was, indeed, to examine the economic impact of hunting, and the social aspect was only an 'additional objective' (Cox et al. 1994: 192). Perhaps therefore the multi-strategy approach, using postal questionnaires (with a response rate of 31 per cent of all subscribers), twelve interviews and two seminars and numerous follow-up conversations and discussions, is significant in yielding additional data. Nevertheless, the study is partial and risks lending itself too heavily to the government's agenda for researching hunting than a concern for theoretical and methodological development of rural research more generally (Hamilton 1990). Nevertheless, Cox and Milbourne's respective approaches stand out among the rash of economic evaluations of hunting's contribution to the UK economy, whereas economic factors have provided the central focus of other studies (Cobham Resource Consultants 1992, Ward 1999) and other contracts commissioned by the Burns Inquiry (Home Office 2000). The issue to emerge within these analyses is multipliers – and to what extent they can be extrapolated. In such cases, the estimates by those in favour and opposed to hunting naturally reflect their own predispositions. Having now considered two of the more recent social science explorations into hunting using qualitative techniques, the chapter now looks at a rural event arising, initially, from the movement to ban hunting but which, as Winter (2003) acknowledges, in the light of FMD came to take on a greater significance in the eyes of some rural protest groups.

Michael Woods (2003)

Woods has conducted a number of explorations of rural politics (Woods 2002, 2003, 2005). Woods (2003) addresses the hunting debate, although this is in a general discussion as to whether a specifically rural social movement can be said to exist. The discussion also draws upon examples of protest in the United States, France and alternative examples within the UK, such as the Farmers For Action fuel blockade. Woods (2003) argues that 'the recent wave of rural protests and campaigns can be shown to exhibit characteristics of a new social movement. However, this does not in itself prove the existence of a "rural movement" ' (Woods 2003: 315). Woods (2003) argues, rather, that the interest groups campaigning in the countryside are too diverse and lack the coherence and identity to be labelled as a rural movement per se. He discusses the Countryside Alliance (CA) (see also Woods 2005 for a detailed history of the history of the CA and its predecessor the British Field Sports Society – BFSS). The CA is the foremost campaigning group for hunting, but Woods also considers how they have expanded their remit to include issues beyond hunting:

> For larger, more formalised, groups such as the Countryside Alliance, the adoption of a holistic 'rural' mantle has been a strategic decision in order to build greater support for a more narrowly focused core concern. In the case of the Countryside Alliance this was the realisation that the single issue of hunting could not mobilise sufficient public support to successfully resist legislation to ban the sport, but positioning hunting as

fundamental to rural life – and consequently, positioning a ban on hunting as an attack of rural identity – could.

(Woods 2003: 316)

Here Woods (2003) importantly bases his argument directly upon the 'insider' accounts of Hart Davis (1997) and George (1999). The process by which the CA came to 'evolve' or redefine itself in terms of an appeal to rural issues more generally is traced:

Most strikingly, a rural movement that is largely led by a one-time paternalistic elite has sought to represent itself as an 'oppressed minority'. This final act completes the process of identity formation and mobilisation in the rural movement – first, supporters are encouraged to think of themselves as 'rural' and connect their particular interests with other 'rural' concerns; second, they are directed to differentiate between 'rural' and 'urban' and to identify the 'urban' as the source of their problems; third, they are told that they are an oppressed minority whose identity is under threat and thus mobilised into collective action.

(Woods 2003: 317)

Woods was interested to trace 'the evolution of the British Countryside Alliance which following the success of its earlier pro-hunting rallies sought to extend its appeal to a wider constituency, including leisure-users' (Woods 2003: 317). So the issue of hunting was expanded to include participants in country activities, such as canoeists and ramblers, as well as those participating in more traditionally perceived country sports. Woods (2003) discusses the CA's own internal debate to engage with 'what is rural'. This serves to unravel distinctions inside this group, for example, between in-migrants and long-term rural residents. It is this point which suggests that the hunting debate was not a rural movement in its own right, as the group itself operates on too diverse a conceptualisation of rurality:

A 'rural movement' cannot therefore be identified as mobilising around any singular 'rural identity'. Rather, the numerous groups concerned represent a range of responses to social and economic restructuring informed by different, and sometimes conflicting, discourses of rurality.

(Woods 2003: 317–18)

Woods also considers the tactics employed by the CA and pro-hunting lobby:

For many groups, including the British Countryside Alliance as well as most family farmer and rural campaign groups in the United States, conventional lobbying and non-confrontational tactics such as petitions and letter-writing campaigns, continue to form a major part of their activities.

(Woods 2003: 318)

Woods (2003) notes that even such conventional tactics are employed with the aim to build support, either internal solidarity or external support, and/or to attract media coverage, the success of which, or lack thereof, can be seen in the passing of the Hunting Act in 2004, which was ultimately not based on the government's own bill, but that proposed and supported by rebel Labour backbench MPs. Woods concludes that:

> The rural movement is characterised most notably by disunity. Yet ... As the continuing consequences of rural restructuring keep rural issues on the political agenda, so too will the rural movement remain as a significant political force.
>
> (Woods 2003: 324)

Woods's (2003) work shows the countryside as a contested space and that the issue of hunting enables new understanding of modern protest and also identity to be raised. The final section of this chapter uses empirical data looking at the messages pro- and anti-hunting lobbies seek to convey and their success in the wake of the Liberty and Livelihood march of 2002. Developing this emphasis upon discourse, the chapter examines Burridge (2006). Burridge (2006) conducts a discourse analysis of the argumentative purposes underpinning the CA's campaign and this allows a nwe look at the substance of Woods's (2003) argument that different messages were present in the march and two means through which they were communicated.

Competing Definitions of 'Nature' and 'Natural' in the Pro- and Anti-shooting Lobbies

An alternative approach to understanding the countryside as a contested space but moving towards a more micro-oriented focus is to look at media representations of pro- and anti-hunting arguments.[4] The respective messages of the pro- and anti-hunting lobbies were translated into the British print media before the ban on hunting came into effect, and the manner in which they make their cases echoes Woods's (2003) point that more than one representation of rurality is again clear. This section looks at such differences and how each group appealed to 'nature' and 'natural' rural ways of life. For example, how do anti- and pro-hunting groups differ in their idealisation of nature and therefore its regulation and protection?

The main players in the hunting debate were the League Against Cruel Sports (LACS), established in 1924, and the International Fund for Animal Welfare (IFAW), established in Canada in 1969. The more 'extreme' organisations, in the sense that their campaigns have had recourse to breaking the law, include the Animal Liberation Front (ALF) and the Hunt Saboteurs' Association (HSA).[5] The largest and most prominent of the anti-hunting lobby the organisation

Campaigning to Protect Hunted Animals (CPHA), which was established in 1996 and incorporates LACS, RSPCA and IFAW. CPHA ran the Deadline 2000 campaign.[6] In these terms, a variety of interest groups are present – all with the common objective of banning hunting.

Cox et al. (1994) made the point mentioned earlier in the chapter that even within hunting there are different forms of participation. The pro-hunting lobby was equally diverse: for example, organisations solely focused upon the protection of hunting and those with more general remits that encompass country sports. Organisations of the former type include 'Action for Hunting' (www.fox-hunters.net) and 'Hunting for Tolerance' (www.huntfacts.com), established in 2002 in direct response to the move to ban hunting. The history of these groups is interesting in that it shows them to be an amalgamation of different organisations. For example, the CPHA's opposite number is the Countryside Alliance (CA), which was established in March 1997 when the British Field Sports Society (BFSS), the Countryside Movement and the Country Business Group merged. The CA, as the organisers of the 'Liberty and Livelihood' march on 22 September 2002, provides the loudest voice of authority for the pro-hunting lobby and their message is used here to summarise the pro-hunting lobby's approach.[7]

The methodological approach applied in this section contains many parallels with Oates's (2002) described in the last chapter. The literatures of these anti- and pro-hunting organisations were accessed via their websites during the year of the march (2002). However, there is more of a focus upon their message rather than the websites as an information resource that guided Oates's (2002) analysis. The websites revealed the philosophies of each lobby through the key issues they draw attention to in support of their stance. They served to implicitly evoke a definition of the countryside and 'nature' and, in doing so, unravelled their respective visions of nature and natural ways of life.

The anti-hunting lobby's approach to refuting the necessity of hunting applied three 'tests': necessity, effectiveness and humaneness (CPHA 'Exposing the Myths', www.banhunting.com). The case is implicitly made that hunting is unnatural, for example, 'cruel and unnecessary sports' and more specifically 'cruel and barbaric' (CPHA, www.banhunting.com). The emphasis upon language reveals that the anti-hunting lobby took the view that hunting transcended civilised behaviour. For example, 'the setting of animal against animal for entertainment' (CHPA, www.banhunting.com) and its inherent perversity lie in its method, namely, the 'slaughter and ritualistic mutilation of an animal' (LACS, News and Media, 9 July 2003, www.league.uk.com/news/).

The anti-hunting lobby's argument that hunting is uncivilised and that 'hunting is cruel, unnecessary and has no place in a modern Britain' (LACS *Campaign Update* Issue 12, February, 2003) is supported by historical comparisons with other, subsequently banned, sports:

Cock fighting, dog fighting and bear baiting are setting one animal on another for the purpose of entertainment. So is hunting.

('Hunters' Nonsense', LACS,
www.league.uk.com/campaigns/hunters_nonsense.htm)

The general theme of cruelty or animal welfare condenses their three means to evaluate hunting (necessity, effectiveness, humaneness). It also served to supersede differences between forms of hunting. Hunting, as Cox et al. (1994) explained (see earlier in the chapter), is a broad term and encompasses hare coursing, the use of terriers to hunt foxes underground and also mink and stag hunting. Whilst acknowledging these differences, in order to focus the discussion the arguments specifically relating to the fox are engaged with here.

In addition to the animal welfare concerns underpinning the anti-hunting lobby's arguments, notions of natural and the natural order are also present in Cox et al.'s (1994) arguments. The anti-hunting literature identifies the social groups taking part in hunting activities, or 'blood sports enthusiasts' (CPHA, www.ban-hunting.com), as including farmers, landowners and gamekeepers as well as those involved with the hunt, either mounted or foot-followers, and their 'rural folklore' regarding the quarry species attacked: for example, the necessity of controlling the fox population – 'individual foxes can cause local difficulties but there is little evidence to support the view that the fox is a significant agricultural pest nationally' (CPHA, www.banhunting.com). Similarly, 'it is not necessary to routinely kill foxes and hunting is ineffective in controlling numbers. And where an individual rogue fox does need to be killed, there are always less cruel alternatives available' (LACS *Campaign Update* Issue 12, February 2003). The fox, it seems, is not at the heart of the problem and, furthermore, foxes are argued to serve a purpose by maintaining the balance of wildlife in the countryside by controlling the rabbit population. The vision of the countryside and its wildlife expounded here is that a 'natural' system of predation in the countryside is more appropriate.

The concept of nature and the natural order is central to the way the hunting issue has become a contested countryside issue. Intervening in the wild animal population levels in the countryside is essential in the view of the hunting community, who present the fox as a dangerous animal that necessitates controlling (culling). In contrast, the anti-hunting lobby appeals to nature's methods of predation. The opinions of the two groups are therefore irretrievably opposed. This is encapsulated by the rejection of the possibility that some forms of hunting (for example, mink) may continue under licence or utilising dogs: 'No Chase. No Kill. No Compromise. Just a Ban' (LACS *Campaign Update* Issue 12, February 2003).

Analysing the websites offers an insight into the conceptualisation of rurality in respect to hunting. In respect to the pro-hunting lobby, the motivations underpinning a desire to hunt are pitched at a variety of levels (recreation, community, environmental management) and hence broader than an appeal to the anti-hunting lobby's 'nature's way'. Most simplistically, the pro-hunting lobby argues that hunting is 'fast and exciting' (www.hounds.org.uk) and that 'hunt followers are there for the rise' (www.hounds.org.uk). More serious, is the rhetoric of 'prejudice and ignorance' that pro-hunting organisations direct at their critics (www.fox-hunters.net). This rhetoric reveals a two-pronged approach to tackling hunting's detractors, one of dislike and one of misinformation. The latter is addressed first.

The logic of the pro-hunting lobby's defence is that the very activities of hunting and also shooting and angling (as will be established later) are misunderstood. As a result of the minimal or misinformation surrounding hunting with hounds, the activity has come to be inappropriately labelled as unnecessary. For example, they cite six adverse consequences: job losses (and generic negative effects upon businesses); destruction of hounds; horse welfare; the quarry species; deadstock (that is, its disposal); and conservation (www.hounds.org.uk/a-facts.htm), alongside alienation from the government (www.hounds.org.uk). The conceptualisation of the quarry species – the fox – by the hunting lobby is considered first. Whilst the pro-hunting lobby seeks to manoeuvre a series of representations of their activities (economic and welfare), the quarry species itself and its position and status in the countryside are focused upon to contrast it with the view of the anti-hunting lobby.

The pro-hunting lobby argues:

> Wildlife management in a man-made environment involves the maintenance, by all available means, of animal populations at levels which can be tolerated by human communities. Hunting is an effective and flexible means of achieving this, and thus can only be addressed meaningfully in the context of other aspects of wildlife management as a whole.
>
> ('Our case for hunting: the facts',
> *CA Campaign Update* Issue 3, October 2002)

Here the appeal is directly made with the conditions of the predator and its prey – in its natural context. The legitimacy that is appealed to here is one of the natural ways of things – hunting is merely an extension of this logic. The philosophical stance that the hunting community uses also appeals to knowledge of the land and its management – the rural way of life. The CA response positions hunting inside the maintenance of the countryside way of life. The way of life they construct is a balance between the managed countryside, the rural business economy and the social community:

> Communities within which hunting takes place derive economic and social benefit from the activity. These are both important components of the concept of utility because they contribute to sustainable development and social capital.
>
> ('Our case for hunting: the facts',
> *CA Campaign Update* Issue 3, October 2002)

The final part of this section examines the extent to which the messages promoted by both lobbies translated into the media coverage of the Liberty and Livelihood march held on 22 September 2002 in London. Methodologically, this is another 'layering' or representation of a rural issue and the importance of looking at such an approach will be considered (Burridge 2006).

The 2002 'Liberty and Livelihood' March[8]

Two contrasting titles were considered here. Both are national newspapers in the UK: the pro-Labour *Guardian* and the pro-hunting *Telegraph*. Following Oates's (2002) terms of 'limited' and 'plenty,' both newspapers offered plenty of coverage. The *Guardian*'s coverage of the event on the day after the march, Monday, 23 September, dominated half of the front page and included a further two pages inside the paper and a political cartoon on the commentary and analysis page (*Guardian*, 23 September 2002). The editorial indirectly addressed the march, with reference to the nation's declining flora and fauna. The *Daily Telegraph*'s coverage similarly dominated, covering three-quarters of the front page, including a large picture. The paper offered additional coverage of the march on four inside pages, two commentaries by *Telegraph* reporters attending the march (a past editor and the current editor) and an editorial. Therefore, immediately, the significance of the pro-hunting march received far more explicit (and implicit) support from the *Telegraph*.

The actual content of the coverage varied considerably between the two papers and they served to introduce new representations of both groups. For instance, the lead article in the *Guardian* caricatured the 'marital bickering' they had overheard taking place between the marchers, 'Oh look, there's Charles and Felicity' (*Guardian*, 23 September 2002). The allusion was brought home by the suggestion that it 'could have been the Henley Regatta. Some had come in full aristo regalia: boys in long socks and knicker-bockers' [*sic*] and the girls who had 'in many instances come straight from their boarding schools to attend the event and were treating it as another fixture in the social calendar' (ibid.: 1). The *Guardian*'s implication was that the marchers did not represent the diversity of rural inhabitants. Furthermore, the salience of the march itself was undermined by the comparison with a regatta – a social event, rather than one with a serious political message. The *Guardian* also highlighted the mixed messages of the pro-hunters in its coverage. This is summarised in table 10.

Overarchingly, the portrayal of hunting in the *Guardian* newspaper rejected the pro-hunting lobby's allusion to hunting's place within the rural way of life:

> If the Countryside Alliance sought to claim that yesterday's march represented the fears of the entire rural community, there were no such pretensions at inclusivity in London's unashamedly elitist clubland.

> (*Guardian*, 23 September 2002: 5)

Table 10 *Guardian* representations of the march's message

- There's an element of cruelty, they're [foxes] vermin, needing control; foxhunting as the only kind way of controlling them
- Rural services (post offices, transport, housing) – 'The important rural issue is the lack of transport' (marcher) (Duncan Smith)
- Rural economy – job losses and supporting farmers – 'It makes no economic sense to ban it' (marcher)
- Urban dictating to the rural – government failing to listen – 'Gay rights, asylum rights, WE want OUR rights' (placard)
- Civil liberties – the right to decide and individual choice – 'Tolerance' 'Live and Let Live' (placards)
- Rural communities and heritage, and 'class bigotry' – 'it's not only toffs here today' (Baroness Mallalieu) (marcher)
- Rising red tape/bureaucracy – the thin end of the wedge – shooting and fishing next

The flavour of the *Telegraph*'s coverage could not be more marked. Their headline '407,791 voices cry freedom' set the tone for the approach of their portrayal of the march and its marchers (the *Daily Telegraph*, 23 September 2002). The rhetoric of the *Telegraph* verged on the flamboyant when the two routes of the march met in central London: 'two tributaries met in the middle of Whitehall to form a giant river of humanity' (*Telegraph* 2002: 1). The *Telegraph*'s clear advocacy of hunting portrayed hunting as being embedded in the very fabric of rural society:

> You could not generalise about these people. No cosy British social snobbery or inverted snobbery helps you out, for the crowds were so socially and geographically diverse. So, too, were the issues that brought them together. For every marcher talking about hunting, there was another telling you about the local bus service, the closing Post Office, the price of lamb, and the greed of the supermarkets.
>
> (*Telegraph*, 23 September 2002: 2)

Borrowing again from Oates's (2002) approach, the topics can be summarised and are represented in table 11.

The vignettes, therefore, were closely aligned with the accounts of the CA organisers. Of course, the *Telegraph*'s affiliation with country sports is long-standing.[9] The differences between the two newspapers' standpoints can also be unravelled in their editorials. The *Telegraph* offered pronouncements from its former and current editors, the *Guardian* made no reference to the march.

This section has explored hunting through an empirical study of the rhetoric of both pro- and anti-hunting lobbies. The 'message' underpinning the broadening of the Countryside Alliance's rhetoric towards a more generalist protection of the countryside has replaced the single-issue focus on hunting of previous rallies (Woods, M. 2002, 2003). It offered a different approach to those undertaken by

Table 11 Themes underpinning the march reported in the *Telegraph*

- Division between town and country
- No countryman in the cabinet – no knowledge of the country
- Liberty and livelihood principles eroded
- Too many laws and 'red tape' already
- Farming misery (post-FMD and BSE)
- Synergy: country living and country sports go hand in hand
- Services: schools, transport, housing and post offices
- Way of life
- A ban would be unenforceable
- Misrepresentation of the countryside by an ignorant government
- Preservation of the countryside
- Prejudice and intolerance

Milbourne (2003a, b) and Cox et al. (1994) in that non-traditional forms of data (the Web and printed media) were used as a resource. However, it complements their findings on the countryside as a contested space. This is a meaning of contested that is not just political (as Woods 2003 explored), but also social in terms of recognising the different communities inside rural areas. This section sought to show that in the case of the two lobbies examined here their differences are incommensurable.

In the latter half of this section the translation of these two communities' expressions of rurality into the printed media was examined. In the case of the two sampled newspapers, the predispositions of each were readily identified. Burridge (2006) offers a more critical and penetrating analysis of the manner in which the media carries a message or definition of rurality and this is discussed next.

Burridge (2006)

Burridge (2006) explored hunting as a means of looking at the processes of argumentation and argumentative strategies employed by the supporters of hunting. He takes the adverts placed in the British media by the CA and 'analyses the rhetorical structure of the posters [to argue that] they are explicitly addressed in interconnected ways to the alleged arguments of the organisation's opponents about who engages in hunting' Burridge 2006: 2). In the same way the previous section showed that how the different lobbies present their case is also directly linked to the arguments of their opponents. Burridge (2006) offers some background discussion as to the claims of the pro-hunting lobby as they appear on their website and in the printed media, but it is the visual medium of the CA's posters that is his primary focus. He explicates his approach:

> I am certainly not examining the posters as instances of what is often termed 'propaganda', but rather more neutrally as instances of argumentation which make use of visual (photographic) and textual elements (which are themselves also obviously visual since they require sight) to make a case in the face of a putative counter-case.
>
> (Burridge 2006: 9)

The posters featured pictures of ordinary-looking members of the public, with headlines such as 'scum', 'pervert' and 'toff' (in red and in capital letters) followed by a question mark and a small paragraph of information on their profession and participation in hunting. Burridge (2006) argues that this is a deliberate rhetorical strategy and the picture and question mark over the label applied to them invites the viewer to note the disjunction. He argues that the contrast between the question and the other elements, regardless of the order in which they are engaged by the viewer, obviously requires both of them to work' (Burridge 2006: 15). That is, the audience (to use Burridge's term) is assumed to have heard the arguments of the anti-hunting lobby (hunters as toffs, for example) and be able to address this misapprehension on the basis of the new material they view in the posters.

Burridge concludes that the posters are part of the CA's campaign to be seen as 'the pursuit of "ordinariness" ' (Burridge 2006: 29). This, he argues, is strategic as 'the claim to be ordinary in such a context is often used to argue that your position cannot be easily dismissed, and you should not receive particular allegedly inappropriate forms of treatment' (Burridge 2006: 31). Burridge's (2006) analysis draws visual material into the variety of methodological accounts examined in this chapter. He links these with the wider claims of the CA and is able to offer a political commentary on both the message of the CA and its medium. He therefore complements the previous studies of hunting by adding another dimension of understanding to the hunting debate as an example of the countryside as a contested space. Having considered examples of the social and media aspects of the hunting debate, the chapter now considers an economic analysis of the hunting debate offered by Ward (1999).

Ward (1999)

Ward (1999) assesses the economic significance of hunting to the UK economy – concluding that the arguments employed by the pro-hunting lobby have overstated their case and therefore 'foxed the nation'. Ward's (1999) scope is also somewhat broader than purely an economic analysis, as he contextualises the pro-hunting lobby's changing rhetorics. Echoing Woods (2003), Ward unravels that the pro-hunting argument has progressively shifted from moral, management and 'way of life' argument towards in the 1990s towards a new emphasis upon the economic contribution hunting makes to the UK economy.

He makes analogies between hunting and bear-baiting, bullfighting and cockfighting, that is, other sports banned in the nineteenth century. The anti-hunting groups are those campaigning for prevention of cruelty to animals. The logic of his argument tackles the debate on four generic levels. At the core of his argument is that economic contributions are dynamic and changing, rather than static. He (1) argues that the claims made by the pro-hunting lobby are unsupportable; (2) addresses the alternatives to hunting; (3) considers the social costs hunting generates; and finally (4) comments on discourse strategies of the economic contribution argument as applied to hunting. All of these points are based upon unravelling the economic contributions.

Ward (1999) acknowledges that the economic impact is difficult to calculate, as the previous chapter on FMD noted. Ward (1999) suggests that knock-on spending is difficult to calculate and it may merely be spent on something also in the rural sector, such as shooting. In relation to the argument that hunting was presenting itself as a way of life, Ward (1999) raises the question as to whether the argument appeals to the rural or to country sports and traditions. The rural, he argues, no longer just equates to geography, and he raises a challenging point as to who should have the right to interfere with activities on private land?

Ward (1999), like Woods (2003), notes the strategic move by rural groups to include economic arguments and discusses the 1997 campaign and the initial moves by the BFSS (the predecessor of the CA). He notes that some figures are associated with all country sports and therefore that there are problems associated with lumping such diverse activities together in order to specifically separate hunting's contribution. Ward (1999) explicates that the data offered by the CA were in fact in the Cobham report, which was commissioned by the Standing Conference on Countryside Sports, clearly a pro-hunting organisation. Ward (1999) further deconstructs the sources appearing in the Cobham report and the report's unreferenced use of BFSS data. For example, Ward (1999) unravels that figure estimates for 1992 were actually derived from 1983 research figures and further that those research data were collated in 1981–2. The question Ward (1999) is raising therefore addresses the issue of multipliers: multipliers which then go on to provide the basis for further extrapolation and certain figures to be reached.

There are, however, a number of problems with Ward's (1999) analysis and the suppositions he makes. For example, whilst it is important to remain mindful of the CA's claim to represent a wide range of rural concerns, this is perhaps taken too far in the separation of hunting from other activities such as point-to-pointing and the somewhat trite observation that hunting horses are used for other purposes as the hunting season is only six months long (Ward 1999: 391).

The problem Ward (1999) highlights in other studies by academic researchers (Winter et al. 1993) in relation to multipliers is a valid one, yet the distinction can be made between the analysis they produced and those conducted by the pro- and anti-hunting lobbies themselves. The problem is, perhaps, a lack of research is more of a concern than the poor research that has resulted from interest groups analyses. Ward then cites the 'limitations on local data sources' (Ward 1999: 392) in Winter et al.'s (1993) analysis. There is a much wider problem of how to incorporate regional and localised characteristics into an analysis – a difficulty that will be encountered by all economic analysts and rural sociologists.

Ward (1999) is not restricted to an interest in the figures, but also their appearance in the campaigning material and speeches of the CA, which naturally draw upon their own research data resources (such as the Cobham studies). Inevitably, a number of CA claims in relation to the economic contribution of hunting are overstated. The same could also be said, therefore, of the anti-hunting lobbies claims, although this is beyond the scope of Ward's (1999) paper. A difficulty here is that Ward (1999) has not contributed his own original research findings to the debate – arguing that he does not wish to contribute to the ever-growing pile. Whilst there are many highly salient points that deconstruct outdated or poorly extrapolated figures, they are not proved to be entirely wrong or replaced with alternative claims or data, i.e. a more accurate analysis. In addition, there are some confusing instances where there is no explication of anti-hunting groups', such as the LACS, data. Yet, when the LACS argues that hunting is in decline, Ward (1999) supports their conclusions with reference to the Cobham Resource Consultants data – data that he has just discredited. This is a danger policy, in that Ward (1999) moves away from purely a economic analysis towards one that engages with moral and social – and even philosophical – issues. This leads to a number of somewhat inappropriate comparisons, such as that between rural school closures having not prompted protest marches on the same scale as the ban of hunting. Rural schools and hunting are not analogous, whereas a later comparison between coal-mining and hunting job losses is more evocative of protest comparisons![10]

Ward (1999) does support some of the findings of other academic commentators on hunting generally, but finds theirs a 'normative' argument and sentimental (Winter et al. 1993, Cox et al. 1994, Cox and Winter 1997, Winter 1998). The attention is placed upon the use of the word 'special', which in this instance is a somewhat poor selection and would be better replaced by distinct or different. The distinction he then goes on to make is somewhat curious, in that he is attempting to refuse to label a particularly 'rural' job as having any intrinsic quality that values it above that of an 'urban' job. Surely the implication is that there are (negative) connotations with activities in rural areas that otherwise could be located in a city, in terms of the pressures that they create in terms of community, amenity and social terms. In addition, perhaps allowing some scope to distinguish between such jobs allows for a more complex reading of a dynamic rural economy – as more complex than first appears – in line with Ward's (1999) initial intention.

Ward's (1999) theoretical model offers a means to unravel the ontological predispositions of his own position. He notes a context of rapid economic change, but does not engage in an analysis of the implications (both positive and negative) of these changes, such as we have seen in earlier rural sociology such as Tönnies and

Newby's work. The theoretical model Ward (1999) employed in this paper is more evocative of the political-economic approach of Marsden. The critical nature of this approach poses several innovative and provocative questions. For example, the notion that the public generally has a legitimate claim to comment on rural concerns (i.e. not just rural people) is interesting. For, indeed, the CPRE is not entirely uninterested in how the future countryside may look and therefore there is a need to look beyond localised concerns. For example, when Ward (1999) appeals to figures that demonstrate how many 'users' the countryside has, there is a need to explicate such use, for there is the same danger of lumping together country sports along with hunting that Ward (1999) resisted earlier. Ward (1999) is here engaging with the diversification of the countryside debate, a highly salient issue for the countryside today. Another term with a high level of prominence is the issue of sustainability. Ward (1999) is able to discuss social, demographic, policy and economic issues in rural areas and also developments in farming, so it is surprising not to see hunting's role in land management for conservation (of non-target species) is not mentioned. This indicates a lack of concern to position hunting in the round. This is surprising in terms of how the FMD epidemic in 2001 demonstrated how significant tourism is to agricultural areas and the rural economy.

This draws to the fore the core dilemma within Ward's (1999) argument, that he himself to all appearances is making his own, subtle normative claims in relation to hunting. For example, that there are alternatives to hunting (such as drag-hunting) does not constitute sufficient support to ban hunting – yet the allusion is clearly made and at length. Attention is directed towards these alternative forms of hunting and the experience that they provide, whilst the experience of 'real' hunting has not received such consideration. Admittedly, Ward (1999) notes that country sports in general have not attracted a great deal of attention and there is, in this light, great scope for research into how people begin to hunt or participate in such activities. In his discussion on the experience of alternative forms of hunting, he does appeal to the subjective experience in his description, but we are not made aware (as Winter does in the Burns Inquiry and Cox does in Cox (2000)) of the author's own position or familiarity with the hunt. This raises question marks about such an omission made regarding such a highly contested field.[11] This leads to instances where LACS and CPHA data are uncritically cited. Because these data are not given the same critical treatment as CRC and CA data, Ward misreads some techniques commonly used in gamekeeping, in this instance seen as feeding the fox population, when the positioning of dead poultry or game is also an important means by which the presence of a fox can be detected (Ward 1999: 398, fn. 7). Another example is the dismissal of BFSS claims that drag-hunting does not provide conservation or community support. Ward (1999) interprets this purely in terms of social benefits and ignores the conservation claim, noting only that farming payments have shifted considerably towards the maintenance of landscape features and wildlife habitats. The conservation card is too significant to dismiss so quickly and requires far more explication than Ward (1999) provides. Finally, in terms of the (mis)application of multipliers, Ward (1999) extrapolates from one year's meet card to suggest that there is little difference between drag-hunts and conventional ones, when Winter et al.'s (1993) data for stag hunting demonstrate the differences between deer hunting and fox-hunting. In further suggesting alternative forms, Ward (1999) argues that ingenuity has been seen within the shooting community and the rise in simulated game shooting. As to the degree that such sports will attract significant audiences, he is perhaps overly optimistic given the disparities between the television coverage between Olympic gold-medal-winning sports.

There is further scope to engage with the particulars of the article, but the general point being made is clear. Ward (1999) does not deconstruct LACS claims about hunting lobby figures to the same extent as he does for CRC figures.[12] He does not acknowledge the differences in hunted species and that (1) nature cannot be left to manage itself and (2) there needs to be an engagement with the very different requirements of hunting each animal (Cox 2001), particularly in the light of the fact that some species are alien to the UK and therefore damaging to that environment (e.g. the American mink). Ward claims that the 1997 bill does not attack these and that the hunting bill is in isolation from other country sports such as shooting and fishing:

> The widely cited figure of £3.8 billion spent on country sports is an estimate of economic activity which includes a whole host of sporting pursuits besides hunting with hounds, none of which were threatened by the proposed legislation.
>
> (Ward 1999: 390)

However, the intentions of the anti-hunting lobby have explicitly been for some time towards shooting as their next target (Cox 2000, citing concerns raised in 1996). Therefore, the lessons of the hunting example are relevant for contemporary debates surrounding country sports. Nevertheless, the main charge of Ward's (1999) paper that the figures appealed to by the country sports lobby are out of date is confirmed by the commissioning of a new study into the contribution of shooting to the UK economy by the Cambridge-based group Public and Corporate Economic Consultants and sponsored by the BASC, the GCT and the CA, the results of which are yet to emerge.

Conclusion

In a context in which the scrutiny placed upon hunting is already beginning to be focused upon country sports more generally,[13] there is a danger that issue-led research may dominate to the detriment of a more holistic placement of country sports inside the rural context and alongside theoretical and methodological developments. This chapter is concerned to avoid such an approach. The hunting debate, as considered here, has served to support the re-conceptualisation of the countryside as a contested space. This is not merely in relation to the ownership of and access to rural areas, but over the very essence of what the rural is and how this is appealed to by opposing groups. The competition and conflict between anti- and pro-hunting lobbies appeal to social, scientific and local knowledge forms of evidence, to the rhetoric of laissez-faire and to the inherent characteristics of 'nature' and what is seen to be natural.

The chapter has reviewed the methodologies of two prominent and contrasting treatments of hunting, finding that political-economy approaches have tended to dominate the research agenda, to the neglect of the individual agency invested in the activity of hunting. Ethnography has a role to play in unravelling the rituals, practices and meanings of hitherto neglected country sports. In turn, these need to be placed in a countryside that is no longer characterised by the occupation community Newby (1977a) identified, but is one with diverse constituents (Milbourne 2003a) and still very powerful and compelling patterns of participation (Cox et al. 1994). The chapter also argues that the contribution of the more recent 'cultural turn' within rural geography in the 1990s, whilst valuable in many respects, has done little to alleviate such an absence of qualitative research into such social forms. The danger here is that the research community responded to the portfolio of research defined by the Burns Inquiry, rather than determining its own research agenda. The lack of ethnographic or anthropological engagements with pro and anti groups could be seen to support such an argument.

In relation to the criticisms levelled at the respective methodologies considered here, an important caveat needs to be made. That is, reflexivity permits an understanding that all methodologies have their own, equally profound limitations and inherent weaknesses (Atkinson 1990) and, as such, are all inherently partial. Nevertheless, there remains the obligation to engage with themes of power and the official sanctioning of some definitions of reality above others (Goffman 1983). Academic researchers, in contentious areas, are in difficult territories as to where to best position themselves. In a context where there is increasing scrutiny by animal rights activists of those engaged in animal testing, there is a need to understand the phenomenon of such protest groups. Animal welfare and rights and their intersections are a research field that has attracted some innovative work by rural geographers, but warrants much more, for example, into the interconnections between animals and society, the relative status of animals and conceptions of nature, 'natural' and the positioning of animals within nature. Chapter 6 takes up the call for a wider portfolio of techniques be employed to engage with the complexities of the rural and suggests a number of techniques that could be useful in complementing existing approaches to engaging with contemporary rurality.

Chapter Summary

The chapter drew upon a sample of government and research council-funded research to examine hunting. It found these to be cognisant of debates taking place in wider sociology and geography. The single issue of hunting contributed to the wider refinement and development of sociological and geographic concepts: for example, understanding the hunting community as a total institution. The chapter suggested that there was scope for a more detailed engagement with the social nuances of hunting and that this would serve to complement the literature on the political and economic aspects of the hunting debate was also discussed.

The idea of the countryside as a contested space provided an ideal framework through which to position different theoretical and methodological studies of hunting. For example, the discussion of the media coverage of the pro- and anti-hunting lobby's messages saw that the very concept of nature was contested and it also allowed the ambiguities within the message of the pro-hunting lobby to be represented. The chapter finally raised a question mark as to whether academic contributions to the hunting debate pursued their own agendas or whether they were excessively influenced by the concerns of the pro- and anti-hunting lobbies and/or funding bodies. This is a theme developed further in the following chapter.

Learning tools

Questions

1. To what extent have political-economic analyses dominated the treatment of the hunting debate?
2. Did the 2002 'Liberty and Livelihood' march constitute a new social movement?
3. How central was the fox to the debates surrounding the banning of hunting with hounds?
4. 'The "Liberty and Livelihood" march was a rural protest, rather than purely about hunting.' Discuss.

Glossary of Emerging Key Terms

a priori: see the glossary at the end of the text.

Drag-hunting: a substitute form of hunting, where no species is pursued. Instead a scented alternative is used to lay a trail that the hunt can ride out to.

Hunting: a term covering a variety of activities. For example, there are a number of hunted species and each form of hunt has a differing practice.

Hunting pink: this refers to the coats worn by members of hunt staff. Confusingly, these are often red (or green).

Nature and natural: a contested term, for example regarding the extent to which the countryside is able to manage itself – nature's way – or whether nature is best perceived as 'red in tooth and claw'.

reflexivity: see the glossary at the end of the text.

The field: the horsemen and women making up a hunting party.

–5–

Game Shooting in the United Kingdom

What would be the situation if there were no shooting or fishing?
H. Piddington, *Land Management for Shooting and Fishing*

The wildlife of today is not ours to dispose of as we please. We have it in trust. We must account for it to those who come after.[1]
King George VI

General Introduction

This chapter offers an applied example of a sociological analysis of a contemporary rural issue that rural sociology can offer. However, unlike the foot-and-mouth disease crisis discussed in chapter 3, which originated in the outbreak in 2001, shooting is a question yet to come to the fore. This chapter therefore takes the opportunity to look at a sample of the existing material surrounding shooting (both academic and interest group-derived) to see how shooting has been approached and studied. It evaluates some of the preoccupations in past and contemporary studies and concludes by offering up a series of questions and points of concern regarding shooting, based on the preceding literature review and on the absences within that literature.

Introduction

The country sport of game shooting has not enjoyed a high research profile in comparison with the country sport of hunting. As Cox et al. wryly note, 'it is tempting to detect the dead hand of political correctness in this absence of a sustained discussion of country sports in the academic literature' (Cox et al. 1996: 1). Yet in more recent times, and in the wake of the hunting ban in the UK, more attention has come to be placed on the possibility of reforming shooting by both the shooting community and those now seeking a ban upon shooting. This chapter seeks to provide an overview or introduction (1) to comment upon the existing research literature and (2) to evaluate absences and biases in this literature so that a more informed picture of UK game shooting in the twenty-first century can be constructed. If shooting is to become subject to reform, then the timing is pressing if new avenues for research a priori[2] of any inherited research agenda are to be established. With this objective in mind, the chapter concludes by posing a series of key research questions that could inform new policy directions for game shooting.

Game Shooting Literature: Key Categories

The academic literature surrounding game shooting, certainly in the past decade, is scarce. However, by broadening the scope to include non-academic literature (which is essential if the arguments of pro- and anti-shooting groups are to be assessed), several alternative bodies of information come to light. Amongst this literature, several subcategories can be distinguished. The main categories are detailed in table 12, with examples.

Table 12 A selection of the game shooting literature

Group	*Research/study*	*Methodology*	*Funding body*	*Focus*
Academic	Piddington (1981)	Questionnaires	CLA	
	Cox et al. (1996)		ESRC (and SCCS)	
	Lorimer (2000)	Qualitative		
	IRS (2006)	Mixed	Welsh Dev. Agency	
Research charity	GCT annual report (summary of publications)	Natural sciences	Various, including DEFRA	Varied: from individual bird to wider land management questions (and issues beyond purely game bird research)
	Tapper (2005)			
Pro	Cobham (1983, 1992)	Economic	SCCS	
	BASC	Natural science		
	PACEC (2006)	Unknown	GCT/CLA/ BASC/CA	
Anti	LACS reports (2005 a, b, c)	Mixed (including visual)	LACS	
Participatory 'guides'	Barnes	Anecdote/ autobiography		Game shooting
	Swan			Rough shooting
	Digweed			Game/clay shooting
	Smith (2004)	Socio-political		Gun control
Related academic	Marvin (2006)	Anthropological		Wild killing
	Hillyard (forthcoming)	Literature review and visual sociology		Gamekeeping work

Of course there is not the scope in this chapter to offer an in-depth analysis of all this material – particularly the ecological work – yet each can be considered for what they do and do not emphasise. The main groupings, unsurprisingly, reflect the main division between pro-shooting organisations (the GCT, the BASC, the NGO and the CA) and those opposed (the LACS, Animal Aid and the RSPCA). The three main bodies – anti, pro and academic research – on game shooting will be considered in turn. Finally, the degree to which the academic community has suffered from an excessive bout of political correctness and whether academic research has approached shooting a priori are evaluated.

Game Shooting: Key Definitions and Focus

In approaching the issues there is a need (much like the term hunting) to understand that shooting is a broad church and that the term represents a wide variety of activities. For the most part, driven and rough shooting of game on the wing (i.e. in flight) will be considered here purely so as to avoid sweeping generalisations that are irrelevant to stalking, for example. Therefore (deer) stalking and wildfowling are excluded; the former is largely focused in Scotland and the latter tends to be a more socially isolated activity. Inevitably, the focus is biased towards England and Wales. Future research is warranted into the role of shooting in Scotland and in other countries, such as Sweden, France and the US. In the latter the right to bear arms and to hunt certainly warrants comparison with the UK context.

Anti-shooting Literature

LACS (2005a)

One of the main opponents of shooting is the LACS. The reports discussed here are disseminated on their website and are used in their campaigns (for example LACS 2004c was sent to the Environment Minister). The league has recently generated a series of LACS reports about the 'bloody business of gamebird shooting' (LACS 2005a, b, c) and concerning game hunting overseas (LACS 2003, 2004b, c). LACS (2005a) will be considered here: its concerns, its methodology and its conclusions.

LACS (2005a) took its focus as methods of predator control (and animal welfare more generally), the species subjected to predator control and the legitimacy of shooting. The methodology targeted the estates of senior figures within the shooting community, namely those associated with the major shooting organisations.[3] Their estates and a number of others (thirteen in England and Wales) were referred to by name. 'Undercover LACS investigations conducted throughout

2004 and the spring of 2005' provided their evidence base (LACS 2005a: 3). In addition to their own new data, they cite the BASC reports and guides (such as the BASC code on snaring) and GCT data.

Their starting point is the scale of predator control currently operating in the UK. They cite the GCT's figures (Robinson 2002 available on the LACS website, although unspecified when accessed) that 4.5 million animals '(and possibility twice as many)' are killed by employees of shooting estates (LACS 2005a: 3). There is no differentiation made between the species of animal killed at this stage. For example, the figures could include rats, foxes, crows, magpies, rooks, feral cats as well as game. The report later specifies such non-targeted species as protected badgers, livestock and household pets. They cite an example of a cat they discovered caught in a snare, although it is unclear as to whether it was a domesticated or feral cat.

It is clear that the focus is therefore upon the act of snaring or predator control as well as – ultimately – the legitimacy of snaring as a practice, the liability of estate owners for their employees' activities (legal culpability[4]) and the banning of fox-hunting below ground under the Hunting Act (2005). Snaring is legal in the UK and the LACS identifies the shooting community's own code of conduct (BASC undated) and associated acts (such as the Wildlife and Countryside Act of 1981) and compares whether guideline recommendations match practice. The first of their reports is divided into three sections: on snaring, bird of prey persecution and fox-hunting below ground. The first two of these are more expressly focused upon game shooting and are considered here.

LACS is clear in its stance on snaring:

> The LACS believes that the use of snares is inherently cruel as even so-called 'humane' snaring (approved snares, regularly checked) will cause an animal distress and severely limit its ability to defend itself against predators. We are not alone in this belief.
>
> (LACS 2005a: 6)

Furthermore, they note that 'even if the code [BASC's code on snaring] could actually address all welfare concerns (which it cannot)' there is also no legal recourse for those who 'flagrantly disregard' the recommended practices (LACS 2005a: 6).

The LACS's argument is based upon their own investigations conducted between 2004 and 2005 and also a number of secondary sources. Their data are difficult to assess, as there is no summary or systematic reporting of what was carried out, how and by what guiding principles. For example, the distances between snares found on estates and livestock or badger setts are on occasion stated whilst not on others. They cite in their footnotes videotaped evidence, which can be taken to support their fieldwork findings. However, it is the extrapolations from that data that, much like Piddington's (1981) from a CLA membership sample, need to be treated with caution. For example, they double the figures of animals killed by employees of shooting estates rather than casting doubt on the accuracy of the figure and surmising it to be higher. They also assume on the basis of their own data (N = 13) that the misuse of snares is widespread.

The secondary data cited in the report are derived from two sources. The first of these are materials that would also be found in social science research, for example citations from the GCT, summaries of relevant legislation and summaries of BASC codes. The second consists of a variety of sources used to back up claims or provide evidence of malpractice. For example, newspaper reports of court cases including evidence cited in the cases themselves, such as witnesses' statements in court. This is for both successful and unsuccessful prosecutions. Also featured is the extensive use of visual materials, such as photographs, but also more generally in the design template for the report, which is 'blood'-splattered. The use of visual material is an interesting one, as the use of visual material for sociological investigations is currently enjoying something of a renaissance. The visual is used here to shock (images of dead predators strung up on a line); as a means of evidence (where snares were set beside steep drops) and archive images of the species that potentially could be caught in snares (such as otters). These are all juxtaposed. The notion that pictures simply reflect reality has long been critiqued within sociology (Pole 2004). Realising that photographs are made as much as taken and also the various ways in which photographs are deployed within LACS (2005a) mean they are part of a broader argument rather than used in any critical or sociological sense.

A further interesting pattern across the report is the shifting terminology. At the outset, the report devotes some time to specifying the details of the BASC snaring code.[5] However, the language further on in the report does not continue to utilise the technical terms in the BASC code. For example, the BASC code states that snares should be firmly anchored by a suitable 'tealer' or stick set firmly in the ground. In the report, cases of unsecured snares are first reported and increasingly from that point onwards referred to only as 'dragpoles'. For example, 'indiscriminate and out of control predator control measures, including more than 70 snares positioned adjacent to gamebird release pens, many without "stops" and many set on dragpoles' (LACS 2005a: 12). That the snares were positioned near release pens containing game birds would suggest they were not indiscriminate and again, the number of incidents (many (p. 12), approximately (p. 12), suggests (p. 13)) is unspecified. In addition, the initial focus upon snares is later expanded to include traps. It is clear that the LACS opposes trapping and snaring in any form, although the main focus of their attack is upon snaring practices. Here we can see that it is not the use of snares that is at issue, it is the wider issue of the legitimacy of predator control.

The LACS's methodology also extrapolates from its findings. For example, 'some snares were set in gaps in fences; this poses a real risk in that the captured animal will hang itself while trying to climb over the fence to get away' (LACS 2005a: 12). This is a nonsensical statement. An animal snared going through a gap in the fence is unlikely to then climb the fence to get away, even in the event that the snare was unanchored. It demonstrates the inconsistencies in the LACS's progressing argument. A further example is their comment that a 'loose interpretation' of the BASC's code statement is that snares should be checked every 24 hours.[6] They calculate that this could leave an animal from 12.01 a.m. on a Tuesday to 11.59 p.m. on a Wednesday – a period of 47 hours and 58 minutes. This is a hypothesis predisposed to assume the worst without reference to evidence of such conduct. Furthermore, snares only checked at sunset would countermand the 24 hours recommendation and therefore some flexibility is needed to reflect the changing seasons.

In summary, it is clear that the LACS reports are not subject to the same level of peer review or standards of research as that of the GCT or studies by the academic community (such as Cox et al. 1996 and IRS 2006). Whilst there is a great deal of fieldwork reported in LACS (2005a), the manner in which the results are related render it impossible to verify or to measure the accuracy of their arguments. Therefore, they remain more akin to research claims than research evidence.

What is clear is that the main motive underpinning the report is not snaring or trapping or even the hypocrisy of shooting estates that have not attended to their own regulatory controls. Rather, the focus is upon a ban upon game shooting. The actual focus has not been upon the practice of game shooting, but rather the work that supports it – land management. A former head of research at the GCT (Dick Potts) noted that game management depends on habitat, food supply and protection. Like a three-legged stool, all need to be in place for shooting to occur (Potts paraphrased in Tapper 2005: 39). What the LACS has attacked is one of these legs – namely the legitimacy of controlling predators. But the role of different species is only secondary within the report, for example, the danger of snaring non-target species. The legitimacy of controlling target species is not expressly discussed. For example, snared animals could 'possibly die if attacked by a predator while restrained' (LACS 2005a: 12). In the case of a rabbit or hare, a predator could be a stoat, weasel or fox. If a fox was snared, it has no predators in the UK countryside. The very question of 'wise use' and 'keeping the balance' is now addressed through the literature of the pro-shooting organisations.

Pro-shooting Commissioned Research

The main body of literature here is Piddington (1981), Cobham Resource Consultants (1983, 1992) and material by the GCT and the BASC. The most recent study, commissioned by the BASC, the CA and supported by the GCT, reported in September 2006 (PACEC 2006).

Piddington (1981)

The Piddington (1981) study is relevant here as it informed[7] the most sustained academic research work exploring shooting (Cox et al. 1996). Piddington (1981) focused on land management for shooting and fishing – or rather the degree to which shooting interests impacted upon land management. The study was commissioned by the Country Landowners' Association (now the Country, Land and Business Association but still known as the CLA) with the support of the then Game Conservancy and carried out by the Department of Land Economy at Cambridge University. Trained as a geographer, Piddington was then an assistant in research in the department. The support of the CLA and the GCT was instrumental in gaining the data collected by the survey (via a poll of CLA members). However, the approach that was adopted by Piddington involves several useful definitions and distinctions, which will be significant later in this chapter and are therefore worth detailing in depth.

Piddington (1981) immediately questions what constitutes game. Ground game includes deer, hares and rabbits (an inclusive definition that contrasts with alternative accounts considered later in the chapter). Other species include French and English partridges, woodcock, grouse and pheasants. Piddington (1981) also addressed fishing, although this is not the focus here. Her fieldwork assessed the extent to which rural land was used for shooting and fishing during the period 1961–76, sporting costs and income, other recreational uses of rural land and their potential conflict with shooting. Finally, she evaluated the contribution of management practices (such as were found) upon landscape and wildlife conservation.

Her methodology included postal surveys (N = 626), further supplemented by interviews drawn from the CLA membership. From this she further 'weighs the information' so as to represent the total membership of the CLA and that of the Scottish Landowners' Federation (south of the Highlands). Collectively, these bodies owned at that time one-third of the agricultural land and private woodland in Great Britain. On that basis, Piddington (1981) claims the generalised conclusions offer a useful insight into shooting in the mid to late 1970s.

The general conclusions of Piddington's study found that 'the incidence of both shooting and fishing was directly related to the size of the property' (Piddington 1981: summary). Larger properties were more likely to have shooting, yet shooting was recorded on 58 per cent of properties. Individual figures varied greatly, both between large and small properties and regionally.

Costs (of laying down shooting) varied from £4 to £45,420 p.a. and income (derived from shooting) from £10 to £57,000. Although the response level to her survey was small for calculating costings at only 25 per cent, she surmised from this figure that £11 million and rather more than a quarter of landowners (not necessarily of the same group as above) provided shooting income details for the same year, with a gross figure of £7 million (with the caveat that some landowners were unable to extract shooting details from general farm or estate finances). A further interesting distinction that Piddington offers relates to more informal shoots and what she terms as costs related to 'in hand' shooting. She defines in hand shooting as 'shooting retained by the landowner for his [*sic*] own use and management' (Piddington 1981: summary). The costs of such shooting relate to the shooting acreage, number of days, total bag (number of head shot) and annual bag.

Piddington's (1981) analysis is very much upon the land management aspects and the economic benefits of shooting. So the figures offered are relevant but somewhat stark. For example, gross costs per head of game on small pheasant shoots (between 251 and 500 acres in size) ranged from 24 pence to 910 pence. Costs per acre ranged from 24 pence to 614 pence and per shooting day from £23 to £307. Income, mainly derived from shooting rents, averaged 80 pence per acre. Therefore, the focus is upon the perceived benefits that game shooting holds for both the landowners and the wider rural economy. What this does serve to high-light are the different levels and costings associated with engaging in game shooting. Piddington's (1981) notion of in hand shooting is a significant one as it distinguishes between 'commercial' and informal participation in shooting – although both of course entail costs. In hand shooting[8] acknowledges shooting that is bought for friends and family or shooting invitations for friends and family. A further interesting point is that 'sales of game were regarded as additional income' (Piddington 1981: summary). The very product, game, in this sense is almost regarded as superfluous in the 1970s context, although Piddington (1981) does raise the question that different species are seen as legitimate stocks to be harvested by landowners or tenants (woodcock and rabbits for example).

A final relevant conclusion, which echoes through to contemporary debates, relates to conflict:

> Owners with fishing were considerably more likely than the average owner to permit other recreational uses to be made of their land. The figures for shooting were not quite so striking. However, with the marginal exception of camping and caravans, the owners of shooting were more likely to allow public access to their land than the average owner. Clearly the conflict between shooting and fishing and other recreations has been exaggerated.
>
> (Piddington 1981: summary)

Her general conclusion in her evaluation of the land management practices associated with shooting (via case studies) revealed that owners underestimated the degree of special management they undertook. For example, they perceived it as normal, rather than special. (The impacts that Piddington (1981) notes include maintenance of landscape and the preservation of a varied habitat for wildlife.) Again, this highlights the significance of informal practices rather than purely financially driven ones:

It appears that owners tend to select sporting tenants for other than purely financial considerations. As a result, sporting rents tend to reflect other than merely financial criteria ... shooting, in particular, generates ancillary employment and thus directly benefits the rural economy.

(Piddington 1981: summary)

The examples of past employment she cites relate to the protection of species (the warrener and fowler, which have now disappeared), but the modern-day gamekeeper continues to find employment.

The overarching conclusion drawn is that 'sporting activities generate management decisions which are beneficial for both the countryside and the rural community, for landscape and for wildlife' (Piddington 1981: summary). Expressed more simply, regarding game birds 'that they can continue to exist is because their habitats are maintained in the face of alternative land uses' (Piddington 1981: 2). Her argument is supported by a straightforward comparison between land management for shooting and for hunting. The distinction between the management practices of a hunting owner and that of a shooting one are that hunting is external (mainly merely allows the hunt across their land), whereas the shooting owner requires land management internal to the property (game cover crop, predator control, copse and woodland planting).

In summary, Piddington's argument is twofold: first, regarding the management of land and, secondly, the attitude towards the game species itself. She notes that 'there is a tendency to believe that wildlife will continue to regenerate naturally despite all man's [*sic*] predations' (Piddington 1981: 5). Tracing game species back historically, she argues that laws protecting game (for example the King's deer) were conservation-based – that is, to conserve natural resources. However, within game species, some are considered vermin rather than game (for example, rabbits, hares and pigeons), whereas pheasants are an alien species introduced by the Romans but disappeared upon their departure as no one preserved the stock and were then reintroduced by the Normans. Therefore, 'conservation of the individual species and maintenance of their habitats are vital for the continuation of both food supply and sport' (Piddington 1981: 4). As the case has been made with rare species in the food chain, rather than 'eat me to save me', the case here was that, without the shooting interest, the pheasant would be unlikely to be found in the UK today. Piddington therefore concludes:

So, mixed with the sporting aspect of taking game and catching fish, there have been the sound economics of both the valuable contribution to the larder and the consideration of the resource, which involved maintaining a suitable habitat.

(Piddington 1981: 3)

In evaluating Piddington (1981) there is no doubt a strong Department of Land Economy, Cambridge University, bias in terms of the studies cited in the report and as a result also in the theoretical preoccupations underpinning the study: for example, farm-based decision-making and the mapping of farm activities in their various forms. Having said this, Piddington's (1981) focus on game does serve to complement the wider picture of land use in the countryside more than has been the case with the piecemeal research on hunting (see chapter 4). The methodological approach underpinning the study also presents a number of concerns: centrally the reliance upon the CLA membership for sampling and the subsequent generalisations made from that sample. This may present a bias towards commercial, large-scale shooting at the expense of landowners with smaller holdings. What role, for example, does in hand shooting play for farmers and their neighbours economically, in terms of support networks and socially?

Some of the secondary aspects of Piddington's study are left underdeveloped. Little mention is made of the contribution of shooting to the rural community, other than the broad brush of offering employment. The social role of shooting, other than the comment that the patronage of shooting rights is not purely based on financial considerations, is secondary. Again, what role does shooting fulfil for community integration or other benefits and how does participation in shooting come about? Finally, the focus upon land management detracts from an engagement with animal welfare concerns involved with rearing (which is a contemporary concern within the shooting community). What she does note is that pheasants are not a native species and the differences between the perceptions of different game species: for example, the metaphor of game as an additional crop (including birds of passage such as the woodcock) whereas some game species are identified as vermin (brown hares and rabbits). The decision to take these species is therefore seen as a right of the tenant or landowner, regardless of whether the sporting aspect is deemed to have a value. Here the very notion of the sporting aspect of taking game 'crops' becomes open to question. For example, the symbolic nature and lore surrounding certain species (white pheasant, woodcock) and the BAP[9] status of the English partridge need to be placed into the equation. Finally, of course, the economic data are in need of updating to reflect the contemporary game shooting scene.

Piddington's (1981) work contributes a holistic approach to the literature on game shooting: the manner in which game shooting was placed historically among changes in agriculture since the Second World War; the broad geographic coverage of the study; and the contrast with fishing that questioned access to private land. The tone of her report is unsurprisingly that of an advocate of shooting or at the very least calls for a considered approach to evaluating game shooting. The line of defence is that of the conservation role shooting fulfils in the countryside and this is admittedly supported by her data. The legacies of the study are the future research questions alluded to from secondary or unanswered questions. These provide a series of concepts and questions to be carried on for future research – most notably the concept of game as a commodity or farming resource like any other.

Cobham Research Consultants (1983, 1992)

The Cobham studies were commissioned by the SCCS, a pro-shooting consortium. The evidence they contain is flawed (see chapter 4's discussion; Ward 1999): most notably, the un-referenced use of BFSS data and that the 1992 publication is reliant upon conjecture from the 1983 data. For data published in the 1980s (admittedly collected in the 1970s), Piddington (1981) offers the more useful account.

Tapper (2005)

There is a great deal of natural science research conducted into 'wise use' of the countryside for game bird populations. Central to this body of literature is the GCT. The GCT consists of scientists with post-doctoral specialism in 'ornithology, entomology, biometrics, mammalogy, agronomics and fisheries science' (Tapper 2005: 3). In a text focused more on social science than the natural, there is not the scope or expertise to engage with the finer nuances of this information. Rather, the GCT somewhat conveniently made available their research findings over the past twenty-five years (in its anniversary year) more accessible in its anniversary publication authored by its research director (Tapper 2005).

The twenty-fifth anniversary of the trust[10] in 2005 does not record its entire history. It was founded seventy-six years ago, its roots in ICI as the owner of Eley shotgun cartridge manufacturers. Eley had identified that the decline in grey partridge numbers would have a deleterious impact upon cartridge sales and established a small research wing to explore this trend. In 2005 their status changed and they acquired charitable status. The approach of the GCT – in the very broadest of terms – has been to promote responsible game management. It undertakes research into the impact of shooting estate land management programmes upon the surrounding wildlife and the beneficial impact upon game stock natural regeneration. It therefore incorporates species welfare as well as habitat research.[11] Its approach is represented through the strapline 'conservation through wise use'.

One of the Trust's most prominent and long-term experiments has been based on a GCT-managed farm in Loddington bequeathed to the GCT (Tapper 2005). The Allerton Research Project owns land in Leicestershire and its Loddington project is central to the arguments the GCT presents. Their Loddington research over the past decade is summarised in Tapper (2005) and also by researchers based on site (Stoate and Leake 2002). The Loddington project has additional significance, as it is run as a commercial farm and as such provides a living experiment, the results of which can and do inform government policy.

The contribution of the GCT to understanding the impact of game management on the countryside cannot be overstated. Their body of research fleshes out some of the arguments in Piddington (1981) regarding the beneficial impact of land management techniques supporting shooting on the wider countryside. Indeed, the quality of their research and its scope far exceed Piddington's study in their impact. Of course, the species the GCT refers to include the songbird population (for example yellowhammers) and also smaller invertebrates (beetles), rather than the targeted predator species the LACS (2005a) focuses upon. In answer to the question that Piddington raises at the outset of her study, 'what would be the situation if there were no shooting or fishing?' (Piddington 1981: 1), the research output of the GCT offers a portfolio of evidence that suggests that the wildlife would be less varied and more rare bird species numbers would decline (Stoate and Leake 2002, Tapper 2005).

Evaluating the contribution of the GCT and the conservation argument (that shooting serves to conserve species and landscapes rather than destroy them) leads to some very difficult questions. First, as we have seen in this chapter, the opponents of shooting dispute this entirely and no research evidence will assuage such a position. In that light perhaps a second, more problematic question relates to a hierarchy of species and society's responsibilities for the welfare and rights of different species within that hierarchy (Wilkie 2005). This addresses LACS's concerns about target and non-target species and also acknowledges the shooting organisations that cite the added value shooting brings to wider bird and associated species numbers. A third, and final, complication to the situation is the issue of the sporting value (to use Piddington's term). The very process of shooting birds – whether specifically reared for that purpose and whether they enter the food chain – as sport is problematic in the same way that hunting was attacked for the perceived pleasure of the kill derived by hunters. These questions will be returned to in the chapter's conclusion following a discussion of the small number of studies and approaches to game shooting applied by academic commentators.

The Academic Research Literature

Cox et al. (1996)

Cox et al. (1996) note that a second reason (alongside political correctness) for the relative neglect of game shooting by academic commentators is that policy concerns drive much academic enquiry. Their own study is an example of research focused upon game shooting, but grounded in the policy questions of the time. In the years that their research was conducted, funded by the ESRC and with an additional contribution from the SCCS, access rights were a key concern.[12]

The research project directors, Cox, Watkins and Winter, adopted a three-pronged approach to the study of game shooting. Alongside property rights and the access issue, shooting's contribution to the English economy and game management (for woodland, landscape and conservation) were addressed. Their methodology followed from and extended Piddington's (1981) approach. They suspected that her data, through her affiliation with the CLA, had led to a bias towards large landowners within her sample. They were therefore concerned to correct for this anomaly in their own resurvey of the content of her survey in order to critically appraise her sample. An additional benefit was that their restudy would also allow for some longitudinal analysis to take place. They conducted postal questionnaires (shooting and non-shooting individuals), a lengthy interview questionnaire (consisting of sixty-six questions), a household questionnaire and a questionnaire for guns.[13]

Immediately, Cox et al. were clear about how to conceptualise shooting:

> The shooting estate does not readily come within the purview of either the production specialists (alternative enterprises) or the consumption specialists (recreation). To think in terms of such a dichotomy is, in this case, quite inappropriate.
>
> (Cox et al. 1996: 1)

In this light they sought to avoid the excessive economic determinism of Piddington (1981) and to raise more sociological questions, such as shooting as sporting recreation and also land management concerns. Their 'socio-economic' study was conceived in the late 1980s, when the economic boom had seen game management enter a new and more intensive phase in some parts of the country (Cox et al. 1996: 2). Rather than a policy-driven approach, they finally sought to comment upon policy implications 'in relation to such issues as access rights and leisure provision, conservation, the regulation of woodland planting and timber production' (Cox et al. 1996: 3).

The geographic areas sampled differed from Piddington's reliance upon CLA membership information, particularly as traditional CLA membership might not have represented the new, more commercialised shoots. The sample areas were defined on the basis of research from UCL that had identified areas representative of rural restructuring and existing areas of expertise within the research team (Watkins on Nottinghamshire) and they revised these on the advice of the GCT in order to include a quintessentially heavily shot-over country. The case study locations were: Buckinghamshire, east and mid-Devon, Cumbria, Nottinghamshire and Gloucestershire. The sample was drawn from the listing of farmers in the *Yellow Pages* (a free directory of businesses distributed in the UK). The postal survey addressed the period August 1990–July 1992 and locations where shooting rights had and had not been used (1429 in the original sample, with a response rate of 50 per cent, therefore N = 712). Seventy-eight interviews were carried out in 1993 across the case study areas and in some cases extra work was undertaken with the maps of the shoot. Contiguous farms were selected in order to offer more detail on the locality. To further offer more localised and detailed understanding of shooting's impact upon the local community, face-to-face interview surveys of residents in two villages from localities in heavily shot-over areas (Gloucestershire N = 78 and Buckinghamshire N = 44). Of a total of 200 individuals contacted, 122 interviews were condcuted (twenty-five were refused).

Finally, the postal survey engaged with the participants of shooting. Sampling was achieved through a gatekeeper (a sporting agent) (N = 74, a response rate of 46 per cent). Places where interviews had taken place were also used as a means to distribute further questionnaires where they knew shooting would be taking place (response rate 11.4 per cent). On such a low rate, Cox et al. somewhat wryly noted 'the exigencies of attempting to insert questionnaires into days characterised by everything from extreme conviviality to appallingly inclement weather, were always likely to be daunting' (Cox et al. 1996: 11). The final figure (N = 118) was treated problematically in terms of its power to generalise more broadly. They also added 'that considerable information has been gleaned from the advertisements and other material in the sporting press' (Cox et al. 1996: 11).[14] They operationalised their watching brief to attend to relevant policy developments and dimensions through attending the meetings of the SCCS, the Game Fair (an annual three-day countryside fair organised by the CLA and held on an English estate) and discussions and meetings with the GCT at their headquarters at Fordingbridge and with staff on the Game and Wildlife Course at Sparsholt College, Hampshire. Formal semi-structured interviews were held with GCT officers, LACS and the CLA.

The Cox et al. (1996) study was therefore ambitious in its scope and breadth. The space is not available to explicate all of their results; indeed, the project team itself was unable to fully analyse their entire data set, due to institutional movements by the project directors (Watkins from the RAC to the University of Nottingham and Winter from the RAC to Cheltenham and Gloucester College of HE). However, their data set offers information not available in the previous studies considered in this chapter.

The attempt to understand shooting's impact upon the local community (both rural and suburban case study locations) was a new addition to research surrounding game shooting. Whilst the sample contained a southern bias (Gloucestershire and Buckinghamshire villages), the results are also somewhat disappointing in that they emphasise the question of access rights, rather than attitudes towards shooting. But, in terms of awareness and participation in shooting, the results are revealing. One-third of the village sample had shot at least once compared with only 11 per cent in the suburban sample (although this figure also includes clay pigeon shooting as well as live quarry species). Eighteen respondents from the village and two suburban residents had shot live quarry. However, 92 per cent of the village and 80 per cent of the suburbanrespondents claimed to be aware that shooting took place in the locality. The processes of gaining awareness were hearing or seeing evidence (guns going off or young pheasants near the road) or taking an interest and watching, and a further group participated as beaters or pickers-up (see descriptions of these terms at the end of the chapter).

In terms of opinions regarding shooting – perhaps the most interesting section of this data set – the results are limited to a single paragraph and table. The question was framed using a variety of categories and is worth replicating (see table 13).

Table 13 Opinions of Shooting

	Village		Suburban		Total	
	No.	%	No.	%	No.	%
In favour	24	31	4	9	28	23
Don't mind	14	18	10	23	24	20
Against	16	21	16	36	32	26
Vermin only	24	31	13	30	37	30
Don't know	0	0	1	2	1	1
Total	78	100	44	100	122	100

Source: Cox et al. (1996: 21).

Cox et al. (1996) note that apathy was greater in the suburban village. What is perhaps more interesting is that, despite lower reports of awareness and participation in shooting, the suburban group is greater in its opposition to shooting and only one respondent indicated that they did not know. This provides an interesting avenue of research to pursue in terms of upon what resources and information public decision-making takes place. The results are open to a number of interpretations. For example, 73 per cent of people do not actively oppose shooting (if in favour, don't mind and vermin only categories are totalled). Alternatively, almost half of people (46 per cent) do not actively support shooting (if against and don't mind categories are totalled). The differentiation between shooting and vermin only shooting is again an interesting one, for this (across both villages) attracts more support (30 per cent) than even those entirely against shooting (26 per cent). Again, the distinctions between species and what is legitimate species management are raised again. Would, for example, shooting of only surplus stock of pheasants and partridges (i.e. wild birds) be legitimate? This asks what element of the game shooting process attracts criticism.

In evaluating Cox et al.'s (1996) contribution, their research provides a broad and important body of research. Whilst information from the landholders exceeds that of rural residents and shooting participants, these two latter interest groups are far more prominent than in the other recent studies considered here. These are vital additions to the debate if the complexities of shooting and its social implications for the UK are to be further researched and understood.

Theoretically, they also pose the challenging question of whether shooting can be perceived as a commodity. Whilst they calculate that gross income from shooting was £22.6 million, less than in Piddington's (1981) figures of £25.8 million, they argue that this is due to the bias towards larger holdings and shooting holdings within her sample. They conclude that 'it would be inappropriate to apply any simple notion of commoditisation to shooting both because of the diversity of the sector and, in particular, because it so completely blurs conventional distinctions between production and consumption' (Cox et al. 1996: 42). They find that the variations that can be found even within a shoot (let days, friends and family days, syndicate days) 'are, at times, almost impossible to disentangle' (Cox et al. 1996).

In respect of the conservation question, they note that not all will be persuaded by such an argument:

> Many conservationists are wholly opposed to the shooting of game on moral grounds. Others consider that the nature conservation benefits of land management associated with shooting outweigh such considerations, although they may dislike the idea of shooting game.
>
> (Cox et al. 1996)

Nevertheless, they conclude, 'the research has shown the extent and type of this management on the survey of farms and estates and shown that it has substantial implications for nature conservation and the appearance of the landscape' (Cox et al. 1996: 57). By management, they refer to the following:

> A managed shoot makes use of local variations in terrain, valleys and hillocks, and draws out contrasts in the landscape with the use of a patchwork of small woods and intervening open areas. This pattern encourages the population of game and enables pheasants to be driven at some height over guns towards another area of suitable shelter. Together with specially planted cover crops and thick hedgerows these areas of woodland provide contrasting cover which allows for a number of possible drives taking account of weather conditions and wind direction. The technical requirements of the pheasant, and other principal game birds, are catered for by specialised forms of land management.
>
> (Cox et al. 1996: 57)

This provides a summary of the generic environmental benefits accrued through game management for the landscape and its wildlife. It also provides some indication of the actual social organisation of a shooting day – a theme that is returned to in the chapter's conclusion.

Cox et al. (1996) contributed one of the most expansive studies of game shooting by academic commentators. It has yet to be matched for its broad approach and the way it is both theoretically informed and policy-relevant.

However, with such a wide remit, some of the finer nuances in the data are neglected. For example, in addressing the costing and expenditure of participants in shooting, these data are explicated but the more social aspects of participation in shooting are not. For example, they phrase an ingenious question at the conclusion of their guns' questionnaire: 'if you could wave a magic wand and change something, anything, what would it be?' (Cox et al. 1996: 118). The result of this open-ended question (with its potential to offer unanticipated directions for the research and to look forward to the future challenges of shooting) is unreported. It is perhaps the dilemmas that beset the project that can be understood to have left some avenues underdeveloped. This is all the more ironic when, in terms of the conclusions they draw, Cox et al. (1996) stand in inverse contrast to the LACS's (2005a) report. Whereas the latter is at pains to over-claim and extrapolate from their data, Cox et al. are almost painfully reticent.

A final comment is warranted on what the project did achieve. Like hunting, game shooting could be described as a 'total institution'. It is a relatively closed world, which creates many challenges for the social scientist in terms of access: not simply access, but an informed access that would be able to construct questions that are knowledgeable and conversant in the forms and phenomenon of shooting. That Cox was a 'card carrying' member of this community (through associations with the gun dog world and the Kennel Club) and an academic should not be underestimated. Their study stands as the most penetrating, methodologically sophisticated and detailed account of game shooting to date. The studies that follow are either snapshots or game shooting is a secondary theme within their analysis.

The Aberystwyth Study (2006)

The Aberystwyth study (IRS 2006) is the most recent study of game research identified in this literature review. The study assessed the economic potential for game shooting in Wales and was commissioned by the Welsh Development Agency. Aberystwyth (specifically the Institute of Rural Sciences) led a consortium of researchers, the exact membership of which is not specified. The research was only a scoping study and as such does not contain referencing as can be found in the other academic literature discussed here. However, the manner in which the very scope of game shooting was evaluated reveals an approach to understanding game shooting – including potential barriers to the development of the game shooting sector in Wales.

In the round, the project perceived shooting to be a 'good thing' for Wales and this informed their approach. For example, the remit of the report included the common emphasis upon economic and environmental impact, but also barriers, best practice elsewhere that could be relevant to the Welsh and the potential to add value to activities already taking place in Wales or associated markets (such as tourism). The Aberystwyth study (IRS 2006) therefore differed in many respects to the other studies discussed here, but as it incorporates new empirical data and is the most recent study identified in game shooting, it will be considered here.

The empirical data collected by the consortium of researchers included in-depth semi-structured interviews with key informants (N = 22, yielding fifty-four themes); desk research economic analysis (using the local multiplier 3 (LM3) approach recently pioneered by the New Economics Foundation); three focus groups; a public opinion questionnaire (N = 159); a small survey of participants sampled at the Midland Game Fair; a snowballing exercise to identify names and addresses of shoots; a postal questionnaire of a sample of commercial shoots; and another postal survey of syndicate shoot captains (sampled through their affiliation with the BASC). The fifty-four themes yielded, whilst throwing up a variety of issues, are a somewhat bricolage approach covering a lot of ground, but none of it well.

Sadly, they have to admit that their focus on game shooting omits a consideration of rabbits, pigeons and foxes, so the question of hierarchies of shot species is absent. Some of their extrapolations are based on estimating the number of rough shooting days using official data on the number of shotgun licences currently held. Whilst they place a caveat on their result that it may be somewhat high (as some guns may be dormant), it served to include vermin shooting (regardless of an earlier statement revealing their intent to exclude this) but ignored clay shooting. The usefulness of their figures – that between 456,098 and 512,012 individual days of game shooting take place per annum in Wales – is highly questionable: they are based on the number of shotgun certificates.

Nevertheless, some of their other methodologies yielded some interesting insights: for example, how game entered the food chain and their note that 'the Game Acts prohibit the sale of game all-year around[15] which makes that sales culture difficult to manage' (IRS 2006: unpaginated). They therefore advocate their reform to reflect new possibilities such as freezing game that were not available when the acts were first conceived.

They concluded that the three strongest scenarios derived through their interviews, then refined into eight scenarios and then discussed in the focus groups were as follows:

- Creation of a 'one-stop shop' for booking shooting holidays in Wales
- Creation of a more holistic game-food market
- The introduction of a shoot-accreditation scheme

The political aspect of shooting was mentioned only in passing – 'in that statutory agencies may have to openly support "shooting" if game management options were to be widened in agri-environmental schemes' (IRS 2006: unpaginated).

However, the introduction of a shoot-accreditation scheme that supports self-regulation and BASC's code of best practice is implicitly referred to. This expressly acknowledges that 'if game shooting is to continue then it's [*sic*] participants and providers both must address the concerns of those who would oppose it' (IRS 2006: unpaginated). This statement is quite interesting in that the report as a whole takes an interest in the economic benefits that can accrue through attracting shooting expenditure to Wales, seemingly, without wishing to take the step to advocate an activity such as shooting. If it is a not a desirable activity, why has the study been commissioned? Is this research reflecting or informing the Welsh Assembly's stance on shooting? The differences between this work and that of the GCT could not be more marked.

The first point is perhaps problematic in the light of the wide variety of shooting that takes place. As Cox et al. (1996) noted, there is a tremendous differential within individual shoots as well as between them. Indeed, in terms of the economic contribution of game shooting to Wales (based on their LM3 analysis), the Aberstwyth study 'suggest that total expenditure on shooting in Wales amounts to at least £56.3 million and possibly as much as £65.5 million' (this includes rough shooting) (IRS 2006: unpaginated). Again, the economic contribution of shooting is acknowledged alongside noting the variety of forms of shooting.

A more contemporary concern is also raised by the report. They comment upon animal welfare concerns, noting the recent debate within the shooting community regarding the raised cage system of egg production. Intriguingly, they also observe:

> The shooting of wild birds (as opposed to reared and released to the wild) was covered by the respondents contributing to this report. Any increase in the shooting capacity would need to be wholly sustainable from a harvest of hatched or migratory birds. Upholding this ethos is of paramount importance to the shooting community.
>
> (IRS 2006: unpaginated)

Here, like Cox et al. (1996), they note the intensification of some areas of the game sector and the rise of commercial shooting. This raises the question of sustainability and rearing, which will be returned to in the chapter's conclusion. Is shooting that only draws upon a sustainable and wild resource or 'crop' legitimate?

Finally, the Aberystwyth report (IRS 2006) offers a series of case study reports, drawn from the data received from the syndicate shoot captains affiliated to the BASC. The level of detail and information across the case studies is variable, reflecting the style that uses each case study to demonstrate a different theme (DIY syndicate; respect to shot birds; and environmental enrichment best practice). The former and the latter have been addressed elsewhere in this chapter, yet respect to shot birds has not. However, they focus solely upon the processing of game meat after the shoot (and how a new, in-house business has been established), rather than the potentially tricky aspects of ensuring that 'the provider has shouldered the ethical responsibility of making full and proper use of the birds that are shot' (IRS 2006: unpaginated). However, in an earlier case study, a shoot captain claims, 'all shot birds are accounted for' (ibid.) This statement needs to be treated problematically in respect of the degree to which it is possible to guarantee the retrieval of all game, regardless of the number of pickers-up or guns' dogs present. This can be for weather-related reasons (a frozen lake making it dangerous to send a dog to retrieve a bird that had landed there) or because birds that have been wounded but fly further before coming down are difficult to mark and trace (for example, a game bird can travel at thirty miles per hour and therefore can travel a considerable distance before dropping). The question of injured or 'pricked' game (see the chapter glossary for a definition) is returned to in the conclusion of this chapter.

The contribution of the Aberystwyth study (IRS 2006) to the game research literature is to introduce an express focus on Wales, to offer a new approach to economic analysis and to raise a few further questions that can be considered in evaluating the future of shooting. Whilst the potential for generalisations is restricted, it reflects how the debate has changed since Cox et al.'s (1996) fieldwork's emphasis upon property access rights. New concerns address animal welfare[16] in rearing practices and also a more prominent economic role of game meat, certainly than in Piddington's (1981) study, in which game meat income was perceived as an additional income.

Marvin (2006), Lorimer (2000) and Smith (2004)

Alternative studies of shooting indirectly relevant to game shooting can be found in the work of Marvin (2006) and Lorimer (2000). Lorimer focused upon stalking in Scotland and addresses the relationship between landownership (the grandee) and participants in stalking (guns). The methodological approach is qualitative in orientation and offers a detailed insight into the processes and experiences – and economic contribution – this activity brings to Scotland. Whilst the explicit focus in this chapter has been upon game shooting, Lorimer (2000) serves as a reminder that very different forms of engagement in country sports take place in the UK and each warrants attention and explication. Indeed, Lorimer has also conducted ethnographic funded research into hillwalking in Scotland (Lorimer and Lund 2003). How shooting and stalking differ as forms of leisure activity would be another interesting direction for research to pursue, much like the insight garnered from Piddington's (1981) comparisons between fishing and shooting.

Marvin (2006) discussed wild killing and paid attention to the different species hunted and reflected upon the social processes involved in their respective deaths. Marvin (2006) serves to differentiate between species and the commitment of the kill associated with them. Drawing upon Ortega y Gasset's work, Marvin (2006) explicates that the possibility of failure in the process of hunting renders the kill itself more significant. There are question marks to be raised about the kind of cross-cultural comparisons Marvin (2006) attempts to make between kills. One of his main subjects is bullfighting, an activity with a strong element of performance and audience that is absent in game shooting. In addition, the very notion of hunting (for example between its UK and US applications) warrants more careful treatment: that is (even within UK hunting, as noted earlier), there are clear differences in form.

Smith (2004) is more focused upon the question of gun ownership and connotations of violence – again the question of the kill but from an alternative angle to that of Marvin (2006). Emotion is also addressed, in a somewhat different manner, in the paper by Smith (2004). Smith (2004) theorises gun control and in doing so provides another dimension to the debate. Whilst only indirectly relevant to a specific focus on game shooting, it raises a number of concepts and some perspective – albeit achieved somewhat through incongruity.

Smith (2004) traces back the history of gun ownership, making a case that this has progressively become the preserve of the nation state. Drawing on Elias's work, Smith (2004) argues that violence's synonymous link with gun control is as relevant today as it was in feudal times, despite its contemporary refinement. It terms of refinement, those owning guns are no longer soldiers or mercenaries in the same sense as in the past; rather he introduces the term sportisation. Sportisation refers to how the use of guns becomes perceived in more sporting terms than with the threat of violence and how this has become self-regulated by organisations representing gun owners (the BASC's code of good shooting practice may be one such example).

What is useful here and may relate to Cox et al.'s (1996) discussion of rural residents' very lack of exposure to or familiarity with game shooting is that guns have become symbols of violence. Smith (2004) argues that this goes some way to understanding the public hysteria associated with gun violence, almost akin to a moral panic. Smith (2004) concludes with a point that is highly relevant in the contemporary climate of increasing critiques of game shooting, that those opposed to shooting only need to win their argument once.[17] Whilst the CA continues to campaign for the repeal of the hunting act, they have been unsuccessful in the eighteen months since the ban came into effect.

The contribution Smith's (2004) analysis makes to understanding game shooting is the symbolic element (guns 'association with violence) and also that gun ownership's relationship with the state has a long history and must be understood in that framework. This is an absence in many discussions of game shooting, where the history of the game laws in the UK is more often the focus (see Price 2002).

Absences within the Research Literature

The chapter has discussed conservation issues, economic and some community impacts, but the social activity – the very interactional processes – have been absent, or only mentioned in passing. The Aberystwyth study (IRS 2006) mentioned that all game is retrieved on a shoot. This is a claim that warrants further research. Cox et al. (1996) mention the convivial atmosphere that can be found at some shoots in passing (whilst explaining a poor response rate), the LACS refers to a few chums visiting a pal in the countryside for a weekend shoot in the preamble to their report (LACS 2005a), but what is shooting as a social experience or process? Whilst the Cox et al. (1996) guns survey reveals the outlay on owning a working gun dog, what does this involve? What impact does being a regular participant in game shooting hold for the everyday social life of a game shot? Is shooting a total institution, as Cox et al. (1994) found in respect of hunting? Or can little difference be found between the attitudes and rituals performed by the regular clay pigeon shot and the game shot? What differences in conservation practices could be seen between these two activities!?

A final comment on the absence of an awareness of the role of land management is warranted. Cox et al. (1996) are the only study of game shooting to attend to the issue of active management. This chapter has shown that some groups contest the need for such management (appealing to nature in its place). Whilst the natural science contribution of the GCT's work to such debates is beyond the remit of this text, what is clear are the differences in rare songbird populations in active management areas such as Loddington. This is achieved on a synergy of feeding; habitat and predator control. The status accorded to different species and their respective roles in the British countryside merit further engagement.

Game Shooting in the UK: Future Directions and Research Questions

The chapter raised the problematic question of a hierarchy of species and society's responsibilities for the welfare and rights of different species within that hierarchy. This relates to the legitimacy of controlling certain species (vermin) to protect others (rare bird populations). Added to this is the issue of the sporting value (to use Piddington's term). The very process of shooting birds – whether or not specifically reared for that purpose and whether or not they enter the food chain – as sport is problematic in the same way that hunting was attacked for the perceived pleasure of the kill derived by hunters. Yet, if vermin or cold shooting were allowed, would, for example, shooting of only surplus stock of pheasants and partridges (i.e. wild birds) be legitimate?

These issues tackle directly what elements of the game shooting process attract criticism. There are several main concerns, drawn from the literature considered here and also from the absences within that literature. They are:

- Animal welfare ('pricking' or wounding)
- Self-regulation (accessibility and conduct)
- Economic distribution of shooting income (to employees of shooting and to the rural economy)
- Game as food (the reform of the Game Acts)
- Game management for landscape conservation

What seem to be at the fore of critiques of shooting are its cultural credentials – that is, how it is perceived and understood more generally. The first three of the points above mention just a few of the points to emerge from the literature discussed in this chapter. They are all interlinked and relate more to the social role of shooting or the social norms and expectations in the shooting field – and the possibility of these being attended to, amended or regulated by new legislation. However, in respect to regulation, can the varied forms of engagement in shooting identified here be separated out for the purposes of analysis? In a more commercial environment than Cox et al. (1996) found, who wins from the commoditisation of game shooting and who loses? A metaphor can help explicate these differences.

A little like cricket spectators, there are a variety of seats available. The champagne set may be found in the members' bar, the waitress-served Pimms in the corporate boxes and gin and tonics in the pavilion whilst self-service lagers are in evidence in the stands. Shooting in a similar way invites different levels (and costs) of participation. A sporting round of fifty clays at a clay ground will cost in the region of £10 (not including cartridges or the hire of a gun); wildfowling a tenner to the 'keeper (not including non-toxic cartridges and decoying equipment if applicable); pigeon shooting in February may involve a nominal £5 towards a shooting organisation or charity; driven game shooting (when bought and not as part of a syndicate) would be unlikely to start at less than £300 for a day (without including tips, lunch, petrol, accommodation, dog and vehicle overheads). Therefore, the Director of Communications for the BASC claim that 'driven shooting is now within the reach of the majority of the population' must be taken with a generous pinch of salt (Graffius 2006: 5). For those shooting twenty days or more a year, that driven game shooting continues to be an exclusive sport is clear.

Perhaps it is this exclusivity that can be used to explain the lack of academic engagement in the social aspects of game shooting. Sociology, with its preference for researching the underdog, may have neglected sports that are exclusive.[18] The rising profile of the sociology of sport makes this all the more surprising. The need to research the social impact of game shooting a priori and before a policy-led agenda is defined is therefore pressing. Indeed, it is a methodological challenge. The LACS (2005a) made full use of visual material in a highly evocative manner. Yet the visual offers one technique to access and conduct a critical analysis of shoots days and its surrounding issues. For example, in the same way that Baerenholdt et al. (2004) use photographs to explicate tourist activities, photographs could offer a means to unravel the roles, relationships and rituals surrounding game shooting. Such research would serve to correct the absences found in the existing literature on game shooting and the current economic and environmental priorities.

Chapter Summary

The chapter has drawn upon a selected literature in order to discuss the current state of play of the literature on game shooting. In recent years, interest group reports have joined the academic literature. The different conclusions of these groups reflect their different orientations towards game shooting. However, the methodologies through which they pursue the collection of research evidence have been shown to markedly impact upon their conclusions.

The academic literature, somewhat disappointingly, continues to be scarce. However, if the net is thrown a little wider, game shooting does relate to discussions in anthropology on wild killing, issues of social class and tourism and gun control. These serve to offer 'perspectives by incongruity' (that is, seeing a given topic from a different angle not considered beforehand) or to complement the traditional concerns of the economic and environmental impact of game shooting. The chapter ends by calling for more interactional research to engage with game shooting's social impact, role and processes. It advocates the use of visual material as one means to access these processes.

Learning tools

Questions

1. To what extent have the different game species been differentiated within the non-academic and academic literature?
2. To what extent have academic researchers approached country sports a priori?
3. How best can sociologists engage in research into the social aspects of game shooting?
4. What is game management? Discuss in relation to some of the benefits and negative consequences of game management for the landscape and for wildlife.

Glossary of Emerging Key Terms

Bag: the number of birds shot on a day's shoot. This will vary, but will decline towards the conclusion of the season.

Beater: individual who flushes game birds from cover towards the guns during a shoot day. The number of beaters usually exceeds the number of guns. They are paid a nominal fee. In the past, beaters have been drawn from the agricultural workforce (Jones 2006).

Cover crop: crop planted for the express purpose of providing cover, protection and food for game birds. Kale, millet, maize, mustard and sorghum are a few examples.

Drive: the process by which an area is progressively cleared of game birds by the beaters towards the guns. When the beaters reach the guns, the drive is over, usually signalled by the blowing of a horn or whistle by the gamekeeper.

Game: pheasants, partridges (French and English), woodcock, red grouse, black grouse, snipe, geese and duck. Brown hares and deer (sika, roe and muntjac for example) are ground game.

Gamekeeper: responsible for rearing and releasing gamebirds and for the organisation of the beaters (the beating line) on a shoot day.

Gun: individual shooting game with a shotgun. There will be between six and ten positioned in a line. It is generally eight or nine. There are some instances where there will be a 'back gun' or guns positioned behind the main line. Some guns will shoot with more than one shotgun (double gunning) and in such an instance will be accompanied by a 'loader' to facilitate reloading of the other gun. Such an assistant to a gun with one shotgun is called a stuffer.

In hand shooting: shooting retained by a landowner for their own personal use or for their friends and family.

Let days: shooting days sold by a shoot or syndicate to paying customers.

Picker-up: individual who uses their dog(s) to collect game, usually at the end of a drive. The gun dogs are highly trained and are generally retrievers or spaniels or breeds which hunt, point or retrieve. The pickers-up are paid a nominal fee, usually more than the beaters.

Pricked game: game that is wounded (that is not killed outright or 'cleanly') by shotgun pellets.

–6–

Representing the Rural: New Methods and Approaches

Introduction

The book began with Hamilton's (1990) argument that rural studies have been somewhat neglected by sociologists. In his analysis of the treatment of the rural in Britain and France he argued that 'there was no "demand" for this sociology – either from the agricultural sector or rural society, but more significantly, none from the [sociological] profession of sociology itself' (Hamilton 1990: 229). The issues considered here, FMD, hunting and game shooting, have demonstrated that sociologists have continued to neglect contentious rural issues. However, it has also shown that rural geography has made important contributions to many of these debates. Where the action is in rural studies is very much in the domain of social, cultural and human geography – and not sociology.

However, the opening chapters on the history of rural sociology and more contemporary issues in rural studies emphasised some of the continuities between sociological concerns and ones that have subsequently been influential within rural geography. The further chapters on the substantive issues of FMD, hunting and game shooting have demonstrated the relevance of social science research for gaining an insight into contemporary rural problems and conflicts. The manner in which social science research has begun to contribute to policy emphasises the degree to which the territory has changed since Hamilton's (1990) original comments.

Nevertheless, there remain several directions, or avenues, that are underdeveloped. The argument here is that these would best serve to complement the existing portfolio of research approaches and theoretical outlooks available to the social scientist, rather than replacing or dominating them. They arise from the preceding analyses of where research absences lie and also in terms of continuing to complement the directions that early rural sociology and more recent geography have pursued. For instance, Newby notes the 'importance of such personally transmitted definitions of the situation' in his early research into rural social relations (Newby 1977a: 426). This is a nuance that ethnographic research approaches are well placed to engage with. In addition, the manner in which Cloke and Perkins (2002) discuss postmodern tourism in New Zealand presents new ways to study the rural.

They argue that photographs come to take on a greater significance in the consumption of the countryside. Their discussion of adventure holidays in New Zealand understands photographs as a form of memento, rather than capturing an essence of nature or rurality, 'so photographs record people's achievements in adventure places for future story-telling' (Cloke and Perkins 2002: 20). The use of the visual to record and understand the rural is therefore another direction for future rural sociologists to explore. The addition of visual techniques to ethnography's critical armoury may be one way to challenge our taken-for-granted perception of rural life and so appreciate the importance of nuances hitherto unseen. The chapter now explores two manners in which the visual can cast an insight into popular perceptions of the rural. The first explores images of farming in children's literature. The second engages in a more ethnographic project that uses photographs as a means to unravel the working practices of one form of rural work – gamekeeping.

Images of Farming in Children's Literature

The call for a visual sociology is not a new one. Fyfe and Law called for an engagement with visualisations and the insights into power relations that they can reveal:

> To understand a visualisation is thus to enquire into its provenance and into the social work that it does. It is to note its principles of inclusion and exclusion, to detect the roles that it makes available, to understand the way in which they are distributed, and to decode the hierarchies and differences that it naturalises.
>
> (Fyfe and Law 1988: 1)

The representation of farming in children's literature can be used as one such case study in order to engage with the portrayal of farming promoted through visual images. The following analysis draws upon research in two public libraries in Nottingham and an infants' school in Darlington in 2002. Specifically, the focus narrows upon the portrayal of technology in images of dairy farming and finds that, whilst benign, the farming community is anachronistically represented in both practice and lifestyle. This indicates a conclusion that popular culture needs to do more than promote a benign nostalgia in its imagery of the farming industry and more accurate images of farming are needed if the Curry Report's (2002) call for a diversified and sustainable countryside is to be achieved.

The value of such an analysis of images, Dingwall et al. note, lies in 'what they reveal about the ideals of a society' and such an approach serving 'as a window on the beliefs and values' of a society (Dingwall et al. 1991: 423). Through their own cross-cultural comparison of parenthood imagery, they argue, 'the same technology can serve to transmit very different symbolic messages' (ibid.). This technique of decoding the visualisations of farming, in order to explore everyday images of farming as represented in children's literature, can be used to study rural culture such as picture books. The challenge is to question the farming technology promoted in images in children's literature, by commenting upon the imagery surrounding farming work and lifestyles. Do images of farming portray current or past farming practices and what statuses are accorded working inside the farming industry? That of the 'prop on a rustic stage' that Newby suggests, or an informed professional? The focus on dairy farming allows these to be engaged with in specific detail – and indeed to the degree to which technology and lifestyle in children's literature bear any relation to a farming industry currently characterised by large-scale agribusinesses.

The preceding chapters have noted the ambiguous status accorded to farming and rural workers in the United Kingdom (Tönnies 1955, Williams 1973, Newby 1977a, 1980, 1985). On the one hand, there is the farming yokel astride his red tractor[1] (Newby 1977a) and living a bucolic life in a rural idyll (Williams 1973), whilst on the other there is a view of an industry only rendered viable through subsidy (Browne 2003) and which is 'devoid of any real sympathy' for its livestock (Woods 1998: 1232). The stereotypes associated with farming and rural lifestyles have been subjected to sociological analysis since the emergence of the discipline. Whereas Tönnies (1955) noted the impact of the rural exodus upon forms of human association, increasing attention has come to be paid to the nature of work and life for those remaining in rural locales. Newby (1977a, 1985) served to mark the distinctions between those working on the land and an urban (and in-migrant rural) population increasingly detached from agriculture. More recently, Milbourne (1997) called for greater attention to be paid to minority groups, such as women and children. The research concerns of sociologists and geographers in their treatment of the rural have therefore moved beyond the study of the impact of the emergence of capitalism to understand the plurality of experiences within contemporary rural settings. The wider framework continues to position farming as a declining economic force in rural areas, as no longer the primary employer: hence the subsequent loss of the occupational communities identified by Newby (1977a). New trends such as in-migration into rural areas and the corresponding out-migration Britain's cities are now experiencing (Urban White Paper 2000) over recent years have not altered the fact that the majority of the population resides in urban or semi-urban areas. It is the implications of the physical separation of an urban population from the everyday realities of rural life that have revealed the continuing status of the rural inside popular culture, above detailing the perspectives of those already occupying rural areas or situations. One such situation, gamekeeping, is considered in the latter half of this chapter.

Williams's (1973) penetrating analysis revealed how the image of the countryside had shifted from that of a location of work, such as agriculture, to a mythical and romantic place in popular cultural imagination. Williams's (1973) critique lay in unravelling the stereotypes associated with the rural – and that they had become evermore shrouded in bucolic nostalgia and included a yearning for an idealised and lost community. For Williams (1973), the countryside has become reified into a picture-postcard rural idyll – tranquil, quiet and delightfully scented. Through this process, the British countryside had become commodified – turned from a reality into a symbol. The insight of Williams's (1973) analysis continues to inform contemporary rural sociology and geography. The commodified and advertised countryside can now been seen through fictional representations (such as Heartbeat country for North Yorkshire) and by reference to television images (Hardy country for Wessex), rather than rural realities described in terms of their amenities or landscapes. Whereas there continues to be a great difficulty in defining the rural (Newby 1980, Hamilton 1990, Cloke et al. 1994), the role of rural images and texts and their status in the UK population's cultural imagination have emerged as a field ripe for analysis. It becomes all the more salient in that 'such writing is rarely carried out with any self-consciously political purpose' as therefore it becomes 'all the more important to monitor it as an indicator of the cultural ground on which explicit reconstructions are seeking to operate' (Dingwall et al. 1991: 443). Popular culture and the manner in which it reflects – or does not – the rapid economic developments of farming in the post-war period that have transformed the industry.

Children's literature is one such site to view whether the state-of-the-art technologies now in place in some dairy farms are portrayed in everyday culture. The visual images contained there open up an important tool for gaining insights into hidden concepts and ideologies in relation to work processes (Strangleman 2004a). The visual can be used to shed light on both the new and the hidden (Bolton et al. 2001) and also old and forgotten practices (Harper 1998, 2002). In narrowing the use of visual images to the specific example of young children's literature, such picture books themselves should not be underestimated, as they 'play an important role in early sex-role socialization because they are a vehicle for the presentation of societal values to the young child' (Weitzman et al. 1972: 1126). Indeed, by definition, the target age group implies that 'picture books are read to children when they are most impressionable' (Weitzman et al. 1972: 1126–1127). Therefore, visual images in picture books construct particular visions of the countryside by supporting a particular message or association and this continues a line of analysis also to be found in geographers' work. For example, the television media's portrayal of rural living is in highly desirable terms and as achieved through rose-tinted portrayals of rural environments, featuring large country houses and Range Rovers (Phillips et al. 2001). Indeed, the challenge becomes to examine whether the portrayal of dairy farming in children's literature and the latest innovations, such as the automated milking system in place at the University of Nottingham's farm, will be featured. The absences in images of the rural and the neglect of certain social groups also warrant critical attention. For example, Weitzman et al.

analysed prize-winning children's literature and concluded that 'the girls and women depicted in these [children's] books are a dull and stereotyped lot' (Weitzman et al. 1972: 1146). They found gender stereotypes prevalent and that 'most women in picture books have status by virtue of their relationships to specific men' (ibid.). The result of this, they argue, is negative as it is 'through picture books [that] girls are taught to have low aspirations because there are so few opportunities portrayed as available to them' (ibid.) The significance for perceptions of rurality may therefore hold equally important implications in terms of the associations they generate.

There is a danger, of course, of viewing children's literature in a simplistic, homogenised way, when the forms of visual styles characterising the genre of children's picture books are highly varied. The imagery can differ in complexity, from the very simple to the use of photographic work. The complexity of the image is, of course, shaped by the age of the target audience in which more complex images are aimed towards older age-groups. However, the style of some cartoons, for instance, invite analogies with eighteenth and nineteenth century artists, such as Gillray and Hogarth, which brings into consideration the purposes underpinning such images. Whilst young children's picture book are unlikely to contain the satirical message Hogarth sought to achieve through *A Rake's Progress*, the work of Williams's (1973) and latter-day rural geographers allows us to see that images are not neutral vehicles of popular culture. The exact method through which such a critical engagement can be achieved is now outlined.

Dingwall et al.'s analysis of images of parenthood in the UK and Japan identified and refined 'four dimensions of the illustration' (Dingwall et al. 1991: 426), which are summarised and applied here:

The nucleus: incorporating the nature of the shot (whether distant or close); where the emphasis lies (such as cropping or trimming of the body).
The mood: this emphasises the focus and lighting of the image (whether clinical or romantic) it is a general or selective image.
The setting: this includes location (indoor or out); analyses the messages of props appearing and whether the image is realistic or stylised in its tone.
The actors: this incorporates social cues (such as age, gender, race, height and marital and social status); relationships between participants in the scene and also between participants and the viewer.

The fourth category of the actor enabled Dingwall et al. (1991) to introduce Goffman's (1979) work on the analysis of domination and subordination in visual images. Goffman's (1979) analysis of gender advertisements considered physical contact and choice of posture to be important indicators defining the situation and he also highlighted the distinction between 'caught', 'candid' and 'fabricated' pictures. One example of this is the role of eye contact in an image as a means of deciphering relationship hierarchies within an image. Dingwall et al. (1991) rein-force the importance of such techniques in revealing the techniques through which 'official' parenthood literature in Japan ascribes parents a pupil, rather than consumer, status. The four categories allow the focus of attention in each image of farming to be challenged and the focus now moves on to young children's picture book images of farming to examine popular conceptions of the country-side; are flat-caps positioned as a form of working apparel or more as a form of dressing up?

Images of Dairy Farming Imagery in Children's Literature

The research explored everyday images of farming in young children's literature and not the text, unless it altered the meaning of the images.[2] Three libraries' col-lections of children's books were studied, two in Nottinghamshire, UK (a central library and a smaller, district library) and one infant school's holdings in Darlington, County Durham, UK. The sampling technique selected every twen-tieth book or, in the case of the latter's much smaller holding, every tenth book. A total of 387 picture books were sampled and thirty-three texts were found to contain images of farming. The sample therefore reflects in many ways the text-books a child would typically be able to access through the public library system and during their first years of formal schooling.

One of the most popular forms of farming emerging from the analysis of the two Nottingham libraries was dairy farming. Ananova's (2003) account of the latest innovations in dairy farming in the UK and Europe describes the introduction of autonomous milking systems, in which the cows present themselves for milking and through which the quota and movement of every member of the herd is mon-itored by computer. In contrast to this technology, the images of dairy farming in the sample represented anachronistic technologies and equipment. The most sophisticated milking technology was a hand-applied milking machine (Tanner and Wood 1995), although this machinery was in use in the mid-1940s (Harper 2001).

In this image, the machine forms the nucleus (the farmer and the three children appearing are positioned towards the machine) and the reader is shown the whole of the farmer, although he is kneeling to attach the machine to a cow. The style of the children's attire reveals a clinical context, in that the children are 'Brownies' learning about the milking process and as the image's style adopts a realistic and highly detailed drawing style, as opposed to a cartoon idiom. The realism of the drawing also presents contradictions. The detail of the milking parlour and the dairy farmer's Wellington boots are all spotless and the floor highly polished, a system that is far removed from the realities of dairy farming, even those featuring automated animal waste cleaning systems.

The old and unfashionable technologies of farming are themes that are continued as sustained through other images of dairy farming appearing in the sample. For instance, a second image (no. 2) takes the form of a simple cartoon and is therefore a less realistic image. The farmer in this case is transporting his milk churns in a horse-drawn wagon (Lacome 1994). The whole of the farmer's body is again shown and he and his horse are the focus of attention. The horse image, for example, is detailed, for example, on the bridle, which contrasts with the simple blocks of colour that feature in the background that are used to depict rolling hills and trees. The old-fashioned use of horse and cart (rather than tractor or tanker) and the featuring of milk churns (redundant in modern dairies for some decades) are out-of-date technologies, despite the book's publication date in the early to mid-1990s.

Both Tanner and Wood (1995) and Lacome (1994) use images that feature working dairy equipment no longer in widespread use (indeed, the milking machine in image no. 1 resembles a churn). The cues in both images indicate attire (they sport a flat-cap and wellingtons), which is practical, yet rendered unnecessary in the clean context in which they both appear, which is visible through the gleaming horse brasses in the background of the first image (no. 1) discussed and through the clean wagon wheels in the more simple cartoon of Lacome (1994).

The appearance of technology (albeit in somewhat anachronistic forms) in these first images is absent in the further images of dairy farming in the sample. A third (no. 3), Watson (1997), is a picture book that uses photographs of dairy farming. The nucleus is once again the farmer, displayed in her entirety, in a more distanced shot of the farmer, outside in a grass field surrounded by her herd. Trees and a hedge can be seen in the distance. The absence of explicit forms of dairy equipment and technology, such as a milking machine, is replaced in this image with a greater emphasis upon the process of farming. The imagery is romantic, as opposed to the clinical and educative tone of the first image. The farmer is shown first-hand interacting with her herd (she is reaching her left hand out to nuzzle one of the cows). Therefore a romantic image is achieved, despite the detail afforded by the use of a photograph, which allows mud to be visible on the cows and on the farmer's wellington boots. Further realism is clearly visible, whilst not at the forefront of the shot, through the identity tags on the ears of several cows. Up-to-date aspects and practices of farming are present in this photographic image in Watson (1997), but this is somewhat submerged under a generally romantic context of husbandry and animal–human contact. The type of dairy farming revealed in this account is further problematised in terms of the 'realities' of farming its use of photographs sustains, as the farmer featured in this text is Helen Browning, a leading member of the Soil Association (a pro-organic campaigning and farming organisation).

A fourth image of dairy farming (Morpurgo and Rayner 1992) employs the most cartoon-like idiom of the sample and is resonant of a Gillray cartoon. One double page spread offers two images involving milking: the one that displays active milking is in image no. 2.

Once again, in both cartoons the attention of the viewer is drawn to the farmer. The farmer occupies the nucleus of both images and, again, his whole body is shown within the cartoon. The cartoon idiom, however, employs props that are again anachronistic dairy farming techniques (hand milking and buckets, rather than sealed churns or tanks). Morpurgo and Rayner's (1992) use of a cartoon idiom also employs speech bubbles. The eye line of the farmer, towards his cow as he milks her, further supports the idea that the farmer is interacting with his cattle in the image. This is the most explicitly anthropomorphic dairy farming image, in which the cows are given human features (smiling faces) and voices (exaggerated eyelashes on the cow and they speak and tease the farmer for singing in the second image). Although the farmer addresses his horse in Lacome (1994), the horse's eye line and still posture and direction (away from the farmer) does not reciprocate to the degree to which the above image does in Morpurgo and Rayner's (1992) imagery.

A final, more general representation of farming, in which dairy cattle appear only within the background, features in Lewis (2000) and the right half that features cattle is featured in a third image that can be contrasted with the first two. This image (no. 3) is a realistic drawing, almost a painting, of the farm at a distance. The viewer's attention is drawn to take in the farm in its entirety, as the distance allows it to encompass the barns, farmhouse, paddocks and a view of several fields behind the farm along the horizon. Unlike the image in Lacome (1994) of the farmer and his horse and cart, the detail of the picture of the farm continues into the background and this enables a herd of eight cattle to be distinguished in one of the fields in the background. Although they are located in the background of the image, it is possible to discern that some of the cattle are grazing. There is also a flock of some dozen sheep in the adjoining field.

The setting of this image is romantic, despite the realistic mood of the drawing itself. This is evidenced by several images of animals and their progeny. The centre-left of the image (not shown) features a cow and her calf standing alongside, at a barn entrance and, more prominently, a ewe and two lambs (one of which is nursing), which are positioned at the forefront of the drawing. This is the only image featuring cattle, that does not feature a farmer, although human presence is detectable through washing hanging out on the line in the middle-right of the image seen in image no. 3.

Human–animal interaction, a feature in most of the images of dairy farming in the sample, is also revealing in that the number of animals in the images tends towards fewer cattle. Only two images in the sample feature a herd of cattle grazing in a field and in one of these images the herd is positioned in the far background or periphery of the image. In Lacome, the clear depiction of a milk load in the centre of the picture consists of three churns on the back of the farmer's wagon, which is not suggestive of the yield of a large herd. Rather, a daily output of three milk churns is suggestive of a small farm possessing a variety of different animals, which was typical of small, family-run farms in the 1940s and 1950s. The small number of animals depicted in the images of dairy farming is shared across the sample; however, the physical settings differ.

The environments appearing across the images are diverse and include inside and out-of-doors settings; they range from a clean and immaculate parlour (Tanner and Wood 1995) to muddied (Watson 1997) and hay-strewn contexts (Morpurgo and Rayner 1992). The professional status of the farmer can also be alluded to, through the props in the image and the bearing of the actors. Tanner and Wood's (1995) spotless milking parlour with rosettes adorning the walls (albeit in the background) contrasts with Morpurgo and Rayner's (1992) action image in which the farmer is the nucleus of the scene, striding across the farmyard and carrying full buckets of milk, which he spills whilst smiling (see the description of image no. 4 below).

Therefore, whilst the props appearing in the images of dairy farming promote a generally positive mood (romantic images of husbandry through animal–human interaction in Watson 1997 and Morpurgo and Rayner 1992), the professionalism of the farmer varies. The imagery is of the jaunty, carefree dairy farmer in the cartoon idiom in Morpurgo and Rayner (1992) (singing and smiling whilst slop-ping milk from his bucket), whilst the clinical realism of Tanner and Wood (1995) promotes a professionally recognised, award-winning model of farming (sug-gested by the rosettes adorning the background walls) using machinery rather than hand-milking. The more general presentation of farming as an occupation and other key features of the wider sample, most notably the same anachronistic model of farming found in the dairy farming images, are now examined via the sample.

Monocultures in Modern Farming

The images of dairy farming in many ways act as an index to the general findings of the sample. The diversity of complexity ranged from the cartoon idiom to highly detailed and realistic images. One difference in the wider sample that contrasted with the subset of the dairy farming images was the centrality of the farmer. The farmer did not always form the nucleus or act as the primary actor in the wider picture books sample and, for example, only adopted a central role in twelve of the thirty-three texts featuring rural and farming imagery. A secondary role for the farmer, for instance, was one story focused around the annoyance of the farmyard animals at a noisy, constantly quacking duck (Rogers and Rogers 1995). However, the activities and props appearing in the general images echoed the findings of the dairy farming images in that they adopted traditional and somewhat anachronistic characteristics. The variety of close and distant images revealed the conventional apparatus appearing in the dairy images, such as livestock housing and environments (stables, barns, pigsties, hen-houses and ponds) and farming equipment, but also anachronistic equipment in other farming industries, such as pitchforks (although building haystacks by hand was practised in the mid-1940s), and horses and carts continued to feature, although outnumbered by tractors (Harper 2001).

The anachronistic portrayal of farming equipment was accompanied by a tendency towards romantic imagery in the activities in which farmers were depicted as being involved: for example, taking part in traditional farming practices, such as collecting eggs (Sloat and Westcott 1999) or driving the tractor (seen in one-third of the sample). These conventional images of farming found across the general sample were, however, countered by a smaller number of texts, that featured more diverse activities. For example, Watson (1997) showed the farmer at the end of the day working at her computer in her office, a somewhat more modern piece of equipment than the milking machine in Tanner and Wood (1995). This image was also exceptional in that it depicted a female farmer. However, this exception in terms of activity and gender was countered by the appearance of only four women clearly performing the role of farmer in the sample, although one of these was again engaged in more diverse activities, such as the hands-on roles of performing practical and less romantic tasks such as oiling machinery, moving muck heaps and worming cows (Osband and Spargo 1993). In the eight images in which other female actors did appear they were ascribed the status of a farming wife. Therefore, while women were not absent in the images, they were for the most part occupying secondary positions in the plot line and were also secondary in the practice of farming when compared with the representations of men.

The caricatures of dress styles in the dairy farming images were repeated in the wider sample. Flat-caps and country headgear, with variations including a deerstalker and a baseball cap, featured in twenty-four of the thirty-three farming images found in the sample. A similar emphasis on practical country wear was evident in the clothing displayed in our sample, including wellingtons and stout boots, dungarees, lumberjack shirts and the highly practical body warmer. Again, like the images of dairy farming, the cartoon idiom did not present the detail of muddy boots or equipment. Therefore, whilst the attire of the farmers in the imagery was detailed enough to distinguish between boots and wellingtons and trousers and dungarees, it did not extend to detail the mud observable in the photograph used in Watson (1997). In addition to stereotypes of farming attire, the average age of farmers in Britain has risen to over sixty years of age so age has emerged as an important issue (Gasson et al. 1998). Recent disasters within the farming industry (such as FMD and BSE) have forced even those children already anticipating a future in farming to reconsider (Nerlich et al. 2005). In contrast to the statistics, using the, admittedly broad, categories of under 30, 30–60 and 60+, the cues in the sample suggested that the majority of images fell into the middle category with twenty-one of our thirty-three samples. Only seven images fell clearly into the 60+ category and all of those in the latter category were presented as able-bodied. The images of farming considered here have served to promote an old-fashioned and anachronistic type of farming; however, the active and out-of-door roles of the farmers do not include any associations of infirmity and avoid the negative connotations ageing holds for a youth-obsessed culture (Biggs 1999). Furthermore, the romantic and positive light in which farming was depicted, for example, through rolling hills and sunshine, predominated and, of the seven images that clearly portrayed farmers as either a hero or a villain, only one defined the farmer as the villain (Waddell and Oxenbury 1991). The general positive image of farming promoted through these sampled picture books is more problematic to evaluate in terms of indicators of prosperity. For example, it is not so readily on view as the display of Range Rovers and large country houses that Phillips et al. (2001) noted in their analysis of rural areas on the television. However, Newby (1977a, b) was at pains to emphasise the poverty, isolation and a lack of basic amenities, such as affordable housing, that can also characterise rural lifestyles. Therefore, whilst prosperity was one of the most subjective categories to define that we included, it was a relevant concept on the basis of Newby's commentaries. Evidence of prosperity included images of large, well-kept farmhouses, the farm employing other staff, farming machinery and a general image of prosperous, well-maintained land and large plots of land. The appearances of indicators of a low social status were not positioned at the forefront of the images. For instance, patched trousers featured in only one account.

Summary

The four dimensions applied here have served to mark out some of the character-istics of authority appearing within the images (men at the forefront, women in secondary roles) and issues of mood (clinical and educative set against romantic examples of animal–human interaction and anthropomorphism). This technique of analysing one form of popular culture, children's books, has been able to distin-guish that even the pictures aimed at the youngest age group (such as very simple cartoons, with large blocks of colour and detail only in the forefront of the picture) are anachronistic in message. The imagery of farming as revealed through this sample promotes and perpetuates a vision of farming more analogous to that of 1940s America (Harper 2001) than farming in the twenty-first century. However, a number of paradoxes within the images also emerge. These include close detailing of non-farming equipment (ornate brasses on a horse's bridle), but sim-plistic drawing elsewhere (on the wheel at the back of the horse cart). Also, the contrast between shambolic farming practices (transporting the milk carelessly) and the degree of cleanliness (the shine on the floor and the professional pride in the display of rosettes) is an internal contradiction within the sample.

The anthropomorphism in many of the images and the anachronistic nature of many of the images, when seen together, echo the critique made by Phillips et al. (2001) by promoting a dreamlike and perfected image of farming practices and lifestyles. The images use their emotive dimensions to evoke a romantic and nostalgic image picture of farming. The benign aura of this nostalgia is lost, however, when children's stories are seen has 'a means for perpetuating the fundamental cultural values and myths' (Weitzman et al. 1972). The size of the sample discussed here prohibits ready generalisations, yet the importance of children's ability to understand the links between farming and food have been highlighted in a recent government inquiry into farming, which highlighted that children are key if the links between farmers and urban residents and, more centrally, food producers and consumers are to be strengthened (Curry, 2002). However, the sampling technique used here does serve to represent the type of library holding and texts available to suburban children and in those terms may indicate the general type of knowledge about farming suburban children may encounter. For, as Dingwall et al. remind us, 'in a culture which plays down individual differences, the cartoon can function as a statement of universal' (Dingwall et al. 1991: 441). This is even more relevant in the light of government guidelines dictat that no library text should be more than five years old, yet the findings here demonstrate that such a policy has not countered the anachronistic and sexist stereotypes that they contain. Initiatives, such as farm visits run by the NFU and Countryside Agency, require a receptive attitude towards farming if the full learning potential of farm visits is to be realised (Rickinson et al. 2003). The visual continues to be one of the key ways in which people are attracted to the countryside, it seems important to be able to represent a diverse countryside which is increasingly characterising Britain's countryside, as opposed to recreating out-of-date, nostalgic images that have been deconstructed briefly here. A more recognisable, contemporary imagery of the countryside should be made available if a diversified rural economy is to prevail and rural tourism (visiting a 'real' countryside) is to prove sustainable.

Visual Sociology: Photo Elicitation and 'Hidden' Work in the Countryside

In contrast to the imagery of farming work in children's literature is the example of 'hidden' forms of work in the countryside more broadly. In the context of post-CAP reform and the direct decoupling of farm payments from scales of production, the new rhetoric surrounding agriculture is that of sustainability and of farming fulfilling a much broader remit for the countryside than that of food production. For example, the emphasis is evocative of a return to a more paternalistic model of farming and stewardship of the land. However, as commentators in rural studies have noted, rural occupations can no longer be seen to be the preserve of farmers or farming, or male-dominated (Milbourne 1997, Little and Morris 2004). There is a call within the sociology of work more broadly to understand the different instances of work that now exist in contemporary society – in both urban and rural environments (Felstead et al. 2005). For example, this includes homeworking, which can potentially be as significant for rural areas as the rise in car-ownership was for rural property prices in the 1960s (Newby 1985).

The diversification of work and the decline of older, industrial-based employment (Strangleman 2004b) create a challenge for the sociologist to be able to engage with where such work takes place and how best to understand it. Strangleman (2004a) further suggests that the use of visual sociology presents one such, neglected, opportunity to study work. It is this latter technique that is used in the final section of this chapter to explicate the working life of one English gamekeeper. It is Harper's technique of 'photo elicitation' that is briefly used to describe how greater insight can be generated into country sports (Harper 2002).

The analysis is based upon a data set created during the 2001–2 shooting season[3] (with some overlap, but representing a full year cycle). It consists of a total of 111 photographs taken in the north-east of England from early July 2001 through to a matter of weeks after the estate's final shoot days. The gamekeeper himself instigated the collection, in order to record his preparations for the shooting season and to demonstrate his activities to his new employers (following the shoot changing hands). The gamekeeper did not personally take any of the photographs, but asked a friend who was also an amateur photographer. The collection was recorded via a process in which the gamekeeper indicated what aspects of his work he wanted to be incorporated (and we shall see that this included rearing, cover crops and release pens). It was the photographer who composed and took the shots.

The background of the collection therefore distinguishes it from Harper's (2002) use of an archive and that of a collection made by a visiting sociologist (Woodward 2003), neither does it represent the imagery one would find of the gamekeeper (www.nationalgamekeepers.org.uk or the pictures from the shooting field found in long-established titles as the *Shooting Times* or *The Field*). The intention here is to attempt to reply to Strangleman's (2004a) argument for greater use of visual techniques to explore previously hidden aspects of work. The photographs and the gamekeeper's explanations[4] of what they represent to (1) engage with some of the myths surrounding gamekeepers' work and (2) see how photographs are a useful medium in unravelling some taken-for-granted aspects of the modern countryside.

Bolton et al. (2001: 503) remind us that, like cartoons or drawing, photographs are made rather than taken and Goffman's (1969) dramaturgical model is useful here. In the case of this collection, the gamekeeper wished to demonstrate to his new employer the 'backstage' preparations that go into running a shoot. That is, the photographs are effectively of what guns (the term used to describe people participating in a day's shooting) who do not run their own shoots will never see. In this case, the photographs provide an opportunity to see a world unseen by all but a handful of people involved with running or working on shoots themselves and, more broadly, a country sport largely dominated by economic analyses (Cobham Resource Consultants 1992). In this sense, the collection discussed here is 'made' not just as proof of work, but also to provide an insight into preparatory stages leading up to the shooting season not celebrated even by those participating in shooting.

The sociological engagement with photographs is itself problematic, for 'paradoxically it may be the very power and ready accessibility of visual images, the apparent transparency of their message, which leads us to dismiss their value as a serious source of data and sociological understanding' (Bolton et al. 2001: 504). Such is the case in relation to this collection, which can be broadly categorised into six main stages or processes engaged with across the summer: hatching; rearing pens; planting cover crops; rearing field; cover crop growth; and release pens. In terms of understanding these pictures, it is not until the features of such shots in the collection are unravelled that a fuller appreciation of the placement and significance of such landscapes is possible. This is akin to Harper's technique of photo-elicitation:

> In the photo-elicitation interview, interview/discussion is stimulated and guided by images. Typically these are photographs that the researcher has made of the subject's world ... A shocking thing happens in this interview format; the photographer, who knows his or her photograph as its maker (often having slaved over creation in the darkroom), suddenly confronts the realization that she or he knows little or nothing about the cultural information contained in the image.
>
> (Harper 1998: 35)

At first glance, one of the most striking aspects of the collection is that people appear in only twelve of the photographs and then often only partially. However, who appears is significant, in that it demonstrates some of the exchange relationships and support systems single gamekeeper estates rely upon. In this case, it includes the keeper's father, father-in-law, a neighbouring farmer and his young daughter. The impression here is that, whilst the gamekeeper works largely in isolation in comparison to the working lives of most urban employees, his own family contributes help at key times of the year: for instance, for the cleaning of rearing pens and for the placing of release pens adjacent to cover crops, both of which are included in the collection.

The number of photographs of the maize cover crops reveals the scale of the gamekeeper's work. Size matters here in this sense in two ways – first the arrangement of the maize in order to make use of the landscape features and also the height of the maize, which is only clear when the keeper appears in one photograph – the only time in which he appears directly facing the camera. Here the gamekeeper demonstrates the tactical placement of maize plots and also the healthy and clear nature of the plots. In a context in which the density and cover offered by the crops will be intrinsic to the birds remaining close by upon release, such issues are revealed to be significant aspects of the gamekeeper's work (Steering Committee for the Code of Good Shooting Practice 2003).

In another image, the keeper can be seen to have strategically positioned the maize to maximise the contours of the landscape. This maize plot is positioned at the top of a rise and therefore birds flying out of the maize will be more challenging birds for shooting than if the maize had been level with the guns. Understanding the role of maize cover, where it is placed and how the quality of the crop itself is significant in many ways for this gamekeeper's work. Therefore, visual techniques have allowed for some of the unseen, backstage aspects of contemporary rural work in the case of gamekeeping to be unravelled. It also shows the diversity of gamekeeping work, beyond the ready association with rearing birds. The romantic associations of game-keeping work (Lawrence 1960) are also defused somewhat by the number of images detailing cleaning the huts in which the birds are initially reared before their release. A number of pictures in the collection (111) illustrated the gamekeeper cleaning with the help of other family members. In these pictures, the tools used by the modern gamekeeper are not those necessarily featured in the more romanticised image of a keeper on the home page of the National Gamekeepers' Organisation (http: //www.nationalgamekeepers.org.uk/). The plus twos (trousers that finish just below the knee) are replaced by shorts, with no shirt, and equipment in the picture includes a mobile telephone and a wallpaper scraper to remove hardened partridge waste from the heaters ('electric hens') that rest above the birds in their pens. That such a task is time-consuming for the keeper is demonstrated in the inclusion of the finished result in the collection: a photograph of a pile of dried partridge waste.

Conclusion

This brief consideration of one photographic data set and the images of farming in children's literature have served to demonstrate the role that visual techniques can bring to an understanding of rural work. There is scope for visual techniques to contribute to deconstructing some of the myths and rituals that surround farming and country sports. The use of ethnographic techniques may allow for a more detailed and sustained understanding of complex rural matters to be reached by challenging taken-for-granted readings of rural work and landscapes. Such data may reveal a more complex picture and not only dispel myths and discourses that are inaccurate but also serve to resolve points of conflict.

The visual here has allowed the role gamekeeping contributes to the countryside to be understood and also to see cultural perceptions of farming through children's picture books. For example, whilst most game crops are readily viewed upon the landscape, the strategy behind their location is perhaps less understood – or rather has disappeared into the normality of the everyday landscape. Therefore, whilst the health of the crop is easily viewed, the importance of its location on the landscape is not so easily interpreted. In this sense, the role of the gamekeeper touches on theoretical concerns to understand the interaction between nature, society and culture in the rural. The visual has been useful for understanding gamekeeping and has brought 'a distinctive contribution to sociological enquiry' (Bolton et al. 2001: 504). Indeed, there is far more scope for the visual to be welcomed into 'mainstream sociological praxis' (Bolton et al. 2001: 505). However, the argument proposed here is that such data are best positioned alongside other techniques in order to be interpreted as fully as possible – the visual provides an important addition to the portfolio of research methods available to the sociologist. For, like all techniques, visual methods have their advantages and disadvantages and are therefore best utilised when they suit the research question concerned. In the current political climate in which visual images are being used as a means to critique country sports, there is a need for the insights visual sociology can bring to engage with other country sports.

Chapter Summary

The final chapter of the book took a more methodological focus and brought the text full circle from the opening theoretical discussions, through three substantive chapters to consider the representation of the rural. The chapter made no claim to offer a definitive means to explore rural issues, but rather recognised, on the basis of the preceding arguments, that rural studies are characterised by paradigms rather than one research culture. It was in that spirit that visual research techniques were advocated in the manner in which they add to the portfolio of research methods available to the social scientist.

Two different examples of the use of visual material to explore rural themes were discussed. Both attempted to challenge the taken-for-granted or previously neglected visual material or forms of work. The chapter concluded that in these instances visual material enabled new insights and questions to be raised and as such complemented the wide variety of methods the text has discussed.

Learning tools

Questions

1. The sub-discipline of rural sociology has been described as 'a problem in search of a discipline'. Have rural studies been too focused on single-issue questions?

2. To what extent can visual studies contribute to our understanding of the rural? Demonstrate your argument with reference to the literature.
3. To what degree are visual methods better than more traditional research techniques? Demonstrate your argument with reference to the literature.

Glossary of Emerging Key Terms

Photo elicitation: the uses of photographs as an aide-memoire in an interview in order to further facilitate the discussion.
Visual sociology: the use of visual images to further aid our understanding of society and social relations. The visual is best used alongside other sociological techniques of investigation.

Conclusion: the Future of Rural Societies and Rural Sociology

The debates engaged with over the preceding chapters have demonstrated the complexity of rural society and rural issues in the twenty-first century. The aim of this text has been to explore the meaning of the rural in contemporary society. It began with Tönnies's writings on the new, emergent discipline of sociology; traced the empirical emphasis introduced by community studies in the 1950s and; the class conflict analyses of Newby's work. Chapter 2 sampled contemporary geography work. It argued that there were some continuities with past rural sociology among the sample of authors analysed but also that contemporary rural geography offered important innovations in the study of the rural.

The third, fourth and fifth chapters then offered a series of UK case studies, through which a selection of literature was analysed. This showed gaps in geographic analyses and the potential for sociology to make a contribution. This series of case studies highlighted that the study of rural matters would benefit from greater sociological engagement. This supports a more general question posed by the text as to whether the rural should once again be on the sociological agenda. The conclusions drawn from the case studies suggest that sociology has much to offer and also that future sociology should be mindful to engage with rural geography in terms of future research practice and innovations in theoretical ideas or new emphases.

The manner in which rural research has been conducted in the literature sampled across the text has given rise to some difficult questions. These relate to issues of theory and method and to continuity and innovation. Chapter 1 served to highlight the consequences of a misappropriation of a rural concept, in this case Tönnies's twin concepts of *Gemeinschaft und Gesellschaft*. This led to a period in the 1950s and 1960s where new research merely sought to document the forms of community associated with *Gemeinschaft* rural societies and rural studies stagnated. However, Pahl's work in returning Tönnies's work to its original ontological emphasis led to a period of theoretical and methodological innovation. Theoretically, this included the emergence of the interaction order as a field worthy of sociological investigation. Methodological developments included an emphasis upon primary fieldwork and the growing recognition of the contribution qualitative research has to bring. Newby's work provided an ideal example of both.

The second chapter examined the late 1970s rural sociology to present-day issues in rural studies more generally. It therefore began at a vibrant time for rural sociology but through the course of the chapter emphasised that sociologists should be aware of the innovations that rural geography offers – such as the commodification of the countryside, its gentrification and the availability of new research techniques such as the visual mentioned in chapter 6. Theoretically, these innovations have been the shift from the traditional equation of the rural with agriculture, but more recent debates have seen a shift from this sectoral approach to a more territorial approach. These territories are theoretically and methodologically rich and Cloke's work on the commodification of rural spaces was held up as an example. With the conclusion of the chapter, rural studies were seen to be flourishing as can be viewed through the number of rural specialisms now characterising rural geography. With this conclusion came an important caveat, for, whilst the study of issues has become more popular in recent times, it is perhaps at the cost of a holistic treatment of the rural. This warrants explication.

The necessarily selective nature of the material considered here prevents any definitive statement for rural sociology, yet the current diversity of theoretical and methodological approaches available to the rural researcher suggests that current rural research is characterised by paradigms rather than one paradigm or system of thought. This was demonstrated in the specific rural issues that were examined through three case study chapters. Whilst the literature sampled in these topics was selective, it served to demonstrate the wide variety of theoretical and methodological approaches open to the rural researcher. The chapters also emphasised that taking single-issue topics of investigation creates the danger of not contributing to or being sufficiently aware of the wider debates regarding theory and method taking place more generally – within both sociology and geography – that is, whether single-issue empirical research serves to further develop and refine more general concepts and debates within sociology and/or geography.

The rise of a more territorial approach to the sociological study of the rural can be seen in its roots. The state of sociology (which is the explicit focus here rather than geography) is that of an established discipline, widely taught across the UK university sector and with a legacy of literature – as we have seen – founded over 100 years ago. The result is a more confident and established discipline than at the time Tönnies or even Goffman was writing. Yet with the expansion of sociology has come a rise in the division of labour within sociology. Where the first students reading for a sociology degree would have encountered a much smaller corpus of literature, the current situation is towards specialisation in sub-fields of sociology – urban sociology, the sociology of health and illness, the sociologies of education and childhood, to name but a few. As a result, holistic sociology is more difficult. The danger becomes to confuse methodological innovations and expansions with theoretical progress and cumulation. Whilst it is clear that the rural remains an important area for themes of conflict and power to be addressed, to what degree has the concept of the rural progressed since Tönnies's time? Considering the lack of sociological engagement with the rural since the 1970s, what progress can be said to have been made? Newby commented that:

> it is possible to exaggerate the lack of theoretical interest shown by rural sociologists and to mistake the inductivist approach which typifies rural sociological research for the absence of any theoretical development.

(Newby 1980: 23)

The situation is further exacerbated by the rise of interdisciplinary research within rural studies. The substantive chapters offered here serve to counter such a suggestion, as they have led to a rich variety of work being produced. The impact of the 2001 FMD epidemic was explored on a variety of levels, from the macro to the micro. Yet interdisciplinary research also gives rise to the question of how such work can be evaluated – and who is qualified to do so. For example, even the closely intertwined fields of rural sociology and geography offer different engagements with postmodernism. Indeed, even within rural sociology, researchers approach their work from different epistemological positions. The same could be said of rural geographers.

Despite such concerns, the wide variety of theories and methods at the disposal of rural research – by both sociologists and geographers alike – has not given rise to methodological anarchism. Cloke echoes C. Wright Mills's notion of the sociological imagination – a geographic imagination. This serves to show that rural studies that bridge these disciplines have recognised the necessity of understanding the contribution of the researcher's imagination to every stage of the research process. This also acts as a mark of research sophistication. For example, the review of LACS in chapter 5 could be accused of applying techniques of evaluation relevant to academic work and therefore inappropriate if applied to research by a political organisation. The very appeal of photographic images or blending of styles within the report (academic-style citations and footnotes) blurs the situation, but Cloke's work enables conflictual issues in the countryside to be addressed and their debates unravelled through notions of commodified rural spaces, the contested countryside and the fractions inside rural communities.

In the context of the reform of the CAP and the decoupling of payments the wide-reaching repercussions for British agriculture and the future of farming need to be researched in social and cultural, as well as economic, terms. Therefore, an awareness of existing research on the current state of the countryside is vital if the CAP reforms and new rural policies are to be targeted effectively. The text has advocated the contribution more interactional and micro-oriented research can make alongside more traditional forms such as political-economic analysis. This was clearly demonstrated through the case of game shooting – and that societal perceptions and concerns need to be taken into account. The SFP system needs to acknowledge the role farming plays in landscape management and also that the very notion of nature and even human–animal relations and hierarchies are contested. Donaldson et al. (2006) imply the opposite, when they mention the number of flowering plants on the fells in the absence of sheep. The lack of grazing caused by the FMD epidemic in the period also led to some pathways becoming overgrown and access problematic (Hillyard forthcoming b). The chapter on game shooting has also highlighted research that has long demonstrated the impact of game management upon the landscape and songbird populations (Stoate and Leake 2002, Tapper 2005).

There is scope for the inductivist approach that Newby employed to penetrate geographic research to the same degree as it has within sociology. Therefore, ethnographic approaches that can be seen to dominate some sub-disciplines of sociology (Hammersley and Atkinson 1995) remain marginal within areas of rural geography. The text finds that there is a future for a sociology of the rural and one such sociology advocated here emphasises the importance of the social actor. Interactionism is also an approach that incorporates the valuable contribution of the postmodern for curtailing sociology's naive realism, but retains a commitment to theoretical refinement and cumulation. Such progress can be achieved through the application of a reflexive, contemporary ethnographic research tradition that allows power and conflict to be analysed at the interactional and meso-institutional level (Hillyard 1999, 2004, forthcoming a). Chapter 6 sought to add the use of visual techniques as a further opportunity for sociologists to render the familiar strange and, indeed, the strange familiar.

The text noted that the number of senior and junior researchers engaged in rural studies bodes well for the future (see the appendix for a summary). Certainly the manner in which some small rural research units or departments have responded to the threat of closure, achieving cost-effectiveness and 'earning their keep' by becoming proactive in their seeking of external, 'soft' funding has served to create a number of successful critical masses of rural research expertise. Cheltenham, Exeter and Newcastle are important examples for the UK and are certainly currently at the forefront of rural research. However, with the shift towards research council funding to support research fellows and assistants, as opposed to permanent HEFCE funding, the situation must be considered to be temporary and at worst potentially precarious. What, for example, in the wake of the RELU research programme will be the career paths of the raft of postgraduate and postdoctoral researchers who have been much in demand over the past few years? Whilst there is increasing flexibility for shifting from outside academia into academic managerial posts or administrative roles in universities (Deem et al. forthcoming), for those unable to secure academic posts who move outside the sector there must be a question mark over the possibilities for their return. Fortunately, the RELU programme has been mindful of such concerns and generated a number of research fellowships. For the current moment, however, the level of prosperity to be found in established rural sociology or rural research departments in the US is yet to be realised in the UK.

In conclusion, some progress has been made towards a definition of the rural, but in contemporary society this must be seen as a working definition and part of a range of perspectives on the rural. Underpinning all of these is the recognition that rural communities are characterised by difference and complexity. Sociologists can take their specialist interests (such as the sociologies of education or work) and apply them more readily to rural concerns in order to engage with these complexities. This would avoid some of the insularity of early community studies work in the 1950s and also enable a sociology of the rural to be more engaged with contemporary debates, issues and trends within rural studies.

Appendix

Rural Sociology Institutional Framework: Critical Masses of Rural Researchers in University Departments/Centres and Institutes; Sociologists with a Periphery Interest in the Rural; Professional Associations; and Rural Journals

University Departments

US and European

Department of Rural Sociology, Cornell University, US.
Agricultural Economics and Rural Sociology, Pennsylvania State University, US.
Department of Rural Sociology, University of Missouri-Columbia, US.
Department of Rural Sociology, Texas A & M University, US.
Department of Rural Sociology, University of Wisconsin-Madison, US.
Rural Sociology Group, Wageningen, The Netherlands.
Centre for Rural Social Research, Charles Sturt University, Australia.

UK

Centre for Rural Economy, University of Newcastle upon Tyne, UK (Lowe, Ward, Donaldson, Thompson, associated Shucksmith and Woodward). Established 1992.
Institute of Rural Studies (Garrod) and Institute of Geography and Earth Sciences (Woods), University of Aberystwyth, UK.
Human Geography Research Group, Department of Geography, University of Leicester, UK (Phillips, Bennett).
Countryside and Community Research Unit, University of Gloucestershire, UK.
Royal Agricultural College, Cirencester, UK.
Centre for Rural Research, School of Geography and Archaeology, University of Exeter, UK (Winter, Reed, Lobley, Jones, Buller, Little, Fish, Cloke).

International and Rural Development Department, Reading University, UK.
Arkleton Centre for Rural Development Research, University of Aberdeen, UK (Bryden).
Rural Restructuring Group, School of Science and the Environment, Coventry University, UK.
Department of Geography (Watkins, Seymour, Morris) and Agricultural and Environmental Sciences (Seabrook), Institute of Science and Society (formerly IGBiS) (Nerlich, Spencer, Wright), University of Nottingham, UK.
School of Sociology and Social Policy, Queen's University Belfast, UK (Shortall).
Department of Geography, University of Wales, Swansea, UK (Halfacree, Gardner, Maxey).

Sociologists with a Periphery Interest in the Rural

Institute for Health Research, Lancaster University, UK (Mort) or Convery in Environmental Management, University of Central Lancashire, UK.
Informatics Collaboratory of the Social Sciences, University off Sheffield, UK (Burridge).
Faculty of Social Sciences, Open University, UK (Neal).
Department of Geographical and Life Sciences, University of Glasgow, UK (Lorimer).

Professional Associations

International Rural Sociology Association
Rural Sociological Society (RSS), US
European Society for Rural Sociology (ESRS)
RuralNet UK (premier membership); http: //www.ruralnet.org.uk/
British Association of IT in Agriculture (BAITA)
European Federation of IT in Agriculture (EFITA)
Rural Economy and Society Study Group (RESSG–UK)
International Rural Sociologists Association (IRSA)
Agricultural Economics Society (AES–UK)

Rural Journals

US and European

Rural Sociology
Sociologia Ruralis

UK

Journal of Rural Studies
Environment and Planning C: Government and Policy
Environment and Planning D: Society and Space

Notes

Chapter 1 'A Problem in Search of a Discipline' (Hamilton 1990: 232): the History of Rural Sociology

1. It is important to note that the period in which the industrial revolution took place is itself contested. See Beckett (1990) for a full discussion.
2. That Tönnies and Simmel enjoy less standing within contemporary sociology is perhaps an indicator of the marginal status of rural sociology within the UK and also that both Simmel's and Tönnies's work has to a greater or lesser degree been poorly translated into English – both analytically and superficially. For Tönnies, this related to the misappropriation of the *Gemeinschaft und Gesellschaft* polarities (see Pahl 1968 and chapter 2). For Simmel, this consisted of the somewhat lumpen and popularist labelling of his sociology as 'formal' (see Frisby 1992 for a detailed discussion of Simmel's contribution) and also the slow emergence of English translations of his work (Craib 1992).
3. Craib (1992), however, is critical of the somewhat dismissive and superficial treatment of Durkheim's methodological approach by Lee and Newby (1983).
4. This title is as it appears in Gerth and Mills's [1948] oft-cited collection of Weber's key works. However, in a remarkable critical edition or essay on the English text of the lecture, Ghosh has commented upon the context of the lecture alongside a programme of the congress to which it was delivered. As a result, Ghosh (2005) elects to rephrase the title of the essay to more accurately reflect its content, preferring 'rural society in its relation to the other branches of society' (Ghosh 2005: 347).
5. See Appendix for the contrast between UK and US rural research centres and departments.
6. They provide a discussion of Littlejohn (1963) as an example of a dynamic study of social class (Bell and Newby 1971: 164–166).
7. This dynamism of change – the economic impact upon the social and then the long-term implications of these social changes over time – is a feature that Newby (1977) himself later seeks to correct, with varying success (Crow et al. 1990).
8. When Williams's (1963). is contrasted with Newby's (1977) six months of

field research and Lacey's (1970) and Hargreaves's (1976) years of field research, the contrast is clear.

9. See the learning tools at the end of this chapter for working definitions of rural sociology and geography.

10. Some would argue that there are still plenty of rural sociologists. Whilst there are admittedly a small number of sociologists concerned with rural issues, the rural is positioned towards the periphery (rather than the centre) of their research concerns.

11. Indeed, much like the sociologist to whom he makes detailed reference, Erving Goffman.

12. Newby (1977a) here draws upon Goffman (1969) [1959] and Goffman (1972) [1956].

13. There is a danger here of following in the footsteps of so many introductory sociology textbooks and viewing Goffman simply as a symbolic interactionist. Whilst it is beyond the remit of this text to engage with the complexities of Goffman's theoretical stance, he is better (though less fashionably) conceptualised as a structural functionalist (see Verhoeven 1993).

14. Delanty's (2003) more recent engagement with community studies is addressed in a later chapter.

15. Parallels can be made with the theoretical developments taking place on the other side of the Atlantic and the 'new' criminologists and the more formal expression of symbolic interactionism (Blumer 1969, Goffman 1969).

Chapter 2 New Issues in Rural Sociology and Rural Studies

1. See the learning tools at the end of chapter 1 for definitions of rural sociology and geography.

2. This is not to suggest that there is an inevitable direction or model of progress underpinning each discipline (or that such 'progress' would be desirable). Both can currently be seen to be characterised by paradigms, rather than one dominant paradigm.

3. Contrasting the British situation with the French, he argued that two theoretical models undercut French rural sociology: one Durkheimian, the other Marxist. British rural sociology exists inside 'a theoretical vacuum' (Hamilton 1990: 228).

4. Hamilton's (1990) construction of sociology during the period of the 1960s and 1970s is one in which echoes commentaries elsewhere. In the sub-discipline of the sociology of education, the functionalist paradigm had given way to very early forms of ethnographic case studies with their ground-breaking remit to explore the impact of social class upon educational attainment (Hargreaves 1967, Lacey 1970, Lambart 1976, 1982). Sociology's orientation towards social class was summed up by Colin Lacey's later observation that

class was like chips: social class was analysed in every study at that time (Lacey and Ball 1979).

5. We can include here the reconfiguration of MAFF into the Department for the Environment, Food and Rural Affairs (DEFRA) and the National Rivers Authority becoming the Environment Agency.

6. Hamilton (1990) provides the example of the rural sociology study group established by Newby and Kenneth Thompson in 1978, which then went on to become the Rural Economy and Society Study Group (under founding chair, Phillip Lowe), which Hamilton argued came to focus on issues, rather than theories or methodologies.

7. Collaborations included his doctoral supervisor (Bell and Newby 1971), an edited collection on research methods (Bell and Newby 1977) and also an introductory textbook (Lee and Newby 1983). That Newby remained in one department, rather than making the career movements that now tend to characterise the professional life of the modern academic, could be argued to have affected the long-term impact of his rural research in that it remained localised and centred in Essex.

8. Indeed, the text acknowledges the influence of discussions held at an SSRC seminar series on stratification (Newby et al. 1978b: 14).

9. The educational background, further education, life-cycle stage and even the socio-economic group of farmers' wives prior to marriage are also considered. The interview approach was therefore put to full use, but was a very different approach from that of more in-depth interview approaches, such as life histories, which are informed by different epistemological goals (Pole and Morrison 2003).

10. The special issue of the *Journal of Rural Studies* reported the findings of an ESRC programme on local governance. 'Essentially the programme was established to examine the development of a system of local governance in the UK in which local authorities found themselves in a variety of relations with other public, private and voluntary sector organizations. The work commissioned under the programme thus directly examined the supposed shift from government to governance and sought to provide new theoretical and empirical resources which would aid this examination' (Marsden and Murdoch 1998: 2). Hence, the relevance of Marsden's concluding article in the journal, which provides an ideal representation of his theoretical stance.

11. For example, continued technological development, such as precision farming.

12. See the glossary at the end of the book for a working definition of ethnography.

13. See the glossary at the end of the chapter for a working definition of postmodernism.

14. See Appendix for indication of the major centres of rural research in the UK.

15. Whilst not considered explicitly in this chapter, their work is touched upon in the following, substantive chapters: for example, Milbourne's work in the hunting debate.
16. For a full explication of postmodernism potential for rural geography see Philo (1993).

Chapter 3 The 2001 Foot-and-mouth Disease Epidemic in the UK

1. It can infect elephants, hedgehogs and rats.
2. To expand upon this, leading livestock breeders, who held influential positions in agricultural societies and Parliament, increasingly supported the slaughter measure, as they frequently sold valuable animals to foreign markets, yet foreign governments, themselves fearing FMD importation, now refused to accept stock unless Britain had been free of FMD for several months. This led to the desire to eliminate FMD as quickly as possible, and the most influential farming groups viewed slaughter as the best means of achieving this.
3. Furthermore, in the UK MAFF had decided nearly twenty years before vaccines were developed that these would never replace slaughter as a means of FMD control in Britain. This was, in turn, partly a result of MAFF's adherence to the ideal of national disease freedom, which dated from the nineteenth century.
4. Rural Development Agencies.
5. This is never more demonstrated than in the £20 million Rural Economy and Land Use (RELU) programme, directed by Professor Phillip Lowe at the Centre for Rural Economy, University of Newcastle. The programme's various calls all share a requirement for interdisciplinary research that unites natural and social science approaches.

Chapter 4 The Hunting Debate: Rural Political Protest and the Mobilisation and Defence of Country Sports

1. Ferreting is included here for want of better categorisation, although it is important to note that the 2004 Hunting Act did not ban ferreting.
2. Campaigning to Protect Hunted Animals (CPHA) was established in 1996 and incorporates the League Against Cruel Sports (LACS), the Royal Society for the Prevention of Cruelty to Animals (RSPCA), the International Fund for Animal Welfare (IFAW) and the Deadline 2000 campaign.
3. 'A place of residence and work where a large numbers of like-situated individuals, cut off from the wider society for an appreciable period of time, together lead an enclosed, formally administered round of life' (Goffman 1961: 11).

4. This section is based on a paper first presented to the European Society for Rural Sociology conference, Sligo, Ireland, in August 2003.
5. Hillyard (2003b) addressed the core concepts and philosophies underpinning specifically more 'mainstream' anti- and pro-hunting campaigns rather than the more extreme organisations.
6. Seeking to ban hunting by 2000.
7. There are, of course, significant differences of opinion both within these organisations (Ward 1999, Woods 2003) and between them (Cox 2000).
8. The 2002 'Liberty and Livelihood' march was preceded by marches in 1997, 1998 and then in 2001 the 'march that never was', which was cancelled due to FMD. The exact numbers and historical background of the CA have been addressed elsewhere (see Woods 2005, chapter 5).
9. For example, the newspaper has for the past three years been the main sponsor of the annual CLA game fair.
10. There is also a comparison made between hunting and the BSE crisis, one that even the CA admits is unjustifiable.
11. Most open to query is that Ward's research underpinning the paper was funded in the research by the LACS to unravel the methodologies applied to economic contributions and hunting. However, Winter (through his role in the Burns Inquiry) stated that he does not personally hunt, Cox (2000) identifies himself as an insider, but notes that 'being a native is not the same as "going native": and the effort to comprehend need not necessarily be accompanied by the suspension of critical faculties' (Cox 2000: 1). The author is similarly an insider, but has never hunted and positioned herself as a participant in shooting (Hillyard 2005). Therefore, what is more the concern is not that Ward is potentially anti-hunting, but that he has not clearly stated his position.
12. And, further, that Cobham's use of unreferenced BFSS data echoes IFAW use of unreferenced data.
13. The seriousness with which the shooting community has viewed its future is indicated by the formation of the campaign for shooting within the Countryside Alliance, alongside the campaign for hunting and, more recently, fishing.

Chapter 5 Game Shooting in the United Kingdom

1. This quote appears above the contents page and editorial to the weekly magazine *Shooting Times* (accessed 13 July 2006).
2. See glossary at the end of the book. However, it is also worth noting that the term has different connotations in philosophy along the lines of an unthinking adherence to an empiricist research approach. A direct translation from the Latin is: from what comes before.
3. Such as the late Earl of Lichfield (former President of the BASC), Sir Edward

Dashwood (former Chairman of the CA Campaign for Shooting) and Andrew Christie-Miller (former Chairman of the GCT).

4. The legality of their own fieldwork is not discussed, For example, they include a photograph of deer. This would have necessitated the presence for an extended period of time on their case study estate. Whether they were invited on to the estate to conduct the research is unspecified.

5. The code is actually a code on fox snaring. This distinction is not mentioned in the LACS report.

6. The BASC themselves recommend every 12 hours.

7. A note of caution is warranted here. Piddington (1981) informed Cox et al. (1996) in the simple sense that they attempted to demonstrate that her survey was atypical (i.e. biased towards large landowners). Their resurvey confirmed this.

8. See the learning tools at the end of this chapter for a definition.

9. Biodiversity Action Plan.

10. As an education and research charity.

11. The history and background of the GCT reveals something of the reasoning behind its specialism in game bird research. Whilst there is a research body within the BASC, the BASC is a political organisation and also does not conduct or explicate its research findings to a degree approaching that of the GCT, whose work appears in peer-reviewed outlets. The GCT also monitors the impact of farming techniques such as the impact of set-aside and field margins and hedgerows upon songbird numbers. The Loddington Project has been instrumental in demonstrating the favourable impact of such measures upon songbird numbers (Stoate and Leake 2002).

12. A future research concern may be the extent to which the new right-to-roam legislation will impact upon shoots.

13. See the end of the chapter for a definition.

14. Whilst it is unclear exactly what this refers to, it could be taken to include adverts for shooting that appear in such national titles as the *Shooting Times* and the *Shooting Gazette* before each season.

15. You can only sell game during the season and for ten days following the close of that species' season.

16. Cox et al. (1996) were cognisant of animal welfare debates, but these were beyond the remit of their project.

17. The current situation, with the Tory party in the ascendancy and with their clear statement in favour of hunting, may perhaps challenge Smith's (2004) view.

18. Again, this echoes the significance of Cox et al.'s (1996) study and accessing this relatively closed world.

Chapter 6 Representing the Rural: New Methods and Approaches

1. The little red tractor image is also celebrated as the motif used to identify British produce for the consumer.
2. A more semiotic or text/image interaction is available elsewhere (Nikolajeva and Scott 2000).
3. The shooting season for partridge is from 1 September to 1 February. The pheasant season commences on 1 October and concludes on 1 February. Most shoots hold their first day a month into the season.
4. During unrecorded interviews.

Glossary of Key Terms

Action research Research that has a political agenda and that intends to make a change as a result of the research, either in the social group studied or through later publication (i.e. radical feminist methodologies that go beyond equal opportunities policies to exclude men.)

Analysis A continuous part of the research process in which the researcher develops initial ideas (Glaser and Strauss's 'sensitising concepts') through their fieldwork and literature review in a cyclical process. Initial ideas develop into first- and second-order concepts ultimately aimed towards theorising.

A posteriori Outcome of (or dependent on) direct experience or observation.

A priori Prior to (and independent of) direct experience or observation (i.e. arm-chair theorising).

Case study A detailed study into one social group using qualitative methods. The social group may be predefined, i.e. a school.

Concepts Abstractions that allow us to order our impressions. Many concepts will be primarily based, or derived, from fieldwork and sociological literature. Concepts can be used to identify similarities and differences between phenomena and classify them.

Consensus theory of truth The notion that the veracity of an account or theory is determinable only through agreement between the researcher and their professional peers, or between the researcher and researched (i.e. subjects).

Constructivism The idea that we (as social actors) construct our worlds. In relation to ethnographic writing, Atkinson (1990) in *The Ethnographic Imagination* argues that, rather than explicating an independent social reality (i.e. accurately showing what's out there), ethnographers actually construct their own accounts of that reality (i.e. their own interpretation or version of it). Interlinks with reflexivity, relativism and Berger and Luckmann's (1966) *The Social Construction of Reality*.

the notion of reflexivity recognises that texts do not simply and transparently report an independent reality. Rather, the texts themselves are implicated in the work of reality-construction. This principle applies not only to the spoken and written texts that are produced and interpreted by social actors, but to the texts of social analysts as well. From this point of view, therefore, there is no possibility of a neutral text. The text –

167

the research paper or the monograph, say – is just as much an artefact of convention and contrivance as is any other cultural product.

(Atkinson 1990: 7)

Deduction The testing of a conceptual or theoretical idea (i.e. hypothesis) by observation in order to confirm or reject that initial idea.

Eclectic Borrowing from a variety of sources. I.e. Erving Goffman is argued to draw from an 'eclectic database' of sources in his writing, including field observations, personal anecdotes, fictional novels, sociological literature, newspapers, autobiographies and made-up examples.

Empathy see *Verstehen*.

Empiricism The supposition (idea) that the only source of valid knowledge is experience. In research terms, empiricism avoids untested theoretical speculation. Has more quantitative connotations that qualitative.

Epistemology Theory of knowledge. In research terms, how methods lead to knowledge of the social world. I.e. a sociology founded on realism would have a different epistemology from one founded on relativism.

Ethnography A collection of research methods that aim to access and study social phenomena qualitatively, with the aim to understand, describe and sociologically interpret those social phenomena. Ethnography primarily involves participant observation, but does not exclude quantitative techniques (although these take a secondary role). Epistemologically, ethnography attaches importance to studying individual interaction and hence the knowledge ethnography subsequently produces contains certain (theoretical) ideas about the nature of the social world. However, whether ethnography constitutes an independent research paradigm, or is an atheoretical research tool, is highly contested.

Ethnomethodology Garfinkel's (1967) *Studies in Ethnomethodology* term ('people's methods') is interpretivist. It critiques mainstream sociology's concept of social structure, aiming instead to investigate how actors construct their world. Actors have to work continuously at making their activities make sense to others, yet, despite this, the way the social world is constructed is entirely taken for granted. For example, 'indexicality' refers to the means by which participants fill in a set of background (common sense) assumptions in order to understand what is going on. 'Glossing' repairs the gaps in indexicality. Based on ideas of social constructivism, ethnomethodology celebrates the individual and the 'awesome' fragility of the social order, as maintained and 'achieved' through every social interaction.

Fetishism When something is taken to extremes. Links with reification. Methods can be said to be fetishised when there is a naive belief that 'doing it properly' will allow the truth to emerge. Marx used the term 'commodity fetishism' to describe how social relations (the exchange of goods) are taken as natural things (and therefore disguise inequality). Therefore, Marx's use has an additional ideological tone.

Grounded theory Glaser and Strauss (1967*) The Discovery of Grounded Theory*. Grounded theory is inductive (i.e. works from the data to the theory). It involves cyclical analysis until the data are exhausted, at which point initial 'sensitising concepts' have been developed (through the course of the research) into first-order concepts and theoretical ideas. The emphasis is upon letting the data speak, and that theory produced through this model will be grounded in data gathered qualitatively. Hence grounded theory tends to be location, or context, specific. It links closely with the notion of reflexivity.

Hawthorne effect When subjects knowing they are being studied affects their behaviour, and hence the research. Named after the industrial plant where it was first observed. In management research terms; anything new works (for a while). I.e. in one case worker productivity improved, even when measures introduced were designed to have the opposite effect.

Hermeneutic circle The notion that no observation or description is free from the observer's interpretation based upon their presuppositions (ideas) and therefore they project their own values, theories, etc. on to phenomena.

Hermeneutics A discipline concerned with the interpretation of literary texts and/or meaningful human behaviour.

Hypothesis A tentative proposal that explains and predicts the variation in a particular phenomenon.

Indexicality see Ethnomethodology.

Inductive theory Theory derived from data; a priori. See Grounded theory.

Infinite regress Reflexivity taken to an extreme. E.g. when you are constantly challenging every assumption to the to the extent that nothing becomes knowable and hence research seems pointless.

Instrumentalism The ends serving the means. Something is instrumental when it is seen to have some practical, pragmatic outcome. This can often be set in a somewhat cynical tone.

Interpretivism Micro-oriented sociology. Includes symbolic interactionism, phenomenology and ethnomethodology. Rejects the notion of invisible structural forces dominating society in favour of an emphasis on individualism. The individual social actor, as a rational choice-making being, is the ultimate constituent of social reality.

Meritocracy In a meritocracy, social positions in the occupational structure would be filled on the basis of merit, not upon ascribed criteria or upon inherited wealth.

Metanarrative A grand scheme, idea or account of how the social world works. Similar to meta-theory.

Methodological imperialism Suggesting one method is the only valid way to gain understanding and knowledge of the social world. Therefore this often contains an underlying ontological (or theoretical) supposition about how the social world works.

Methodology The study of methods (or procedures) used in a discipline to gain warranted knowledge. Echoes reflexivity. Basically thinking and reflecting about methods.

Multi-strategy research Burgess's (1984) *In the Field* term. Also called triangulation. When different methods are used to verify the findings of other methods. However, as methods are used within an overall research strategy, it is hard to see how results could ever clash startlingly.

Naturalism This term can have two opposed meanings: (1) That the methodologies of the natural and physical sciences (i.e. physics) provide a blueprint that should be followed by the social sciences; (2) The necessity to investigate human action in its natural or everyday setting and that the researcher must avoid disturbing that setting.

Nominalism The notion that what people take to be an external objective reality has no real existence independent of people's cognitive efforts. Basically, there is nothing really 'out there'.

Objective Impartial, detached, impersonal, unbiased and unprejudiced. Links in with positivistic ideas of research and value-freedom, based on a scientific notion of research.

Ontology The study of, or an idea about, the essence of phenomena and the nature of their existence. Realist ontology is therefore different from relativist ontology. Not to be confused with epistemology, but your ontology defines your epistemology, i.e. your ideas about how society works will affect they way you go about collecting knowledge (researching) the social world.

Paradigm A distinctive perspective that proposes a conceptualisation or explanation of phenomena (i.e. a way of looking at a phenomenon). If it is a paradigm, it has been adopted into mainstream modes of thinking (i.e. become a popular way of thinking). Kuhn (1970) *The Structure of Scientific Revolutions* saw only one paradigm being dominate at one time until criticism led to a dramatic shift to an alternative paradigm that accounted for such criticisms. In sociology, numerous paradigms of thought exist, although there have been shifts in popularity, e.g. functionalism was mainstream in the 1950s; interpretivism rose in the 1960s. Quantitative techniques of research were dominant (to the detriment of ethnography) up until the mid-1960s.

Pedagogy The art of teaching, and thinking reflexively about what epistemology (or ideas) teaching is based upon.

Phenomenology Another strand of interpretive sociology, phenomenology is more extreme than symbolic interactionism, but less so than ethnomethodology. Phenomenology makes no assumptions about the existence or causal powers of social structures, but rather emphasises the human character of social interaction. Analysis and description of everyday life is phenomenology's main aim.

Like constructivism, everyday knowledge is creatively produced by individuals who are also influenced by the accumulated weight of institutionalised knowledge produced by others. (Ethnomethodologists would criticise this position.)

Positivism An approach that emphasises the use of methods presumed to be used in the natural sciences in the social sciences.

Postmodernism A rejection of certainty and an emphasis on pluralism. Borrows from Lyotard's notion of the loss of 'centre'. Historian Keith Jenkins in *On 'What is History?'* offers a useful definition:

> there are not – and nor have there ever been – any 'real' foundations of the kind alleged to underpin the experiment of the modern; that we now just have to understand that we live amidst social formations which have no legitimising ontological or epistemological or ethical grounds for our beliefs or actions beyond the status of an ultimately self-referencing (rhetorical) conversation.
>
> (Jenkins 1995: 7)

Realism There is a real social and natural world existing independent of our cognitions, which we can neutrally apprehend though observation. Basically, the belief that there really is an independent reality 'out there'.

Reflexivity The monitoring by an ethnographer of his or her impact upon the social situation under investigation at every stage of the research process (i.e. not just in the field). This may be called situational reflexivity and can be contrasted with epistemological reflexivity, where the observer attempts hermeneutically to reflect upon and articulate their own assumptions deployed in interpreting fieldwork observations. See Atkinson's (1990) quote under Constructivism. Interlinks with notions of epistemology and, ultimately, ontology.

Relativism The notion that how things appear to people and individuals' judgement about truth are relative to their particular paradigm or frame of reference. Ultimately, everything is as valid as the rest and a rejection of the notion that the 'truth is out there'. The opposite to Realism.

Reliability A criterion that refers to the consistency of the results obtains through research.

Sociological imagination C. Wright Mills's (1959) book *The Sociological Imagination*, later adapted by Paul Atkinson (1990) *The Ethnographic Imagination*. This recognises that research is a creative act (see Constructivism). The ethnographer (as usually the only researcher involved in their study) plays a central role in the entire research. Therefore, their own abilities to be imaginative and resourceful will define the quality of that research.

Symbolic interactionism Part of interpretative sociology, holding that individuals' interaction makes up society, rather than individuals' being governed by external controls, such as social structures. Blumer (1969) *Symbolic*

Interactionism and Mead (1972) *Mind, Self and Society* are key texts. Mead conceived of society as an exchange of gestures that involve the use of symbols. Symbolic interactionism is thus the study of the self–society relationship as a process of symbolic communication between social actors. Therefore, symbolic interactionists (such as Erving Goffman) do not reject notions of structure outright.

Theory By definition, theory is general. A formal definition would be: a formulation about the cause-and-effect relationships between two or more variables, which may or may not have been tested. Sociological theory attempts to explain our everyday experience of the world.

Triangulation see Multi-strategy research.

Validity The success of a test in measuring correctly what it is designed to measure. A self-referencing (and therefore problematic) definition of validity is to ask whether the research has achieved what it set out to do.

***Verstehen* (understanding)** A term used to refer to explanations of the actions of subjects by understanding the subjective dimensions of their behaviour. Ethnography aims to gain rich, thick understanding (*Verstehen*) of social phenomena; to see from the researched perspective and make the strange familiar. A Weberian term.

References

Ananova (2003) 'Self-milking cows boost dairy farm production' [http://www.ananova.com/news/story/sm_786100.html?menu accessed 7 July 2003]

Anderson, I. (2002) *Lessons to be Learned Inquiry*. London, Stationery Office. July [http: //archive.cabinetoffice.gov.uk/fmd/fmd_report/report/index.htm]

Atkinson, P. (1990) *The Ethnographic Imagination*. London, Routledge.

Atkinson, P., Delamont, S. and Hammersley, M. (1993) 'Qualitative Research Traditions', in Hammersley, M. (ed.) *Qualitative Research Traditions in Educational Research: Current Issues*. Milton Keynes, Open University Press.

Baerenholdt, J.O., Haldrup, M., Larsen, J. and Urry, J. (2004) *Performing Tourist Places*. Aldershot, Ashgate.

Baker, P.J., Harris, S. and Webbon, C.C. (2002) 'Effect of British hunting ban on fox numbers', *Nature* 419: 34–35.

Ball, S.J. (1981) *Beachside Comprehensive. A Case-study of Secondary Schooling*. Cambridge, Cambridge University Press.

BASC (undated) *Code of Practice: Fox Snaring*. Wrexham, BASC.

Beckett, J.V. (1990) *The Agricultural Revolution*. Oxford, Blackwell.

Bell, C. and Newby, H. (1971) *Community Studies: an Introduction to the Sociology of the Local Community*. London, Allen and Unwin.

Bell, C. and Newby, H. (eds) (1977) *Doing Sociological Research*. London, Allen and Unwin.

Bell, M. (1994) *Childerley: Nature and Morality in a Country Village*. Chicago, University of Chicago Press.

Bennett, K. and Phillipson, J. (2004) 'A plague upon their houses: revelations of the foot and mouth disease epidemic for business households', *Sociologia Ruralis* 44(3): 261–284.

Berger, P. and Luckmann, T. (1966) *The Social Construction of Reality*. Harmondsworth, Penguin.

Bernard, M., Phillipson, C., Phillips, J. and Ogg, J. (2001) 'Continuity and change in the family and community life of older people', *Journal of Applied Gerontology* 20(3): 259–278.

Biggs, S. (1999) *The Mature Imagination: Dynamics of Identity in Midlife and Beyond*. Buckingham, Open University Press.

Blake, A., Sinclair, M.T. and Sugiyarto, G. (2002) 'Quantifying the impact of Foot and Mouth Disease on tourism and the UK economy'. Nottingham University, Business School: http: //www.nottingham.ac.uk/ttri.

Blumer, H. (1969) *Symbolic Interactionism: Perspective and Method*. Englewood Cliffs, NJ, Prentice-Hall.

Bolton, A., Pole, C. and Mizen, P. (2001) 'Picture this: researching child workers', *Sociology* 35(20): 501–518.

Bourdieu, P. (1973) 'Cultural reproduction and social reproduction' in Brown, R. (ed.) *Knowledge, Education and Cultural Change*. London, Tavistock.

Brown, R. (ed.) (1973) *Knowledge, Education and Cultural change: Papers in the Sociology of Education*. London, Tavistock.

Browne, A. (2003) 'Thunderer: Your country needs you: don't buy British', *The Times*, 14 April.

Burgess, R.G. (1983) *Experiencing Comprehensive Education*. London, Methuen.

Burgess, R.G. (1984) *In the Field*. London, Routledge.

Burridge, J. (2006) ' "Hunting is not just for blood-thirsty toffs": the Countryside Alliance, Heteroglossia, and Stake Inoculation', paper presented to the British Sociological Association conference, Harrogate, April.

Campbell, D. and Lee, R. (2003) ' "Carnage by computer": the blackboard economics of the 2001 foot and mouth epidemic', *Social and Legal Studies* 12(4): 425–459.

Cloke, P. (ed.) (2003) *Country Visions*. Harlow, Pearson.

Cloke, P. (2005) 'Deliver us from evil? Prospects for living ethically and acting politically in human geography', *Progress in Human Geography* 26(5): 587–604.

Cloke, P. and Little, J. (1997) *Contested Countryside Cultures*. London, Routledge.

Cloke, P. and Perkins, H. (1998) 'Cracking the canyon with the Awesome Foursome: representations of adventure tourism in New Zealand', *Society and Space* 16: 185–218.

Cloke, P. and Perkins, H.C. (2002) 'Commodification and adventure in New Zealand tourism', *Current Issues in Tourism* 5(6): 521–549.

Cloke, P. and Thrift, N. (1987) 'Intra-Class Conflict in Rural Areas', *Journal of Rural Studies* 3(4): 321–333.

Cloke, P., Doel, M., Matless, D., Phillips, M. and Thrift, N. (1994) *Writing the Rural: Five Cultural Geographies*. London, Paul Chapman.

Cloke, P., Goodwin, M. and Milbourne, P. (1998a) 'Inside looking out; outside looking in. Different experiences of cultural competence in rural lifestyles', in Boyle, P. and Halfacree, K. (eds) *Migration into Rural Areas: Theories and Issues*. Chichester, Wiley.

Cloke, P., Phillips, M. and Thrift, N. (1998b) 'Class, colonisation and lifestyle strategies in Gower', in Boyle, P. and Halfacree, K. (eds) *Migration into Rural Areas: Theories and Issues*. Chichester, Wiley.

Cloke, P., Milbourne, P. and Widdowfield, R. (2000) *Rural Homelessness*. Bristol, Policy Press.

Cloke, P., Crang, P. and Goodwin, M. (2005) *Introducing Human Geography*, 2nd edn. London, Arnold.

Cobham Resource Consultants (1983) *Countryside Sports: Their Economic Significance*. Oxford, Cobham Resource Consultants.

Cobham Resource Consultants (1992) *Countryside Sports: Their Economic Significance*. Oxford, Cobham Resource Consultants.

Coffey, A. (1999) *The Ethnographic Self*. London, Sage.

Consortium of Social Science Associations (COSSA) (2005) 'COSSA holds Capitol Hill briefing on future of rural America', *COSSA Washington Update*. 24(6): 1–2.

Convery, I., Bailey, C., Mort, M. and Baxter, J. (2005) 'Death in the wrong place? Emotional geogaphies of the UK 2001 foot and mouth disease epidemic', *Journal of Rural Studies* 21: 99–109.

Countryside Alliance (2004) Press Release: '59% say keep hunting – Advertising Standards Authority accepts no majority for a ban on hunting', 2 June http: //www.countryside-alliance.org/news/04/040602pers.html [19 August 2004]

Cox, G. (2000) ' "Listen to us!" Country sports and the mobilisation of a marginalized constituency', paper presented to The Contested Countryside conference, Rural History Centre, University of Reading, Reading, UK, 18 September.

Cox, G. (2001) 'The right way for animal welfare: just how should we relate to animals?' in Sissons, M. (ed.) *A Countryside for All: the Future of Rural Britain*. London, Vintage.

Cox, G. and Winter, M. (1997) 'The beleaguered "Other": hunt followers in the countryside', in Milbourne, P. (ed.) *Revealing Rural 'Others': Representation, Power and Identity in the British Countryside*. London, Pinter.

Cox, G., Hallett, J. and Winter, M. (1994) 'Hunting the wild red deer: the social organization and ritual of a "rural" institution', *Sociologia Ruralis* XXXIV(2–3): 190–205.

Cox, G., Watkins, C. and Winter, M. (1996) *Game management in England: Implications of Public Access, the Rural Economy and the Environment*. Cheltenham, Countryside and Community Press.

Craib, I. (1992) Modern Social Theory. London, Harvester.

Crow, G. and Allan, G. (1994) *Community Life: an Introduction to Local Social Relations*. London, Harvester Wheatsheaf.

Crow, G., Marsden, T. and Winter, M. (1990) 'Recent British Rural Sociology', in Lowe, P. and Bodiguel, M. (eds) *Rural Studies in Britain and France*, trans. H. Buller. London, Belhaven Press.

'Cull MAFF' (undated) http: //cullmaff.com/demands.htm [accessed 16 May 2003]

Curry, D. (2002) *Farming and Food – a Sustainable Future*, Report of the Policy

Commission on the Future of Farming and Food, January, HMSO, Cabinet Office. http: //www.cabinet-office.gov.uk/farming

Deem, R., Hillyard, S. and Reed, M. (forthcoming) *Management Knowledge and the University*. Oxford, Oxford University Press.

Delanty, G. (2003) *Community*. London, Routledge.

Dingwall, R. (2004) 'The sociology of measurement', paper presented to 'Caught between Science and Society: Foot and Mouth Disease' workshop, 19 November, University of Nottingham, Nottingham, UK.

Dingwall, R., Tanaka, H. and Minamikata, S. (1991) 'Images of parenthood in the United Kingdom and Japan', *Sociology* 25(3): 423–446.

Donaldson, A. and Woods, D. (2004) 'Surveilling strange materialities: categorization and the evolving geographies of FMD biosecurity', *Environment and Planning D: Society and Space* 22: 373–339.

Donaldson, A., Lowe, P. and Ward, N. (2002) 'Virus-crisis-institutional change: the foot and mouth actor network and the governance of rural affairs in the UK', *Sociologia Ruralis* 42(3): 201–214.

Donaldson, A., Lee, R., Ward, N. and Wilkinson, K. (2006) 'Foot and mouth – five years on: the legacy of the 2001 foot and mouth disease crisis for farming and the British countryside', *Centre for Rural Economy Discussion Paper Series* No. 6, February.

Durkheim, E. (1984) [1893] *The Division of Labour in Society*. Basingstoke, Macmillan.

Felstead, A., Jewson, N. and Walters, S. (2005) *Changing Places of Work*. Basingstoke, Palgrave.

Follett Report (2002) *Infectious Diseases in Livestock. Scientific Questions Relating to the Transmission, Prevention and Control of Epidemic Outbreaks of Infectious Disease in Livestock in Great Britain*. Report of the Royal Society Inquiry, July [http: //www.royalsoc.ac.uk/inquiry/index.html]

Frankenberg, R. (1957) *Village on the Border: a Social Study of Religion, Politics and Football in a North Wales Community*. London, Cohen and West.

Frankenberg, R. (1969) *Communities in Britain: Social Life in Town and Country*. Harmondsworth, Penguin.

Frisby, D. (1992) *Sociological Impressionism: a Reassessment of Georg Simmel's Social Theory*, 2nd edn. London, Routledge.

Fulcher, J. and Scott, J. (2003) *Sociology*, 2nd edn. Oxford, Oxford University Press.

Fyfe, G. and Law, J. (1988) 'Introduction: on the invisibility of the visible', in Fyfe, G. and Law, J. (eds) *Picturing Power: Visual Depiction and Social Relations*. London, Routledge.

Game Conservancy Trust (GCT) (2005) *Review: a Full Report of the Activities of the Game Conservancy Trust and Game Conservancy Limited*. Fordingbridge, Hampshire, Raithby Lawrence.

Garfinkel, H. (1967) *Studies in Ethnomethodology*. Englewood Cliffs, NJ, Prentice-Hall.

Gasson, R., Errington, A. and Tranter, R. (1998) *Carry on Farming: A Study of How English Farmers have Adapted to the Changing Pressures on Farming*. Wye, Wye College, University of London.

George, J. (1999) *A Rural Uprising. The Battle to Save Hunting with Hounds*. London, Allen.

Ghosh, P. (2005) 'Max Weber on "the rural community"' a critical edition of the English text', *History of European Ideas* 31: 327–366.

Gibbons, S. (1986) [1932] *Cold Comfort Farm*. Harmondsworth, Penguin.

Glaser, B. and Strauss, A. (1967) *The Discovery of Grounded Theory*. New York, Aldine de Gruyter.

Goffman, E. (1961) *Asylums: Essays on the Social of Mental Patients and Other Inmates*. Harmondsworth, Penguin.

Goffman, E. (1969) [1959] *The Presentation of Self in Everyday Life*. Harmondsworth, Penguin.

Goffman, E. (1972) [1956] 'The nature of deference an demeanour', in Goffman, E. (1972) *Interaction Ritual*. Harmondsworth, Penguin.

Goffman, E. (1979) *Gender Advertisements*. Cambridge, Mass., Harvard University Press.

Goffman, E. (1983) 'The interaction order', *American Journal of Sociology*. 89(1): 1–53.

Goffman, E. (1997) *The Goffman Reader*. Oxford, Blackwell.

Goldthorpe, J.H., Lockwood, D., Bechhofer, F. and Platt, J. (1968a) *The Affluent Worker: Industrial Attitudes and Behaviour*. Cambridge, Cambridge University Press.

Goldthorpe, J.H., Lockwood, D., Bechhofer, F. and Platt, J. (1968b) *The Affluent Worker: Political attitudes and behaviour*. Cambridge, Cambridge University Press.

Graffius, C. (2006) 'Syndicate shoots' success' News report, *Shooting Times* 29 June.

Guardian (2001) 'Special report: foot and mouth disease'. [http//www.guardian.co.uk/footandmouth]

Hamilton, P. (1990) 'Sociology: commentary and introduction', in Lowe, P. and Bodiguel, M. (eds) *Rural Studies in Britain and France,* trans. H. Buller. London, Belhaven Press.

Hammersley, M. and Atkinson, P. (1995) *Ethnography: Principles in Practice*. London, Tavistock.

Hargreaves, D.H. (1967) *Social Relations in a Secondary School*. London, Routledge.

Harper, D. (1998) 'An argument for visual sociology', in Prosser, J. (ed.) *Image-based Research: A Sourcebook for Qualitative Researchers*. London, Falmer.

Harper, D. (2001) *Changing Works: Visions of a Lost Agriculture*. Chicago, Chicago University Press.

Harper, D. (2002) 'Changing works: eliciting accounts of past and present dairy farming', Contexts: Understanding People in their Social Worlds. 1(1): 52–58.

Harris, S. (1993) *The Red Fox – Friend or Foe? What the Experts Say*. London, League Against Cruel Sports.

Hart Davis, D. (1997) *When the Country Went to Town*. Ludlow, UK, Excellent Press.

Hillyard, S.H. (1999) 'Goffman's reflexive imagination', in Walford, G. and Massey, A. (eds) *Studies in Educational Ethnography, Volume 2: Explorations in Methodology*. Stamford, Connecticut, JAI Press.

Hillyard, S.H. (2003a) 'An exploration of the dialectic between theory and method in ethnography'. Unpublished PhD thesis, University of Warwick, Coventry.

Hillyard, S.H. (2003b) 'Bunny-huggers and toffs: media representation of the pro and anti hunting lobbies', XX Congress of the European Society for Rural Sociology: 'Work, Leisure and Development in Rural Europe Today'. 18–22 August 2003. Sligo Institute for Technology, Sligo, Ireland.

Hillyard, S.H. (2004) 'The case for partisan research: Erving Goffman and researching inequalities', in Jeffrey, R.A. and Walford, G. (eds) *Studies in Educational Ethnography Volume 5: Ethnographies of Educational and Cultural Conflicts: Strategies and Resolution*. Stamford, Connecticut, JAI Press.

Hillyard, S.H. (2005) 'Keeping the balance': hidden work in the British countryside', paper presented to the Institute for the Study of Genetics, Biorisks and Society, University of Nottingham, Nottingham, UK 20 June.

Hillyard, S.H. (2006) 'Cull MAFF!: the mobilisation of the farming community during the 2001 Foot and Mouth Disease (FMD) epidemic', in Herbrechter, S. and Higgins, M. (eds) *Returning (to) Community*. Amsterdam, The Netherlands, Rodopi. (Critical Studies series.)

Hillyard, S.H. (forthcoming a) ' "As relevant as banning polo in Greenland" (George 1999: 41). The absence of ethnographic insight into country sports in the UK', *Qualitative Research* 7.

Hillyard, S.H. (forthcoming b) 'Divisions and divisiveness and the social cost of foot and mouth disease: a sociological analysis of FMD in one locality', in Döring, M. and Nerlich, B. (eds) *From Mayhem to Meaning: the Social and Cultural Impact of Foot and Mouth Disease in the UK in 2001*. Manchester, Manchester University Press.

Home Office (2000) *Report of the Committee of Inquiry into Hunting with Dogs in England and Wales*. The Stationery Office, London.

Institute of Rural Studies (IRS) (2006) *The Economic Potential for Game Shooting in Wales*. Aberystwyth Institute of Rural Studies, University of Wales Aberystwyth, with Richard Garner Williams, Socio-Economic Research Services (SERS) Ltd.

Jenkins, K. (1995) *Re-thinking History*. London, Routledge.

Jones, David S.D. (2006) 'Beating – a peep into the past', *Keeping the Balance: the Official Magazine of the Gamekeepers' Organisation*. Summer Issue: 37–38.

Jones, O. (1997) 'Little figures, big shadows: country childhood stories', in Cloke, P. and Little, J. (eds) *Contested Countryside Cultures*. London, Routledge.

Kuhn, T. (1970) *The Structure of Scientific Revolutions*. 2nd edn. Chicago, Chicago University Press.

Lacey, C. (1970) *Hightown Grammar: the School as a Social System*. Manchester, Manchester University Press.

Lacey, C. and Ball, S.J. (1979) 'Perspectives on education', Wakefield, Yorkshire. Educational Productions [a taped discussion between Colin Lacey and Stephen Ball, Sussex University].

Lambart, A.M. (1976) 'The Sisterhood', in Hammersley, M. and Woods, P. (eds) *The Process of Schooling: A Sociological Reader*. London, Routledge.

Lambart, A. (1982) 'Expulsion in context: a school as a system in action', in Frankenberg, R. (ed.) (1982) *Custom and Conflict in British Society*. Manchester, University of Manchester Press.

Lawrence, D.H. (1960) *Lady Chatterley's Lover*. Penguin, Harmondsworth.

League Against Cruel Sports (LACS) (2003) 'Wild about killing: a LACS investigation into how British travel companies enable sport hunters to slaughter some of the world's most threatened species' (December) [http: //www.bloodybusiness.com/reports/wild_about_killing.pdf accessed 28/6/6

League Against Cruel Sports (LACS) (2004a) Press Release: 'Countryside Alliance "59 % say keep hunting" poll "misleading" ' http: //www.league.uk.com/news/latest_news/2004/jun2004/ca_poll.htm June, 2004. [accessed 23/06/04]

League Against Cruel Sports (LACS) (2004b) 'Wild about killing 2: a special investigation into African trophy hunting' [http: //www.league.uk.com/investigations/Wild_about_killing_2.pdf accessed 28 June 2006]

League Against Cruel Sports (LACS) (2004c) 'The myth of trophy hunting as conservation: a League Against Cruel Sports submission to Environment Minister, Elliot Morley MP' (December) [http: //www.bloodybusiness.com/trophy_hunting/The%Myth%of%20Trophy%20Hunting%20as%20Conservation.pdf 28 June 2006]

League Against Cruel Sports (LACS) (2005a) 'The killing game: out of control predator control, the first in a series of LACS reports about the bloody business of gamebird shooting.' (May) [The date of LACS (2005a) is not stated in that publication, but is referred to in LACS (2005c) footnote 1.] [http: //www.bloodybusiness.com/commercial_shooting/index.html accessed 28 June 2006]

League Against Cruel Sports (LACS) (2005b) 'The killing game 2: bred to be wasted, the second in a series of LACS reports about the bloody business of

gamebird shooting' (August) [http: //www.bloodybusiness.com/commercial_
shooting/index.html 28 June 2006]

League Against Cruel Sports (LACS) (2005c) 'The Killing Game 3: the money
pits, the third in a series of LACS reports about the bloody business of game
shooting' (December) [http: //www.bloodybusiness.com/commercial_
shooting/index.html 28 June 2006]

Lee, D. and Newby, H. (1983) The Problem of Sociology: an Introduction to the
Discipline. London, Hutchinson.

Leyshon, M. (2002) 'On being "in the field": practice, progress and problems in
researching young people in rural areas', *Journal of Rural Studies* 18: 179–191.

Leyshon, M. (2004) 'Making the pub the hub: power, drinking and rural youth', in
Little, J. and Morris, C. (eds) *Gender and Rural Change*. Aldershot, Ashgate.

Little, J. (2003a) ' "Riding the rural love train": heterosexuality and the rural community', *Sociologia Ruralis*, 43(4): 401–417, October.

Little, J. (2003b) 'The value of qualitative research', Address to the DEFRA Rural
Data Seminar, The Conference Centre at Church House, London, UK 16
October.

Little, J. and Morris, C. (eds) (2004) *Critical Perspectives in Rural Gender
Studies*. Aldershot, Ashgate.

Littlejohn, J. (1963) *Westrigg: the Sociology of a Cheviot Parish*. London,
Routledge.

Lockwood, D. (1958) *The Blackcoated Worker*. London, Allen and Unwin.

Lodge, D. (1984) *Small World*. London, Penguin.

Lorimer, H. (2000) 'Guns, game and the grandee: the cultural politics of deer-
stalking in the Scottish Highlands' *Ecumene* 7(4),: 431–459.

Lorimer, H. and Lund, K. (2003) 'Performing facts: finding a way over Scotland's
mountains', in Szerszynski, B., Heim, W. and Waterton, C. (eds) Nature
Performed: Environment, Culture and Performance. London, Blackwells.

Marsden, T. (1986) 'Property–state relations in the 1980s: an examination of land-
lord-tenant legislation in British agriculture', in Cox, G., Lowe, P. and Winter,
M. (eds) (1986) *Agriculture: People and Policies*. London, Allen and Unwin.

Marsden, T. (1997) 'Reshaping environments', *Transactions of the Institute of
British Geographers* 22, 473–487.

Marsden, T. (1998) 'Creating competitive space: exploring the social and political
maintenance of retail power', *Environment and Planning A*, 30: 481–498.

Marsden, T. (1998b) 'New rural territories: regulating the differentiating rural
spaces', *Journal of Rural Studies* 14(1): 107–119.

Marsden, T. (1999) *The Condition of Sustainability*. London, Routledge.

Marsden, T. (2000a) *Consuming Interests: the Social Provision of Foods*. London,
Taylor and Francis.

Marsden, T. (2000b) *Rural Sustainability*. London, Town and Country Planning
Tomorrow Series No. 4.

Marsden, T. and Murdoch, J. (1998) 'Editorial: the shifting nature of rural governance and community participation', *Journal of Rural Studies* 14(1): 1–4.

Marvin, G. (2006) 'Wild killing: contesting the animal in hunting', in The Animal Studies Group (eds) *Killing Animals*. Urbana: University of Illinois Press.

Mead, G.H. (1972) *Mind, Self and Society*. Chicago, Chicago University Press.

Milbourne, P. (1997) 'Introduction: challenging the rural: representation, power and identity in the British countryside', in Milbourne, P. (ed.) *Revealing Rural 'Others': Representation, Power and Identity in the British Countryside*. London, Pinter.

Milbourne, P. (2003a) 'Hunting ruralities: nature, society and culture in "hunt countries" of England and Wales', *Journal of Rural Studies* 19: 157–171.

Milbourne, P. (2003b) 'The complexities of junting in rural England and Wales', *Sociologia Ruralis* 43(3): 289–308.

Mills, C.W. (1959) *The Sociological Imagination*. New York, Oxford University Press.

Mort, M., Convery, I., Bailey, C. and Baxter, J. (2004) *The Health and Social Consequences of the 2001 Foot and Mouth Disease Epidemic in North Cumbria*. [www.lancs.ac.uk/fss/ihr/research/healthandplace/foot&mouth.htm accessed 23 May 2005]

National Audit Office (2002) *The 2001 Outbreak of Foot and Mouth Disease*. HC 939 Session 2001–2002. London, Stationery Office.

Nerlich, B. (2004) 'War on foot and mouth disease in the UK in 2001: towards a cultural understanding of agriculture', *Agriculture and Human Values* 21(1): 15–25.

Nerlich, B. and Döring, M. (2005) 'Poetic justice? Rural policy clashes with rural poetry in the 2001 outbreak of foot and mouth disease in the UK', *Journal of Rural Studies* 21: 165–180.

Nerlich, B., Hamilton, C. and Rowe, V. (2002) 'Conceptualising foot and mouth disease: the socio-cultural role of metaphors, frames and narratives', metaphorik.de: http: //www.metaphorik.de/02/nerlich.htm

Nerlich, B., Hillyard, S. and Wright, N. (2005) 'Stress and stereotypes: children's reactions to the outbreak of foot and mouth disease in the UK in 2001', *Children and Society* 19: 348–359.

Newby, H. (1977a) *The Deferential Worker: a Study of Farm Workers in East Anglia*. London, Allen Lane.

Newby, H. (1977b) 'In the field: reflections on the study of Suffolk farm workers', in Bell, C. and Newby, H. (eds) *Doing Sociological Research*. London, Allen and Unwin.

Newby, H. (1978) 'The rural sociology of advanced capitalist societies', in Newby, H. (ed.) *International Perspectives in Rural Sociology*. Chichester, John Wiley.

Newby, H. (1980) 'Rural sociology', *Current Sociology* 28(1): 1–117.

Newby, H. (1985, updated edition) *Green and Pleasant Land? Social Change in rural England*, updated edn. London, Wildwood House.

Newby, H., Bell, C., Rose, D. and Saunders, P. (1978a) 'Maintaining the deferential dialectic', in Newby, H., Bell, C., Rose, D. and Saunders, P. *Property, Paternalism and Power*. London, Hutchinson.

Newby, H., Bell, C., Rose, D. and Saunders, P. (1978b) *Property, Paternalism and Power. Class and Control in Rural England*. London, Hutchinson.

Nikolajeva, M. and Scott, C. (2000) 'The dynamics of picturebook communication', *Children's Literature in Education* 31(4): 225–239.

Oakley, A. (1974) *The Sociology of Housework*. London, Martin Robertson.

Oates, B. (2002) 'Foot and mouth disease: informing the community?' *Informing Science* June: 1197–1207.

Pahl, R.E. (1965) *Urbs in Rure: the Metropolitan Fringe in Hertfordshire*. London, Geography Department, London School of Economics and Political Science.

Pahl, R.E. (1968) [1966] 'The rural–urban continuum', in Pahl, R.E. (ed.) (1968) *Readings in Urban Sociology*. Oxford, Pergamon.

Pahl, R.E. (1975) *Whose City?* Harmondsworth, Penguin.

Pahl, R.E. (2005) 'Are all communities communities in the mind?' *Sociological Review* 53(4): 621–640.

Phillips, M., Fish, R. and Agg, J. (2001) 'Putting together ruralities: towards a symbolic analysis of rurality in the British mass media', *Journal of Rural Studies* 17: 1–27.

Phillipson, J., Bennett, K., Lowe, P. and Raley, M. (2004) 'Adaptive responses and asset strategies: the experience of rural micro-firms and foot and mouth disease', *Journal of Rural Studies* 20: 227–243.

Philo, C. (1993) 'Postmodern rural geography? A reply to Murdoch and Pratt', *Journal of Rural Studies* 9(4): 429–436.

Piddington, H. (1981) *Land Management for Shooting and Fishing*. Cambridge, Department of Land Economy.

Pole, C. (2004) 'Visual research: potential and overview', in Pole, C. (ed.) *Seeing is Believing? Approaches to Visual Research*. Amsterdam, Elsevier JAI.

Pole, C. and Morrison, M. (2003) *Ethnography for Education*. Maidenhead, Open University Press.

Pole, C., Mizen, P. and Bolton, A. (1999) 'Realising children's agency in research: partners and participants?' *International Journal of Social Research Methodology: Theory and Practice* 2(1): 39–54.

Price, C. (2002) 'Game laws in the UK', paper presented to the Standing Conference on Countryside Sports, London, July.

Private Eye (2001) 'Not the Foot and Mouth Report: everything Tony Blair didn't want you to know about the biggest blunder of his premiership', edited by Christopher Booker, with research by Richard North. November.

Public and Corporate Economic Consultants (PACEC) (2006) *The Economic Contribution of Game Shooting to the UK Economy*. Cambridge, PACEC.

Redfield (1947) 'The folk society', *American Journal of Sociology* 52: 292–7.

Rees, A.D. (1950) *Life in a Welsh Countryside: a Social Study of Llanfihangel yng Ngwynfa*, 2nd edn. Cardiff, University of Wales Press.

Rickinson, M., Sanders, D., Benefield, P., Dillon, J. and Teamey, K. (2003) *Improving the Understanding of Food, Farming and Land Management amongst School-age Children: A Literature Review*. London, Department for Education and Skills and the Countryside Agency. Research Report RR422 (May).

Rock P. (1979) *The Making of Symbolic Interactionism*. London, Macmillan.

Rural Sociological Society (RSS) (2005) *Challenges for Rural America in the Twenty-first Century*. University Park, PA, Rural Sociological Society.

Sassoon, S. (1999) [1928] *Memoirs of a Foxhunting Man*. London, Faber and Faber.

Scott, A., Christie, M. and Midmore, P. (2004) 'The impact of the 2001 foot-and-mouth disease ourbreak in Britain: implications for rural studies', *Journal of Rural Studies* 20:1 1–14.

Shilling, J. (2004) *The Fox in the Cupboard*. London, Viking.

Simmel, G. (1971) [1903] 'The metropolis and mental life', in Simmel, G. (1971) *On Individuality and Social Forms*, edited by Donald Levine. Chicago, Chicago University Press.

Smith, S. (2004) 'Theorising gun control: the development of regulation and shooting sports in Britain', unpublished paper, University of Leicester.

Stacey, M. (1960) *Tradition and Change: a Study of Banbury*. Oxford, Oxford University Press.

Steering Committee for the Code of Good Shooting Practice (Countryside Alliance, Shooting Times, BASC, NGO, Game Farmers' Association, Scottish Landowners' Federation, CLA and GCT) (2003) *The Code of Good Shooting Practice*. Wrexham, BASC.

Stoate, C. and Leake, A. (2002) *Where the Birds Sing: the Allerton Project: 10 years of Conservation on Farmland*. Fordingbridge, GCT.

Strangleman, T. (2004a) 'Ways of (not) seeing work: the visual as a blind spot in *WES*?' *Work, Employment and Society* 18(1): 179–192. March.

Strangleman, T. (2004b) *Work Identity at the end of the Line? Privatisation and Culture Change in the UK Rail Industry*. London, Palgrave.

Tapper (2005) *Nature's Gain: How Gamebird Management has Influenced Wildlife Conservation*. Fordingbridge, GCT.

Thomas, W.I. (1928) *The Child in America*. New York, Alfred Knopf.

Tönnies, F. (1955) [1887] *Community and Association: Gemeinschaft und Gesellschaft*. trans. Charles Loomis. London, Routledge.

Urban White Paper (2000) Our Towns and Cities: The Future – Delivering an Urban Ranaissance. London, HMSO.

Verhoeven, J. (1993) 'An interview with Erving Goffman, 1980', *Research on Language and Social Interaction* 26(3): 317–48.

Ward, N. (1999) 'Foxing the nation. The (in)significance of hunting with hounds in Britain', *Journal of Rural Studies* 15: 389–403.

Ward, N., Donaldson, A. and Lowe, P. (2004) 'Policy framing and learning the lessons from the UK's foot and mouth disease crisis', *Environment and Planning C: Government and Policy* 22: 291–306.

Weber, M. (1970) [1904] 'Capitalism and rural society in Germany', in Gerth, H.H. and Mills, C. Wright (eds) (1970) [1948] *From Max Weber: Essays in Sociology*, Chapter XIV: London, Routledge. (Based on a lecture delivered in 1904.)

Weitzman, L.J., Eifler, D., Hokada, E. and Ross, C. (1972) 'Sex-role socialization in picture books for preschool children', *American Journal of Sociology* 77(6): 1125–1150.

Wilkie, R. (2005) 'Sentient commodities and productive paradoxes: the ambiguous nature of human–livestock relations in Northeast Scotland', *Journal of Rural Studies* 21: 213–230.

Williams, R. (1973) *The Country and the City*. London, Chatto & Windus.

Williams, W.M. (1956) *Gosforth: The Sociology of an English Village*. London, Routledge.

Williams, W.M. (1963) *A West Country Village: Ashworthy: Family, Kinship and Land*. London, Routledge.

Wilmott, P. and Young, M. (1960) *Family and Class in a London Suburb*. London, Routledge.

Winter, M. (1998) 'The rural economy', in White-Spundner, B. (ed.) *Our Countryside*. Cambridge, Pearson.

Winter (2003) 'Responding to the crisis: the policy impact of the foot–and–mouth epidemic' *Political Quarterly* 74(1): 47–56.

Winter, M., Hallett, J., Nixon, J., Watkins, C., Cox, G. and Glanfield, P. (1993) *Economic and Social Aspects of Deer Hunting on Exmoor and the Quantocks: Research Report to the National Trust*. Cirencester, Centre for Rural Studies.

Wirth, L. (1938) 'Urbanism as a way of life', *American Journal of Sociology* 37: 49–66.

Woods, A. (2002) *A Manufactured Plague: The History of Foot-and-mouth Disease in Britain*. London, Earthscan.

Woods, M. (1998) 'Mad cows and hounded deer: political representations of animals in the British countryside', *Environment and Planning A* 30(7): 1219–1234.

Woods, M. (2002) 'Was there a rural rebellion? Labour and the countryside vote in the 2001 general election', in Bennie, L., Rallings, C., Tunge, J. and Webb, P. (eds) *British Elections and Parties Review, Volume 12, The 2001 General Election*. London, Cass.

Woods, M. (2003) 'Deconstructing rural protest: the emergence of a new social movement', *Journal of Rural Studies* 19(3): 309–325.

Woods, M. (2005) *Contesting Rurality: Politics in the British Countryside.* Aldershot, Ashgate.

Woodward, R. (2003) 'Looking at militarised landscapes', paper presented to the Rural Economy and Society Study Group conference, 'Critical Turns, Rural turns: Critical (Re)Appraisals, 16–18 September, University of Newcastle.

Wright, N. (2004a). Mapping the language of rural landownership: property, class and rurality. University of Gloucestershire, unpublished PhD.

Wright, N. (2004b) 'Valuing foot and mouth: a call for the relocation of the politics of modeling', paper presented to 'Caught between Science and Society: Foot and Mouth Disease' workshop, 19 November, University of Nottingham, Nottingham, UK.

Wright, N. and Nerlich, B. (2006) 'Use of the deficit model in a shared culture of argumentation: the case of foot and mouth science', *Public Understanding of Science* 15: 331–342.

Young, J. (1971) *The Drugtakers: the Social Meaning of Drug Use.* London, Paladin.

Young, M.F.D. (ed.) (1971) *Knowledge and Control: New Directions in the Sociology of Education.* London, Collier-Macmillan.

Image references

Lacome, J. (1994) *I'm a Jolly Farmer.* London, Walker Books.

Lewis, K. (2000) *Little Lamb.* London, Walker Books.

Morpurgo, M. and Rayner, S. (1992) *Martians at Mudpuddle Farm.* London, A. & C. Black.

Osband, G. and Spargo, B. (1993) *Farmer Jane.* London, Penguin.

Rogers, E. and Rogers, P. (1995) *Quacky Duck.* London, Orion Children's Books.

Sloat, T. and Westcott, N.B. (1999) *Farmer Brown Goes Round and Round.* London, Dorling Kindersley.

Tanner, G. and Wood, T. (1995) *Farming.* London, A. & C. Black.

Waddell, M. and Oxenbury, H. (1991) *Farmer Duck.* London, Walker.

Watson, C. (1997) *A Day in the Life of a Farmer.* London, Franklin Watts.

Index